JESUS, GNOSIS AND DOGMA

JESUS, GNOSIS AND DOGMA

RIEMER ROUKEMA

t & t clark

Published by T&T Clark International
A Continuum Imprint
The Tower Building, 11 York Road, London SE1 7NX
80 Maiden Lane, Suite 704, New York, NY 10038

www.continuumbooks.com

First published as *Jeazus, de gnosis en het dogma* by Uitgeverij Meinema, Zoetermeer. Translated from the Dutch by Saskia Deventer-Metz.

British Library Cataloguing-in-Publication Data
A catalogue record for this book is available from the British Library

ISBN: 978-0-567-06480-6 (Hardback)
          978-0-567-46642-6 (Paperback)

Typeset by Free Range Book Design & Production Ltd
Printed and bound in Great Britain by CPI Antony Rowe, Chippenham, Wiltshire

Author's note
As a rule, for biblical quotations I use the New Revised Standard Version, and for quotations from the Gospel of Thomas: April D. DeConick (2007), *The Original Gospel of Thomas in Translation: With a Commentary and New English Translation of the Complete Gospel*. London, New York: T&T Clark.

Contents

Preface   xi

1   Introduction   1
     1.1   Jesus as source of inspiration   1
     1.2   Jesus considered historically and theologically   3
     1.3   Who is Jesus? Reactions of Peter, Matthew
         and Thomas   9
     1.4   Outline and explanation   14

2   Jesus' Origin and Identity   18
     2.1   The letters of Paul   18
     2.2   The Gospel of Mark   24
     2.3   The Gospel of Matthew   32
     2.4   The Gospel of Luke   36
     2.5   The Gospel of John   39
     2.6   Evaluation of the New Testament data   44
     2.7   The Gospel of Thomas   45
     2.8   Cerinthus and the Ophites   49
     2.9   The Gospel of Judas   51
     2.10   Theodotus   53
     2.11   The Tripartite Tractate   55
     2.12   Comparison of the New Testament and
         other writings   58

3.   Jesus' Teaching   60
     3.1   The Gospel of Mark   61
     3.2   The Gospel of Matthew   63
     3.3   The Gospel of Luke   65
     3.4   The Gospel of John   67

3.5	Evaluation of the New Testament data	70
3.6	The Gospel of Thomas	71
3.7	The Gospel of Judas	80
3.8	The Gospel of Mary	82
3.9	The Tripartite Tractate	84
3.10	Other teachings of Jesus after his death and resurrection	85
3.11	Comparison of the New Testament and other writings	86
4	**Jesus' Death, Resurrection and Exaltation**	**88**
4.1	The letters of Paul	88
4.2	The Gospel of Mark	92
4.3	The Gospel of Matthew	95
4.4	The Gospel of Luke and the Acts of the Apostles	96
4.5	The Gospel of John	97
4.6	Evaluation of the New Testament data	100
4.7	The Gospel of Thomas	102
4.8	Cerinthus and the Ophites	103
4.9	The Gospel of Judas	104
4.10	Theodotus	104
4.11	The Tripartite Tractate	107
4.12	A tradition about Simon of Cyrene	108
4.13	Comparison of the New Testament and other writings	110
5	**Interim Conclusions and New Questions**	**114**
5.1	Interim conclusions	114
5.2	New questions	118
6	**Jewish Christianity**	**121**
6.1	Testimonies of church fathers about Jewish Christians	122
6.2	The Pseudo-Clementine writings	125
6.3	An ancient form of Christianity?	127
6.4	Conclusion	130
7	**Did Jesus Have a Secret Teaching?**	**132**
7.1	Jesus' unwritten teachings in the 'catholic' church	133
7.2	Private teachings in the synoptic gospels	135
7.3	Private teachings in the Gospel of John	139
7.4	A secret teaching after all? Conclusion	141

8   Does Jesus as LORD and Son of God Fit into Early Judaism?   145
    8.1   The Old Testament   146
    8.2   Philo of Alexandria   151
    8.3   Other early Jewish writings   154
    8.4   Conclusion   160

9   Jesus and the Dogma of God's Trinity   164
    9.1   God the Father, the Son and the Holy Spirit in
          the New Testament   164
    9.2   The Father, the Son and the Holy Spirit in
          gnostic writings   167
    9.3   Some church fathers from the second century   168
    9.4   Adoptianism   173
    9.5   Modalism   175
    9.6   Tertullian of Carthage   177
    9.7   Origen of Alexandria   179
    9.8   Arius   182
    9.9   The Nicene Council   185
    9.10 Conclusion   187

10 Conclusions and Evaluation   191

Bibliography   199

Index of Passages   217

Index of Names and Subjects   229

I dedicate this book to the memory of my mother,
Sjoukje Roukema-Tom (1927–2006)

Preface

This work is in a way a sequel to my earlier book *Gnosis and Faith in Early Christianity: An Introduction to Gnosticism*, from 1999. Still, it may be read separately, even though sometimes I will refer to this earlier study. At times it will be apparent that I have slightly readjusted my view, for example with regard to the question as to whether Jesus had a secret teaching. I have made some small corrections to the Dutch text for this English edition.

I thank my colleagues Hans-Martin Kirn and Bert Jan Lietaert Peerbolte for their constructive comments on an earlier version. I learned a great deal from the meetings of the Gnosticism Working Group in Heerde led by the retired professors Abraham P. Bos and Gerard P. Luttikhuizen. In the final phase, my student Helma Lubbers carefully assisted me in adapting the references of the Dutch text to the English version, in making the bibliography, the indices, and in proofreading. Lily Burggraaff witnessed the writing of this book at first hand and stimulated me in doing so.

CHAPTER 1

Introduction

1.1 *Jesus as source of inspiration*

The stream of books and articles about Jesus of Nazareth is endless. Not only Bible scholars and other theologians publish their findings about Jesus, but historians, journalists and novelists do so as well. Among the authors are not only Christians, but also agnostics, atheists and others who do not belong to a Christian church. Coming from all possible directions of thoughts, time and again people try to describe who Jesus was during his life, what he revealed to a group of insiders after his death, what his role was in history, or how one can believe in him nowadays. Films, radio and television programmes and numerous websites can be added to the printed publications. Even though the magnitude and influence of the Christian churches have diminished in the Western world, the interest for the person standing at the base of Christianity has not in the least disappeared. Furthermore, it is striking that less common characteristics of Jesus are not shunned. In a few best-selling novels, Jesus is portrayed as the partner of his disciple Mary Magdalene,[1] and in another book it was presumed that Jesus was identical to Julius Caesar.[2] The American psychologist Helen Schucman wrote *A Course in Miracles*, consisting of more than eleven hundred pages which, as she claims, were dictated to her by Jesus.[3] Various other authors wrote similar works with messages

1 Marianne Fredrikson (2003), *According to Mary Magdalene* (English translation by Joan Tate). Charlottesville VA: Hampton Roads; Dan Brown (2003), *The Da Vinci Code*. London: Bantam Press.
2 Francesco Carotta (2005), *Jesus was Caesar: On the Julian Origin of Christianity*. Soesterberg: Aspekt.
3 Helen Schucman (1976), *A Course in Miracles*. Mill Valley: Foundation for Inner Peace.

1

attributed to Jesus.[4] Books such as *The Jesus Sutras*[5] (about Chinese Christianity from the seventh to the eleventh centuries) and *The Muslim Jesus: Sayings and Stories in Islamic Literature*[6] have also appeared. Not only in the Bible and in Christianity is Jesus honoured, but also in the Koran and in later Islamic traditions; there he is seen as an important prophet.

The fact that in the twentieth century important manuscripts dating back to early Christianity have been found has stimulated the interest for and research after the 'historical Jesus' tremendously. In particular, the discovery of the Gospel of Thomas, published in 1959, was sensational. This document contains a collection of sayings attributed to Jesus of which a great deal were unknown in the past. Other sayings are related to the Biblical gospels, but are formulated differently. Some authors think, or at least suggest, that the Gospel of Thomas gives a more reliable image of Jesus' teachings than the Biblical gospels. Because the Gospel of Thomas has often been related to the gnostic movement in early Christianity, the consequence has been drawn that Jesus stood close to the later gnostics. He would have been a teacher who gave insight in the gnosis, i.e. knowledge, of the origin and destiny of mankind. In the gnostic view, the human being has something divine in himself, which originates from the high spheres of the eternal light. What matters in this life, is to obtain insight into the source of one's divine essence so that thanks to this insight, one can return to the high kingdom of light after one's earthly life. In the Gospel of Thomas, Thomas counts as Jesus' disciple par excellence who had more insight into Jesus' secret teachings than the other disciples.[7] Another discovery, made just a few years ago, concerns the Gospel of Judas. Worldwide, this text has been given an exceptional amount of attention. The document was published in translation in 2006. It describes Jesus as a teacher who came to bring secret knowledge about God and mankind, for which most of his disciples were not ready. According to the New Testament gospels, Judas, one of Jesus' disciples, delivered him to his adversaries. In the Gospel of Judas this is also described, but at the same time he prevails as Jesus' most inquisitive disciple, though not an infallible one. Only Judas would have known that Jesus descended from the high reign of Barbelo. Barbelo was a designation of the divine mother who originated from God the Father.[8]

---

4   Roman Heiligenthal (2006), *Der verfälschte Jesus: Eine Kritik moderner Jesusbilder* (3rd edn). Darmstadt: Wissenschaftliche Buchgesellschaft.
5   Martin Palmer (2001), *The Jesus Sutras*. New York: Ballantine Publishing Group.
6   Tarif Khalidi (2001), *The Muslim Jesus: Sayings and Stories in Islamic Literature*. Cambridge MA: Harvard University Press.
7   For literature on the Gospel of Thomas see sections 1.3 and 2.7.
8   For literature on the Gospel of Judas see section 2.9.

In early Christianity the point of view that Jesus had initiated a few of his disciples into a secret gnosis, which the other disciples could not accept, was not generally shared. In what often is considered the mainstream of early Christianity, Jesus was believed to be the Christ and the Son of God who had taught people how to live in accordance with God's will. He had healed many sick people and freed those possessed by evil spirits. He had announced the coming of God's kingdom, but was imprisoned and condemned to an ignominious death on a cross. However, his first followers testified that on the third day after his death he had appeared to them and continued teaching them. Jesus' life, death, resurrection and appearances meant to them that in this way he had realized salvation from sin and death. They expected him to return from heaven and establish the kingdom of God. In the final judgement, which God was to pronounce over the world, those who believed in Jesus and had been baptised, would be saved from perdition.

This view of Jesus was accepted in 'orthodox', 'catholic' Christianity[9] and found its temporary conclusion in the council of Nicaea in 325 CE. Here the belief was confirmed that Jesus Christ as the Son of God also is God, just as the Father through whom he was begotten from eternity. In the same breath, belief in the Holy Spirit was mentioned. This is the dogma of God's trinity, which is well known, even though it is difficult to explain. It is clear that the orthodox and catholic church had a rather different view of Jesus than the gnostics of the first centuries.

1.2 *Jesus considered historically and theologically*

In this book, I want to work out where these various views on Jesus in early Christianity come from and how they can be assessed. Furthermore, I want to make a distinction that is not always considered although it is very important. Even though I realize that one may criticize the terms I choose to use – for lack of better – I want to differentiate between what can be said about Jesus *historically* on the one hand, and what can be said about him *theologically* on the other. With *historically*, I mean that which, after careful study, can be dug up from the oldest written evidence about Jesus. I immediately admit that there is no unanimity about the question as to what, historically speaking, can be established about Jesus. The views vary from utmost sceptical to very optimistic. I will presently return to this matter. What can be said *theologically* about Jesus concerns the question as to what Jesus of Nazareth has to do with God, and what one can possibly believe or think about him, not only in the past but also in the present time.

---

9   For the term 'catholic' see section 1.4.

As this book is about Jesus and God and other heavenly powers, it might as a whole easily be considered a theological book. In theology, various disciplines can be distinguished, such as Biblical studies, church history, systematic theology and practical theology. Considering this, the term 'theology' has a broad meaning. In the contrast between 'historical' and 'theological', however, I use the latter term in a more narrow sense. In this contrast, 'theological' does not indicate the academic study of the sources, history and practice of Christianity, but refers to one's religious preference. Theology (*theologia* in Greek) in the narrow sense concerns the question how we can speak (*logia*) about God (*theos*).

The observation that no unanimity exists about the question as to what, historically speaking, is indisputable about Jesus, raises the question of whether the contrast between 'historical' and 'theological' has any point to it. After all, every author is inevitably inclined towards letting his or her theological or philosophical outlooks play a part in judging 'historical' facts. It is inevitable that someone who studies Jesus and early Christianity is in part led by personal 'theological' preferences. Pure objective historical knowledge does not exist, because this knowledge is always coloured by a subjective element.

This applies not only to contemporary researchers, but also to ancient sources that deal with people and events in antiquity. The authors of the gospels were not neutral historians – these do not really exist – but evangelists. They wanted to report Jesus' life, death and resurrection and, in doing so, spread their view of Jesus and arouse faith in him. This means that the gospels, those not included in the Bible as well, have both an historical and a theological side. The theological side reflects the convictions of the authors. Their theological views can, of course, be historically researched, as they give insight into the way in which the authors and their sympathizers believed in Jesus. Thus there appears to be an overlap between the concepts 'historical' and 'theological' as well. First of all, there is the appearance of the 'historical' Jesus. Secondly, accounts have been made of this that bear witness to the theological convictions of the authors. At the same time – and thirdly – their theological views give insight into the historical development of belief in Jesus: this is the overlap between both concepts. In the fourth place, there is the question what people of our time can theologically say and believe about Jesus.

As already noted, there is no unanimity about the historical reliability of the oldest evidence of Jesus. Rudolf Bultmann, for example, interpreted many of Jesus' sayings in the synoptic gospels of Matthew, Mark and Luke as products of the early church. He supposed that in the first decades of the Christian movement, words of the Christian prophets who had spoken in the name of Jesus, were attributed to the instruction

Jesus gave during his life on earth.[10] In this line of thought, the American *Jesus seminar* concludes that merely a minor part of Jesus' teaching in the New Testament gospels originates from himself.[11] Although criteria have been drawn up for the investigation of the 'historical Jesus', a lot depends upon the way in which they are applied. John P. Meier sums up five criteria which he considers to be the most important.[12] In the first place, he names the criterion of embarrassment. A saying of Jesus that could embarrass the early church, for example that he, as 'the Son', did not know when the end of the world would come (Mark 13:32), has a good chance of originating from Jesus himself. Because the first Christians considered Jesus to be divine, they would never come up with such a saying themselves. Secondly, Meier names the criterion of discontinuity. This means that words of Jesus that do not fit with early Judaism and earliest Christianity – for example, that one may not swear an oath (Matthew 5:34, 37) – really originate from him. Meier points out, however, that this criterion is difficult to apply, as our knowledge of early Judaism and earliest Christianity is limited. Furthermore, Jesus has also surely made many statements that do exactly fit with early Judaism and earliest Christianity. The third criterion is that of multiple attestation. When, independently of each other, various sources contain one and the same tradition they probably go back to Jesus himself. But here Meier also makes a critical note. It is, after all, possible that a tradition arose very early in the church and was hence borrowed by various authors. Fourthly, he names the criterion of coherence. What corresponds with the sayings of Jesus that are recognized as authentic, has a good chance of being trustworthy as well. Meier remarks, however, that the earliest Christians may have created sayings that faithfully echoed Jesus' own 'authentic' words, but did not really originate from him. The fifth criterion is that of Jesus' rejection and execution. Jesus incited opposition, and therefore he was crucified. An image of Jesus too sweet and innocent is no longer about the historical Jesus.

This enumeration proves that Meier has something to say against several of these criteria, which he considers to be the most important. Consequently, it is hard to make a reasonable case for a saying attributed

10 Rudolf Bultmann (1970), *Die Geschichte der synoptischen Tradition* (8th edn). Göttingen: Vandenhoeck & Ruprecht; see the index at 'Gemeinde' (p. 407).
11 Robert W. Funk and Roy W. Hoover (1993), *The Five Gospels: The Search for the Authentic Words of Jesus.* New York etc.: Macmillan; James M. Robinson (2005), *The Gospel of Jesus: In Search of the Original Good News.* San Francisco: HarperSanFrancisco.
12 John P. Meier (1991), *A Marginal Jew: Rethinking the Historical Jesus I. The Roots of the Problem and the Person.* New York etc.: Doubleday, pp. 167–177. He discusses five other criteria on pp. 178–183.

to Jesus as genuinely originating from him against someone taking up a very sceptical position. James D. G. Dunn approaches this question differently. He argues that the gospels demonstrate that, after a period of oral tradition, there was a concern to put down in writing how Jesus was remembered. Speaking strictly historically, we can no longer go back to the person of Jesus himself, because we only have written testimonies of the oldest recollections of him. Dunn is moderately optimistic about the reliability of the core of the oral traditions about Jesus and of their written accounts.[13] Along this line of thought, Richard Bauckham has investigated the function of eyewitnesses in ancient biographies and in the New Testament gospels. Opposed to the trend in New Testament research, he argues that the gospel writers refer to eyewitnesses according to well-known patterns. He maintains that Jesus can only become known thanks to their testimonies and he shares Dunn's opinion that these are relatively reliable.[14] Pope Benedict XVI goes even further. In his book about Jesus, he also starts from the reliability of the New Testament gospels, but omits a weighing of the historical sources. He states that Jesus as described in the New Testament gospels is the true 'historical' Jesus.[15] His book can best be read as a *theological* – but not a historical – study of Jesus' importance.

I personally appreciate Dunn's approach, although undoubtedly criticism can be expressed about his method.[16] In what follows I will show how I assess the various traditions about Jesus historically and theologically. The distinction between a historical and a theological approach towards Jesus entails that one's theological beliefs do not necessarily have to coincide with that which can be made historically acceptable. To make clear how working with this difference functions, I will give four examples.

Historically speaking, it is in every way plausible that Jesus was baptized by one John – named the Baptist – in the river Jordan.[17] An argument for the reliability of this tradition is the embarrassment which it evokes.[18] The authors of the gospels regarded Jesus as God's Son, so

13 James D. G. Dunn (2003), *Jesus Remembered*. Grand Rapids MI, Cambridge: Eerdmans, pp. 335–336.
14 Richard Bauckham (2006), *Jesus and the Eyewitnesses: The Gospels as Eyewitness Testimony*. Grand Rapids MI, Cambridge: Eerdmans, pp. 114–147; 472–508.
15 Joseph Ratzinger Benedict XVI (2007), *Jesus of Nazareth*. New York: Doubleday.
16 Birger Gerhardsson (2005), 'The Secret of the Transmission of the Unwritten Jesus Tradition'. *New Testament Studies*, 51, 1–18.
17 See Matthew 3:13–17, Mark 1:9–11, Luke 3:21–22 and the Gospel of the Ebionites (translation in J. K. Elliott (2005), *The Apocryphal New Testament: A Collection of Apocryphal Christian Literature in an English Translation* (reprint). Oxford: Clarendon Press, p. 15).
18 Meier, *A Marginal Jew*, pp. 168–169.

why should he have to undergo the baptism, which meant that his sins were to be forgiven? Because of this anomaly, the Gospel of Matthew elaborately explains why Jesus had to be baptized. In the Gospel of Luke, Jesus' baptism is scarcely mentioned and in the Gospel of John, it is completely omitted.[19] So there is no good reason to cast doubt on the reliability of this tradition, which seemingly puts Jesus on one line with all others who were baptized. But the sound of a heavenly voice – meaning the voice of God – which said to Jesus, 'You are my Son, the Beloved; with you I am well pleased' or 'You are my Son, today I have begotten you,'[20] falls outside of the normal order. This does not imply that Jesus and John never heard this voice, but it is more of a mystical experience which, in historical aspect, stands less solid than the fact that Jesus was baptised by John. Yet we can establish that according to the gospels, Jesus was designated as God's beloved Son at the beginning of his public appearance. So it is a historical fact, pointing to their *theology*, that the gospel authors, according to an old tradition, considered Jesus as God's Son. But whether Jesus really is the Son of God is a question of belief about which we can only speak theologically. A historian cannot definitely answer this question on grounds of historical arguments, because then he would be exceeding his competence.

A second example: according to the gospels of Mark (10:45) and Matthew (20:28), Jesus said that he came as the Son of Man 'to give his life as a ransom for many'. This testifies to the view that Jesus' death on the cross did not overtake him as a tragic and senseless fate, but served as a sacrifice to God by which 'many' (mankind) would be redeemed and would receive forgiveness of sins.[21] Albert Schweitzer, being a liberal theologian, was decidedly convinced that Jesus really said this, and in my opinion he certainly could have been right about this.[22] Yet, it cannot be ruled out that this statement was put in Jesus' mouth later, after his life on earth. This would imply that this interpretation of Jesus' death originated with his first disciples and was later attributed to Jesus himself. Dunn too, who in general is reasonably positive about the reliability of the Biblical gospels, regards it as probable that the words 'ransom for many' are an elaboration of the core tradition.[23] So, strictly historically speaking, it cannot be determined with certainty that Jesus has said this in such a way; this statement about the meaning of his death might have originated

---

19 Cf. John 1:32–34.
20 Respectively, Mark 1:11 and Luke 3:22 according to manuscripts that may contain Luke's oldest text; see section 2.4.
21 Cf. Mark 14:24; Matthew 26:28.
22 Albert Schweitzer (1977), *Geschichte der Leben-Jesu-Forschung* (reprint). Gütersloh: Gerd Mohn, pp. 442–444 (2nd edn. 1913: Tübingen: Mohr Siebeck).
23 Dunn, *Jesus Remembered*, pp. 812–815.

in earliest Christianity. In theological respect, however, a Christian may
agree with it.

A third example: In our time, many people are appealed by the Gospel
of Thomas. Partly, this is because all sorts of traditional Christian points
of view, such as Jesus' redemptive death as a sacrifice for our sins and his
resurrection from the dead, are absent. The Gospel of Thomas asserts a
claim to Jesus' secret teaching or hints at it.[24] It tells about the heavenly
origin and destination of man, knowledge of one's self and inner renewal.[25]
Jesus is the teacher of wisdom and gnosis. Saying 108 promises that the
one who drinks from his mouth – which means consumes his teaching
– shall become as he is. The intuitive feeling of a reader that the view of this
gospel on Jesus, God and mankind appeals to him or her can be called a
'theological' preference. This preference, however, does not automatically
infer that this teaching attributed to Jesus is historically reliable and thus
goes back to Jesus himself. It may also have been ascribed to him by
Christians who had developed their own outlook on Jesus.

A fourth example: from the gospels of Matthew, Mark and Luke it can
be deduced that Jesus had announced that God's kingdom would dawn
within the near future and that he himself, as God's Son, would come on
the clouds from heaven.[26] That Jesus had indeed aroused this apocalyptic
expectation is confirmed by Paul's first letter to the Thessalonians. This is
probably the earliest letter we have of Paul, dating from about 50 CE. He
suggests that he counts on witnessing these events himself.[27] Therefore it is
quite likely, historically speaking, that Jesus as an apocalyptic preacher has
announced this in such a way. But since the last decades of the first century
CE Christians have been asking themselves if these events would take place
within the near future or if they would ever occur.[28] As a consequence,
in the Gospel of Thomas this kind of apocalyptic expectation cannot be
found. When in this document Jesus speaks about the coming of God's
kingdom, usually something heavenly, mystical or something spread out
over the earth is meant.[29] Even though the expectation that heaven and
earth shall pass by is mentioned a few times in the Gospel of Thomas

---

24 E.g., Gospel of Thomas *heading*; 1; 2; 5; 13.
25 E.g., Gospel of Thomas 3; 22; 29; 49; 50; 67; 84.
26 Matthew 16:28; 24:30; 24:34; 26:64; Mark 9:1; 13:26; 13:30; 14:62; Luke 9:27;
    21:27; 21:32; cf. Acts 1:11.
27 1 Thessalonians 4:15–17; see also Romans 13:11–12; 16:20; 1 Corinthians 7:29;
    15:51–52; James 5:8; Revelation 1:7; 22:20.
28 This is reflected in Matthew 24:49; 25:5; 2 Peter 3:4, and in the decrease of the
    apocalyptic expectation in several later writings of the New Testament, such as the
    epistles to the Ephesians (cf. 1:10; 1:21; 2:7; 4:10), the Colossians (cf. 1:5; 3:4) and the
    Pastoral epistles (cf. 1 Timothy 4:1; 6:15; 2 Timothy 3:1; 4:1; 4:3; Titus 2:13).
29 E.g., Gospel of Thomas 3; 22; 46; 49; 54; 82; 99; 113.

(11, 111), Jesus' announcement of the near coming of God's kingdom and of his own coming on the clouds is not included. This certainly was for a theological reason. The view of the near apocalyptic coming of God's kingdom and of Jesus apparently did not fit in with the image of Jesus that the compiler of this gospel had in mind. But however difficult this element of Jesus' teaching may have been to justify, it really did belong to it in historical aspect, even though it did not come true at that time.

1.3 *Who is Jesus? Reactions of Peter, Matthew and Thomas*

To give an idea of matters that will come up for discussion in this book, here a foretaste of what awaits us is given. As stated earlier, the difference between a 'historical' and a 'theological' approach is not always made. For example, in Elaine Pagels' book *Beyond Belief: The Secret Gospel of Thomas*, published in 2003, she does not pay attention to this difference.[30] She describes how, in the first centuries of our era, various interpretations of Jesus' teachings existed, and how, in the fourth century, with the help of Constantine, the first Christian emperor, the 'orthodox' outlook gained the advantage. A great part of her book is dedicated to the gospels of John and Thomas. She believes on the one hand that the Gospel of John has a lot in common with the Gospel of Thomas, but on the other hand that it was written to oppose the Christians who referred especially to Thomas.[31]

In theory, it is possible indeed that the author of the Gospel of John in part reacted to Christians who particularly orientated themselves to Thomas. This might be the reason why Thomas was described as a sceptic in the Gospel of John (11:16; 14:5). According to this gospel, Thomas was not there when the other disciples were sent out by the risen Jesus and they were given authority to forgive sins or not forgive them (20:19–25). Even though, according to the Gospel of John (20:26–29), Thomas afterwards acknowledged the risen Jesus as 'Lord and God', this gospel could be explained in such a way that Thomas did not deserve to be considered the apostle par excellence. However, according to Raymond Brown, a great authority on the Fourth Gospel, reacting to Thomas Christians was but one of the motives of the Gospel of John and the writer reacted to many more early Christian groups in his environment.[32] Ismo Dunderberg has carefully studied the many and very different theories about the

30 Elaine Pagels (2003), *Beyond Belief: The Secret Gospel of Thomas*. New York: Vintage Books.
31 Pagels, *Beyond Belief*, pp. 33–41; 57–58.
32 Raymond E. Brown (1979), *The Community of the Beloved Disciple: The Life, Loves, and Hates of an Individual Church in New Testament Times*. New York, Mahwah: Paulus Press, pp. 71–88 (85).

relationship between the gospels of John and Thomas. He concludes that these books originated independently of each other.[33] In my opinion, his conclusion deserves support indeed. But even if it were correct that the Gospel of John reacts, among other things, to a group of Thomas Christians, this does not necessarily mean that this group had access to the Gospel of Thomas as it came to light in the twentieth century. We will see that this gospel, in the form and extent in which we know it now, is often secondary to the New Testament gospels. From this it can be deduced that the collection as it is now known has been compiled later than the canonical gospels, supposedly some time in the second century.

Pagels also compares the Gospel of Thomas to the synoptic gospels of Matthew, Mark and Luke. As an example of her method, I will examine her review of an important passage in these gospels, where Jesus asks his closest disciples who people say he is. His disciples answer, 'Some say that you are John the Baptist, others say that you are Elijah, still others say that you are one of the prophets.' Upon which Jesus asked, 'But who do you say that I am?' Peter answered according to the Gospel of Mark, 'You are the Christ.' According to Matthew, Peter's answer was a little longer, 'You are the Christ, the Son of the living God,' and according to Luke, Peter's answer ran, 'The Christ of God.'[34] Starting from the Gospel of Mark, generally considered as the oldest of these three, we can conclude that at the moment of Jesus' question Peter had come to realize that Jesus was the expected Christ or Messiah. In the gospels of Matthew and Luke, in which the Gospel of Mark is included to a large extent, this answer has been enlarged or slightly altered.

Pagels subsequently compares this description of the synoptic gospels with the form this narration took in the Gospel of Thomas 13. There, Jesus' question runs, 'Compare me to someone and tell me whom I resemble.' Peter responds, 'You are like a righteous messenger.' Pagels remarks that this phrase may interpret the Hebrew term Messiah ('anointed one') for the Greek-speaking audience whom Thomas addresses. I think the difference is greater than she suggests, but I will not go further into that now. Then Matthew states, 'You are like a wise philosopher,' which Pagels regards as a term used instead of the Hebrew rabbi, in language any Gentile could understand. Thirdly, Thomas answers, 'Master, my mouth is wholly incapable of saying whom you are like.' Jesus answers to this, 'I am not your master, because you have drunk, and have become drunk from the same stream which I measured out.' According to this

33 Ismo Dunderberg (2006), *The Beloved Disciple in Conflict? Revisiting the Gospels of John and Thomas*. Oxford: Oxford University Press.
34 Matthew 16:13–16; Mark 8:27–29; Luke 9:18–20 ('Christ' may also be translated as 'Messiah').

account, Jesus then took Thomas aside and spoke three words to him. Afterwards, when Thomas' companions asked him what Jesus had said, Thomas said to them:

> If I tell you even one of the things which he told me, you will pick up stones and throw them at me; and a fire will come out of the stones and burn you up.[35]

Pagels explains that, according to this gospel, Jesus reveals things to Thomas that are so mysterious that they cannot be written down, not even in this gospel filled with 'secret sayings'.[36] This means – thus can be inferred – that, according to the Gospel of Thomas, only Thomas is initiated into Jesus' secret teaching. Jesus' other disciples, such as Peter and Matthew, do not know Jesus' actual instruction and could not bear it.

Pagels clearly demonstrates how the version of the Gospel of Thomas differs from those of the synoptic gospels. My objection toward her discussion of this conversation is, however, that she pretends that the version of the Gospel of Thomas can make just as much claim to historical reliability as the synoptic gospels. It is, however, much more probable that the version of the Gospel of Thomas is a polemical reaction to the account which – in three different but much-related versions – occurs in the synoptic gospels.[37] In these three gospels, Peter gives the 'correct' answer, corresponding to the important position attributed to this apostle in early Christianity. That, in contrast to the synoptic gospels, Gospel of Thomas 13 also mentions an answer of Matthew can be interpreted as a reference to the gospel carrying his name. The fact that Matthew in Gospel of Thomas 13 indeed gives an answer, though not the best one, can thus be understood as an implicit criticism of the Gospel of Matthew. We may conclude that the version of Gospel of Thomas 13 comes from

35 Pagels, *Beyond Belief*, pp. 41–47 (47).
36 Pagels, *Beyond Belief*, p. 47. See section 2.7 for the view that the three things – or: words – refer to the name of the LORD, 'I-am who I-am' (Exodus 3:14). In that case Jesus would have revealed himself to Thomas as Yahweh.
37 Cf. Risto Uro (2003), *Thomas: Seeking the Historical Context of the Gospel of Thomas*. London, New York: T&T Clark, p. 92, who concludes that Gospel of Thomas 13 may be described as a 'cultural translation' of a story like the one in Matthew 16:13–20; Larry W. Hurtado (2003), *Lord Jesus Christ: Devotion to Jesus in Earliest Christianity*. Grand Rapids MI, Cambridge: Eerdmans, pp. 461–462, who calls Gospel of Thomas 13 a '*consciously polemical adaptation* of the Synoptic tradition' (italics Hurtado); and Reinhard Nordsieck (2004), *Das Thomasevangelium: Einleitung – Zur Frage des historischen Jesus – Kommentierung aller 114 Logien*. Neukirchen-Vluyn: Neukirchener Verlag, p. 72, who argues that Gospel of Thomas 13 has undeniably been influenced by the oral, but not by the written tradition on Peter's confession.

a community not orientated to Peter or to the Gospel of Matthew, but to the apostle Thomas. This story was rewritten in reaction to the version of the synoptic gospels, and not Peter, let alone Matthew, but Thomas was given a leading part.[38] (To avoid misunderstanding, it must be noted that the Gospel of Thomas was not written by the apostle Thomas himself, but was later compiled by others who affixed his name to it. Also, the title given to the Gospel of Matthew since the second century does not guarantee that the apostle Matthew actually wrote this gospel.)

This explanation obviously raises the question of whether or not the description of the synoptic gospels is historically reliable. After all, it is conceivable that it was thought up afterwards that Peter gave the 'correct' answer in order to justify the important position he occupied in early Christianity. Indeed, in the historical-critical research of the gospels, Bultmann, for example, alleged that this tradition is based on legend.[39]

However, this critical view has also been disputed. As Dunn points out, Mark has precisely noted where this event took place, namely when Jesus and his disciples were on their way to the villages of Caesarea Philippi; these are located north-east of Galilee. Such an exact location is an argument for the reliability of this tradition. Dunn also points to the fact that Peter, shortly after this conversation, was called 'Satan' by Jesus, because he was not setting his mind on divine things but on human things. Jesus said this because Peter wanted to prevent him accepting his forthcoming suffering and death (Mark 8:31–33). It is difficult to imagine that the evangelist just made up this conflict between Jesus and Peter and Jesus' severe rebuke of this important apostle. Again, this is an argument in favour of the view that Peter's confession of who Jesus is goes back to a reliable tradition. Furthermore, Dunn points out that the Gospel of John describes a similar event. After many followers of Jesus in Galilee had turned away from him, he asked his twelve disciples,[40] 'Do you also wish to go away?' Of the twelve, Peter answered, 'Lord, to whom can we go? You have the words of eternal life. We have come to believe and know that you are the Holy One of God' (John 6:67–69). Remarkably enough, according to the oldest, nearly complete manuscript of the Gospel of John (from around 200 CE) Peter's answer is, 'You are *the Christ*, the Holy One of God,' and other manuscripts read, 'You are the Christ, the Son of God' or 'You are the Christ, the Son of the living

---

38 See Bauckham, *Jesus and the Eyewitnesses*, p. 236, for this explanation of Matthew's role in this saying. Aside from being named as author of this gospel, Matthew, after all, plays – as opposed to Peter – no significant role in early Christianity.

39 Bultmann, *Geschichte der synoptischen Tradition*, pp. 275–278.

40 By the way, Pagels, *Beyond Belief*, p. 60, incorrectly writes that the Gospel of John never mentions 'the twelve'. See also John 20:24.

God.' However, we can regard these versions of Peter's confession as adaptations that must harmonize his statement with the other gospels. Still, this proves that in early Christianity already, the event in John 6:67–69 was considered to be the same as the one told in the synoptic gospels. Apart from these, the Gospel of John has also preserved a recollection of this striking conversation. Dunn concludes therefore, that it is very probable that in Mark 8:27–30 we see recalled an episode within Jesus' mission in which the issue of his Messiahship was raised.[41]

However, in her discussion of the various versions of this episode, Pagels completely bypasses the question of historical reliability. Although she does not explicitly state that the version of the Gospel of Thomas is, in historical respect, at least as reliable as the version of the Gospel of Mark, she does suggest this. Her sympathy for the faction that was inspired by the Gospel of Thomas is obviously reflected in her book. Here, her *theological* preference speaks, and she has the right to cherish this preference. Unfortunately, she does not point out that in *historical* respects, the version of the Gospel of Thomas is secondary to the synoptic gospels.[42]

Reinhard Nordsieck remarks in his commentary on the Gospel of Thomas that advancing Thomas is not only secondary in relationship to the confession and position of Peter, but also in relationship to the saying preceding Gospel of Thomas 13. There, it so happens to be James who is introduced as the most important leader of Jesus' disciples. In Gospel of Thomas 12, Jesus' disciples ask him who their leader will be after he will have left them. Jesus' answer reads:

No matter where you came from, you should go to James the Righteous One, for whose sake heaven and earth exist.[43]

'James the Righteous One' certainly is the one who, according to the Acts of the Apostles and the letters of Paul, had a leading position in the

---

41 Dunn, *Jesus Remembered*, pp. 644–645.
42 It regularly turns out that she mainly puts forward from this gospel what appeals to her, e.g., 'Thomas' gospel encourages the hearer not so much to *believe* in Jesus, as John requires, as to *seek to know God* through one's own, divinely given capacity, since all are created in the image of God', and 'that the divine light Jesus embodied is shared by humanity, since we are all made "in the image of God"' (*Beyond Belief*, pp. 34; 40–41; italics Pagels). But she does not emphasize the strangeness of this gospel, which appeals less to Western people; e.g., that relatively few are chosen by God, that they are to lead their lives as solitary individuals and ought to live in celibacy. See section 3.6.
43 Translation April D. DeConick (2007), *The Original Gospel of Thomas in Translation: With a Commentary and New English Translation of the Complete Gospel*. London, New York: T&T Clark, p. 80.

Jewish Christian church of Jerusalem.[44] Thanks to a casual remark of Paul, we know that he was 'the brother of the Lord', which means that he was the brother of Jesus.[45] This is confirmed by the Jewish historian Flavius Josephus, who also states that the high priest Ananus had this James stoned on the accusation of his violating the law of Moses.[46] This execution took place in the year 62 CE. The Gospel of Thomas 12 legitimates the leading position of James in the circle of Jesus' disciples by making Jesus say that when he would have left them, they should go to James, apparently to acknowledge him as their leader. This conversation certainly did not really take place,[47] but it does confirm that James, the brother of Jesus, was an important leader in early Jewish Christianity. In this light, however, it is strange that directly after this, in Gospel of Thomas 13, neither James, nor Peter nor Matthew, but Thomas was introduced as Jesus' most initiated disciple. This brings Nordsieck to the conclusion that Gospel of Thomas 13 originates from a later phase than the traditions in which either James, or Peter, or another apostle was regarded as the most important leader.[48] Therefore, there is no historical ground for the suggestion that we can infer from Gospel of Thomas 13 that Thomas was really initiated by Jesus into a secret knowledge for which the other disciples such as Peter and Matthew were not ready.

1.4 *Outline and explanation*

After this foretaste of what, among other things, will be discussed in this book, here follows an outline of the following chapters. In chapters 2–4, we will examine more elaborately the views on Jesus that appeared in the New Testament and other – often called gnostic – early Christian writings. Chapter 2 is devoted to Jesus' origin and identity, chapter 3 to Jesus' teaching, and chapter 4 to his death, resurrection and exaltation. Since the early Christian literature of the various traditions is too voluminous to discuss as a whole in the book I had in mind, I will only discuss a selection of it. From the New Testament, I will first examine those letters of Paul of which it is generally accepted that they have been written (or, in fact, dictated) by Paul himself.[49] This regards the letter to the Romans, two

---

44 Acts 15:13; 21:18; 1 Corinthians 15:7; Galatians 1:19; 2:9; 2:12.
45 Galatians 1:19; it follows that this James is also mentioned in Matthew 13:55 and Mark 6:3.
46 Flavius Josephus, *Jewish Antiquities* XX, 200 (LCL 456).
47 Thus Nordsieck, *Thomasevangelium*, p. 68.
48 Nordsieck, *Thomasevangelium*, pp. 72–74.
49 On the basis of critical investigation not all of the letters in the New Testament attributed to Paul are recognized as 'authentic'; this means that a number of these

letters to the Corinthians, the letters to the Galatians, to the Philippians, and the first letter to the Thessalonians. The letter to Philemon is generally attributed to Paul as well, but it is of no importance to our topic. Because Paul has little to report about Jesus' teaching, a section about his letters is not included in chapter 3. Further on, I will consider the four New Testament gospels, and in chapter 4 some details from the book of Acts will be reviewed. I will always begin with the Gospel of Mark, because this gospel – as has been noted already – is generally regarded as the oldest of the three synoptics. Because I do not strive for completeness, I will leave fragments of other gospels not included in the New Testament and without a 'gnostic' character out of consideration.[50]

After an evaluation of the New Testament data, I will continue with a selection of gnostic literature, among which I also consider the Gospel of Thomas,[51] and a few testimonies of church fathers about gnostics. I will always comment upon the Gospel of Thomas, the Gospel of Judas and the extensive *Tripartite Tractate* (Nag Hammadi Codex I, 5). Chapters 2 and 4 discuss what Irenaeus of Lyons and Clement of Alexandria have to say about Cerinthus, the Ophites and Theodotus. These gnostics are missing in chapter 3, however, because, in the accounts of their beliefs, the church fathers wrote little of Jesus' teaching. Instead, I will discuss the Gospel of Mary and some other gnostic teachings that Jesus after his death and resurrection was believed to have given. Chapter 4 includes a separate gnostic tradition about Simon of Cyrene. This selection of gnostic – or related – literature is somewhat random. After all, there is no canon of the most authoritative gnostic works. I realize that I have left out many other writings such as the *Apocryphon of John*,[52] but I have not striven for completeness. The selection has also been determined by the popularity of the gospels attributed to Thomas, Judas and Mary. The intention is that these writings, together with the remaining testimonies, are somewhat representative. Chapters 2 to 4 are concluded with a comparison between the New Testament and the other, gnostic writings.

Chapter 5 contains a few preliminary conclusions from the comparison between the New Testament traditions about Jesus and the gnostic

letters have likely or perhaps been written by pupils of Paul in his name. This concerns the letters to the Ephesians, the Colossians, the second letter to the Thessalonians and the letters to Timothy and Titus. Other letters in Paul's name not included in the New Testament are the third letter to the Corinthians, the letter to the Laodiceans and Paul's correspondence with the philosopher Seneca.

50 Such as fragments of 'Jewish Christian' gospels (see section 6.1), other papyrus fragments and the Gospel of Peter (see Elliott, *The Apocryphal New Testament*, pp. 3–25; 31–45; 150–158).

51 See section 3.11.

52 The *Apocryphon of John* was discussed in my book of 1999, *Gnosis and Faith in Early Christianity: An Introduction to Gnosticism*. London: SCM Press, pp. 36–49.

documents. Afterwards, a few new questions are raised for discussion. At that time there also was a 'Jewish Christianity', which the New Testament mentions only indirectly. Chapter 6 deals with the question of what to think of the 'Jewish Christian' view of Jesus, which deviates in many ways from that which can be read about him in the New Testament. And what of the impression, not only conveyed by the New Testament and gnostic documents, but also given by the church fathers, that Jesus shared a secret instruction with just a few of his disciples? This is the theme of chapter 7. The next two chapters lead to the final conclusions. Chapter 8 deals with the Old Testament and early Jewish background of the belief in Jesus as the Son of God, the Word and even as the LORD, Yahweh. Chapter 9 examines the views on Jesus in relation to God the Father, as they were developed in catholic Christianity, up to and including the council of Nicaea. Although in the Nicene Creed not only Jesus Christ but also the Holy Spirit are mentioned in the same breath as God the Father, I will not concern myself here with the position of the Spirit in the dogma of God's trinity. In the decades after this council, intensive thought and dispute have been given to this matter, but this is not the theme of this book. Chapter 10 contains a concluding evaluation of the multiplicity of views on Jesus in the first centuries that were passed in review.

I have hesitated about the question of how I would represent the name of God, in the Hebrew Bible written as YHWH. In many Bible translations this name is rendered as 'LORD'. Although this translation goes back to a very old tradition, it may be criticized since it sounds offensively dominant and masculine. However, the Hebrew consonants YHWH are, printed as such, unpronounceable. Were I to add the vowels and continually write Yahweh, it might perhaps offend those who, in accordance with the Jewish tradition, do not want to pronounce this name. Because in the quotes from the Old Testament found in the New Testament, the name YHWH is represented as the Greek *Kurios*, which means 'Lord', I have after all chosen to record the Hebrew name accordingly, namely as LORD or the LORD, in capital letters. Whenever 'Lord' is written (with one capital and three lower-case letters), it refers to the Greek *Kurios*, and when 'LORD' is written this is a rendering of YHWH. By way of exception, however, I will sometimes note this name in full, with vowels.

For that matter, I just wrote about 'quotes from the Old Testament found in the New Testament', as if the Old Testament was already available as a complete canon in the first century of the Christian era. At that time, however, this was not yet the case.[53] For that time, the designation 'the Old Testament' is an anachronism, but if one does not want continually

---

53 See, e.g., Lee M. McDonald (2007), *The Biblical Canon: Its Origin, Transmission, and Authority*. Peabody MA: Hendrickson, pp. 186–189.

to use long-winded wordings, one cannot do without anachronisms. This is also true for the New Testament of which, originally, no complete canon existed. However, its outlines did become clearer in the second, third and fourth centuries.[54]

Another choice in need of some justification concerns the manner in which I indicate the diverse Christian factions. Because I do not only strive for a theological account, but also, and even in the first place, for a historical description, it is in no case fitting continually to speak of 'the Christian church' and 'the heretics'. In the aspect of the history of religion, Valentinian gnostics, for example, were also Christians, because they appealed to Christ and were baptized in the name of the Father, the Son and the Holy Spirit. It has become common to designate the early 'catholic' ('general') church as 'mainstream Christianity'. But although Celsus, a second-century critic of Christianity, spoke of the 'great Church',[55] little can be said with certainty about the numbers. An objection to the term 'catholic' can be that at first this was not commonly used for the type of Christianity that gradually became to be so called in the course of the second and third centuries.[56] For that matter, neither the designation 'gnostic' was as generally used in the second and third centuries for such traditions as it is nowadays.[57] Because anachronistic designations cannot always be avoided, I will still sometimes speak of 'catholic' Christianity and – as far as it applies – designate the other factions and their writings with the term 'gnostic'.

54 See Riemer Roukema (2004), 'La tradition apostolique et le canon du Nouveau Testament', in A. Hilhorst, ed., *The Apostolic Age in Patristic Thought*. Leiden: Brill, pp. 86–103.
55 In Origen, *Against Celsus* V, 59 (SC 147).
56 J. N. D. Kelly (1972), *Early Christian Creeds* (3rd edn). New York: Longman, pp. 384–386.
57 See Michael A. Williams (1996), *Rethinking 'Gnosticism': An Argument for Dismantling a Dubious Category*. Princeton NJ: Princeton University Press.

CHAPTER 2

Jesus' Origin and Identity

To determine what we can, historically and theologically, say about Jesus, we shall now look more closely at the question of who Jesus was and where he came from. The Gospel of Luke 3:23 states that Jesus was about thirty years old when he was baptized by John the Baptist in the river Jordan. The three synoptic gospels describe that after this took place, he spent time in the wilderness in preparation for the task awaiting him. Afterwards, he began to wander about in Galilee with his message that the kingdom of God was at hand.[1] This probably took place in the year 28 CE.[2]

Regarding the question of who Jesus was and where he came from, much more has been said in early Christianity. We will begin to examine the New Testament, because this includes the oldest testimonies. Afterwards, 'gnostic' and related sources will come up for discussion.

2.1 The letters of Paul

The earliest Christian documents that we have at our disposal are the letters of Paul; in section 1.2 we noted that probably the oldest of these is his first letter to the Thessalonians, generally regarded as dating from around 50 CE. The remaining letters known to be by him date from the 50s of the first century. The letter to the Philippians might be an exception, as it could have been written around 62 CE.

Paul pays exceptionally little attention to the life of Jesus in his letters; he never mentions Jesus' baptism nor the beginning of his appearance.

---

1 Matthew 3:13–4:17; Mark 1:9–15; Luke 3:21–4:15.
2 Gerd Theissen and Annette Merz (1997), *Der historische Jesus: Ein Lehrbuch* (2nd edn). Göttingen: Vandenhoeck & Ruprecht, p. 186.

It is, however, possible to conclude from a few of Paul's texts how he thought about Jesus' origin. In his letter to the Galatians (generally dated around 56 CE[3]) he writes, 'But when the fullness of time had come, God sent his Son, born of a woman, born under the law' (Galatians 4:4). With this text, Paul does not give the impression that he is saying something completely new to the Galatians, because in that case he would have to justify this statement, which he does not do at all. He does not deem it necessary to explain that he is referring to Jesus as the Son sent forth by God, nor from where God has sent his Son. Some scholars understand this expression to mean that God sent forth his Son in the same way that he sent forth Moses and the prophets to the people of Israel;[4] this means that God has given them a special task and it does not say anything about the place from which they have been sent. But because Paul mentions the sending of the Son of God even before he makes mention of his birth, he will certainly have intended that the Son of God was with God before he was sent forth to be born as man.[5] Because Paul undoubtedly shared the Old Testament conception that God lives in heaven,[6] we can conclude that, in his view, God's Son also originated from heaven and that he already was there before he came to earth.[7] The theological term for this is 'pre-existence'. We must note, however, that Paul does not state that God's Son already carried the name of Jesus in heaven (or in his pre-existence). Paul mentions no speculation whatsoever about the nature of Jesus' pre-existence.

Moreover, Paul states in Galatians 4:4 regarding Jesus' origin that he is 'born of woman' and 'under the law'. After having first referred to Jesus' divine origin, he subsequently names his earthly origin. He considers it unnecessary to elucidate Jesus' earthly origin by mentioning, for example, the name of Jesus' mother or his place of birth. Paul's

3 The view that the letter to the Galatians was written in 48 or 49 is less likely; in that case it would not have been addressed to the ethnic Galatians in the north of the Roman province Galatia (in present-day Turkey), but to the inhabitants of the south of this province. For this view, see for example H. N. Ridderbos (1953), *The Epistle of Paul to the Churches of Galatia: The English Text with Introduction, Exposition and Notes.* Grand Rapids MI: Eerdmans, pp. 22–35.

4 Thus James D. G. Dunn (1998), *The Theology of Paul the Apostle.* London, New York: T&T Clark, pp. 277–278, who refers to Exodus 3:12–15; Judges 6:8; Psalm 105:26; Jeremiah 1:7; 7:25, etc.; see also James D. G. Dunn, *Christology in the Making: An Inquiry into the Origins of the Doctrine of Incarnation.* London: SCM Press, pp. 38–44.

5 Cf. Romans 8:3, where Paul writes that God sent his Son in the likeness of sinful flesh; there he uses the verb *pempein*, whereas in Galatians 4:4 he uses *exapostellein*.

6 See, e.g., Psalm 115:16; Ecclesiastes 5:1; Romans 1:18.

7 See, e.g., Franz Mussner (1974), *Der Galaterbrief.* Freiburg: Herder, pp. 271–272; Joachim Gnilka (1994), *Theologie des Neuen Testaments.* Freiburg: Herder, p. 24; Hurtado, *Lord Jesus Christ*, pp. 118–119.

statement that Jesus is born 'under the law', means that he is born in a Jewish environment in which one lived in obedience to the law of Moses. Paul reminds the Galatians of Jesus' birth 'under the law' to point out the purpose of this: in order to redeem those who were under the law, so that we might receive adoption as children (Galatians 4:5). Paul was engaged in a fierce controversy with the Galatians concerning the position of the law of Moses, because, in his opinion, they wrongly wanted to subject themselves to all sorts of requirements of this law. It can be deduced from this letter that after Paul, other (so-called 'Jewish Christian') preachers had tried to persuade the Galatians to live according to the Mosaic law, and apparently with success. A drastic measure was, for example, that they made circumcision compulsory for non-Jewish men in the Christian church. With this letter, Paul wants to convince the non-Jewish Galatians that, if they want to believe in Jesus Christ, the literal maintenance of all kinds of regulations from the law of Moses does not fit in with this. The thoroughness with which he demonstrates this, stands in clear contrast to the conciseness of the formulation with which he, without further explanation or justification, designates Jesus as 'the Son of God' and alludes to God who sent his Son.[8] This proves that in the Galatian congregations, this was not a topic to be brought up for discussion.

A text in Paul's letter to the Philippians (dating from about 54 or 60–62) also testifies to Jesus' origin, but in completely different terms. Many exegetes think that Paul quotes a hymn here, but this opinion is not shared by everyone.[9] Paul admonishes the congregation that the same mind be in them that was in Jesus Christ and describes him thus,

> who, though he was in the form of God,
> did not regard equality with God
> as something to be exploited,
> but emptied himself,
> taking the form of a slave,
> being born in human likeness.
> And being found in human form,
> he humbled himself
> and became obedient to the point of death –
> even death on a cross. (Philippians 2:6–8)

The most probable explanation of this description of Jesus Christ is that he first, in his pre-existence with God, was equal to God, and that he

---

8   See also Galatians 1:16; 2:20.
9   Gordon D. Fee (1995), *Paul's Letter to the Philippians*. Grand Rapids MI: Eerdmans, pp. 39–46; 192–194, is not convinced that Paul quotes an older hymn.

subsequently 'emptied' himself, pointing to his descent from heaven to earth, where he became equal to man, and lived as a servant. To this must be added that this text has also been explained with regard to Jesus' life on earth, where he lived as a second Adam, created in God's image. On this point of view, differing from the first Adam, Jesus did not want to be like God (cf. Genesis 3:5) and humbled himself as a servant.[10] Exegetes such as Gordon D. Fee and Larry W. Hurtado discuss this interpretation, but do not consider it to be plausible. It is indeed more probable that Paul points to Christ's coming from his pre-existence, after which he became equal to man.[11] If this explanation is correct, then it seems that Paul in this letter also assumes Jesus' divine and heavenly origin. If, furthermore, it is correct that Paul here quotes an existing hymn, it can be deduced that, even before Paul wrote his letter, the outlook existed that Jesus originated from God and that he, before his earthly existence, was equal to God.

A third text, in which Paul mentions Jesus' human origin and thereby at the same time designates him as the Son of God, appears in the salutation of his letter to the Romans (dating from 56 or 57 CE). There he writes that the gospel that he proclaims, concerns

> his (namely God's) Son, who was descended from David according to the flesh and was declared to be Son of God in power according to the spirit of holiness by his resurrection from the dead, Jesus Christ our Lord. (Romans 1:3–4)

Because various terms of this passage do not return in any of Paul's letters, exegetes think that he used an older confession here. Given the reference to the lineage of David, the king of Israel, and since 'the spirit of holiness' is a Hebrew formulation that Paul does not use anywhere else in his letters, it is supposed that this confession originates from Jewish Christians in Palestine for whom Hebrew was a familiar language.[12] In this confession it is twice stated that Jesus was God's Son. Differentiation is made between his human origin ('according to the flesh') from the lineage

---

10 Thus Dunn, *Christology in the Making*, pp. 114–121; Dunn, *The Theology of Paul the Apostle*, pp. 281–288. The expression 'in the form of God' would then be equivalent to 'in the image of God' (Genesis 1:26–27).

11 Fee, *Philippians*, pp. 202–203; Hurtado, *Lord Jesus Christ*, pp. 119–123; see also Martin Hengel (1976), *The Son of God: The Origin of Christology and the History of Jewish-Hellenistic Religion*. Philadelphia: Fortress Press, pp. 1–2; Bert Jan Lietaert Peerbolte, 'The Name above all Names (Philippians 2:9)', in George H. van Kooten, ed. (2006), *The Revelation of the Name YHWH to Moses: Perspectives from Judaism, the Pagan Graeco-Roman World, and Early Christianity*. Leiden: Brill, pp. 187–206.

12 See, e.g., Otto Michel (1977), *Der Brief an die Römer* (14th edn). Göttingen: Vandenhoeck & Ruprecht, pp. 72–73.

of David,[13] and his spiritual identity ('according to the spirit of holiness') as the Son of God, who arose form the dead and is dressed with power. Here it is not written, as it is sometimes assumed, that Jesus has become God's Son since his resurrection from the dead, but that he has since then been indicated as 'God's Son *in power*', meaning that he obtained a higher, more powerful position after his resurrection from the dead.[14] In comparison with the two texts of Paul that we previously discussed, it is remarkable that this text does not point to Jesus' pre-existence.

A few other texts from Paul's letters confirm that he himself assumed Jesus Christ to be pre-existent with God the Father before he appeared on earth as a human being. In 1 Corinthians 8:6 he writes,

> yet for us there is one God, the Father, from whom are all things and for whom we exist, and one Lord, Jesus Christ, through whom are all things and through whom we exist.

Of this statement too, it is assumed that Paul quotes a traditional formula.[15] However this may be, if Paul casually writes, without further explanation, that everything came into being through the Lord Jesus Christ, this implies that, in his view, God created the world with the assistance of Jesus Christ, which points to his pre-existence.[16] Furthermore, Paul declares in 1 Corinthians 10:4 that the rock from which the Israelites drank water in the wilderness was Christ himself. Therefore, they drank their 'spiritual drink' from Christ. So Paul assumes that the pre-existent Christ travelled along with the Israelites.[17] In 2 Corinthians 8:9, he writes, in an appeal to give generously to an offertory for the congregation of Jerusalem,

> For you know the generous act of our Lord Jesus Christ, that though he was rich, yet for your sakes he became poor, so that by his poverty you might become rich.

From this text too, we can deduce that Paul points to Jesus' riches when he was with God in heaven, prior to becoming poor by becoming man.[18]

---

13 This tradition also occurs in Matthew 1:1–16; Luke 1:27; 1:32; 2:4; 3:23–31.
14 See, e.g., James D. G. Dunn (1988), *Romans 1–8*. Dallas TX: Word Books, pp. 5–6; 11–16.
15 Wolfgang Schrage (1995), *Der erste Brief an die Korinther (1Kor 6,12–11,16)*. Solothurn, Düsseldorf: Benzinger Verlag, Neukirchen-Vluyn: Neukirchener Verlag, pp. 221–222.
16 Schrage, *Der erste Brief an die Korinther (1Kor 6,12–11,16)*, pp. 243–244; Hurtado, *Lord Jesus Christ*, pp. 123–124.
17 See Exodus 17:6; Numbers 20:7–11, and Schrage, *Der erste Brief an die Korinther (1Kor 6,12–11,16)*, p. 394.
18 See Margaret E. Thrall (2000), *The Second Epistle to the Corinthians II*. London, New York: T&T Clark, pp. 532–534.

This tour through a few of Paul's letters shows in the first place that, without further explanation, Paul could allude to Jesus' heavenly origin as something that, in his view, was not under discussion. Secondly, it shows – and this is confirmed by other texts from his letters[19] – that Paul could designate Jesus as the Son of God without having to explain or defend this as something new. Because his 'undisputed' letters date from the 50s (with perhaps an extension to 62 CE), it follows that the designation of Jesus as the Son of God, historically speaking, goes back to the 40s at least.

In chapter 8 we shall deal with the question of from where this idea of Jesus as the pre-existent Son of God derived. With regard to Jesus' identity, there is however another surprising designation to be found in Paul's letters. It happens several times that Paul quotes an Old Testament text about the LORD (Yahweh) and applies this to Jesus.[20] In Romans 10:13, he cites Joel 2:32, 'Everyone who calls on the name of the Lord shall be saved.' From Romans 10:9, it turns out that by 'the Lord' Paul means Jesus in this context, while Joel means the LORD God. In Romans 14:11, Paul writes, 'As I live, says the Lord, every knee shall bow to me, and every tongue shall give praise to God.' This is a free quotation from Isaiah 45:23, where the prophet speaks in the name of the LORD. However, in Paul's argument, he means Christ when he writes 'Lord' (see Romans 14:8–9). Philippians 2:9–11, which is the second part of the hymn that we encountered before, alludes to the same text from Isaiah 45:23. Here, Paul writes,

Therefore God also highly exalted him
and gave him the name
that is above every name,
so that at the name of Jesus
every knee should bend,
in heaven and on earth and under the earth,
and every tongue should confess
that Jesus Christ is Lord,
to the glory of God the Father. (Philippians 2:9–11)

19 Romans 1:9; 5:10; 8:3; 8:29; 8:32; 1 Corinthians 1:9; 15:28; 2 Corinthians 1:19; 1 Thessalonians 1:10. In the letters in Paul's name that have probably been written by a pupil of Paul, the designation 'the Son (of God)' for Jesus seldom occurs: only in Ephesians 4:13 and Colossians 1:13.
20 See David B. Capes (1992), *Old Testament Yahweh Texts in Paul's Christology*. Tübingen: J. C. B. Mohr.

According to numerous commentaries, 'the name that is above every name' is an allusion to the name Yahweh (or LORD).[21] This is confirmed by the end of this hymn, which says that Jesus Christ is Lord to the glory of God the Father.

Another Old Testament quote in which the Lord is named and which is applied to Jesus, is 1 Corinthians 1:31, 'Let the one who boasts, boast in the Lord,' which refers to Jeremiah 9:22–23 in the Greek translation. David B. Capes declares that in still two other passages Old Testament texts about Yahweh are applied to Jesus. 1 Corinthians 2:16 reads, 'For who has known the mind of the Lord so as to instruct him? But we have the mind of Christ,' and 1 Corinthians 10:26, 'the earth and its fullness are the Lord's.'[22] We must add, however, that other Old Testament quotes in which the LORD is named, are applied by Paul to God 'the Father'.[23] This shows that he is not consistent in his identification of the LORD with Jesus. In our discussion of the gospels, we shall see, however, that this identification, which sometimes occurs in Paul's writings, is not just limited to his letters.

2.2 *The Gospel of Mark*

The Gospel of Mark is generally assumed to have been written in the 60s of the first century or round about the year 70 CE. It is widely accepted to be of later date than the undisputed letters of Paul. This gospel teaches its readers apparently little about Jesus' origin, birth and baptism. It starts with a short description of the ministry of John the Baptist and his announcement of the coming of Jesus; John then speaks about Jesus as someone stronger than he himself, who will baptize with the Holy Spirit (1:1–8). Subsequently, Jesus' baptism by John in the river Jordan is described; afterwards the heavens opened and the Spirit descended upon him as a dove and a voice came from heaven and spoke, 'You are my Son, the Beloved; with you I am well pleased' (1:11). Because the voice from heaven obviously means the voice of God, Jesus is, according to this account, declared to be God's beloved Son at the moment of his baptism. This corresponds with the letters of Paul, insofar as in those Jesus is also called God's Son. The Gospel of Mark offers no opinion on whether Jesus is being regarded as God's Son from that moment and therefore adopted as God's Son at his baptism, or whether he actually was so beforehand.

---

21 See, e.g., Fee, *Philippians*, pp. 221–222.
22 Capes, *Old Testament Yahweh Texts*, pp. 136–149; Cf. Isaiah 40:13; Psalm 24:1.
23 Romans 4:7–8; 9:27–29; 11:34; 15:9–11; 1 Corinthians 3:20; 2 Corinthians 6:18.

Differing from the later Gospels of Matthew and Luke, the Gospel of Mark tells nothing about the circumstances of Jesus' birth. Only in Mark 6:1–3, mention is made of the residents of Jesus' home town, saying of him in surprise, 'Is not this the carpenter, the son of Mary and brother of James and Joses and Judas and Simon, and are not his sisters here with us?' The readers know from Mark 1:9, which tells that Jesus came from Nazareth in Galilee, that Jesus' hometown is Nazareth.[24] It is remarkable that in Mark 6:3 Jesus is called the son of Mary and that his father is neither mentioned here, nor in the rest of the Gospel of Mark. No suggestion is made, however, that there was something special about Jesus' birth.

After Mark's account of Jesus' baptism, he continues with a short record of Jesus' stay in the wilderness and of his preaching of the imminent kingdom of God (1:12–15).

Even though this gospel does not contain specific stories of Jesus' origin, it does give some indications of his very special identity. In addition to the account of Jesus' baptism, Jesus is designated as the Son of God on a few other occasions. However, for this designation we cannot point to Mark 1:1, even though it reads, according to most manuscripts, 'The beginning of the good news of Jesus Christ, the Son of God'. The words 'the Son of God' are not present in all manuscripts, and a comparison of the manuscripts shows us that the version without these words is the most original.[25] Of importance, however, is Mark 3:11, which reads that the unclean spirits cried out to Jesus, 'You are the Son of God', and Mark 5:7, where a possessed man cried out, 'What have you to do with me, Jesus, Son of the Most High God?' These incidents remind the reader of the exclamation of a possessed man in Mark 1:24, 'What have you to do with us, Jesus of Nazareth? Have you come to destroy us? I know who you are, the Holy One of God.'[26] We see that according to the Gospel of Mark the demons knew of Jesus' divine origin and authority.

In the story of Jesus' transfiguration, which tells that Moses and Elijah appeared to him and to three of his disciples, a voice came out of the cloud and spoke, 'This is my Son, the Beloved; listen to him' (9:7). The voice out of the cloud is surely intended as the voice of God, who thus, according to this gospel, confirms what was also said to Jesus at his baptism.

---

24 This is confirmed by Mark 1:24, where a possessed man addresses Jesus as 'Jesus of Nazareth'. This designation also occurs in Mark 10:47; 14:67; 16:6.

25 Bart D. Ehrman (1993), *The Orthodox Corruption of Scripture: The Effect of Early Christological Controversies on the Text of the New Testament*. New York, Oxford: Oxford University Press, pp. 72–75; Bruce M. Metzger (1994), *A Textual Commentary on the Greek New Testament* (2nd edn). Stuttgart: Deutsche Bibelgesellschaft, United Bible Societies, p. 62.

26 For the title 'the Holy One of God' compare John 6:69, where Peter calls Jesus thus; see section 1.3.

According to Mark 13:32, Jesus said about the horrors of the end
of this world and about his own coming, 'But about that day or hour
no one knows, neither the angels in heaven, nor the Son, but only the
Father.' Some exegetes believe that it is hardly conceivable that Jesus
spoke about himself as 'the Son' in the absolute sense. They, therefore,
think that this saying originated from the early church.[27] Others think
that Jesus perhaps did say this, but that he spoke of 'the Son' in the
sense of 'the Son of Man',[28] a term which he, according to this gospel,
regularly used to describe himself (the last time in 13:26), and which
we will examine further. The objection to the latter opinion is that 'the
Son' is found nowhere else as a shortened form of 'the Son of Man',
and that 'the Son' in Mark 13:32 is named in contrast to 'the Father',
meaning God the Father, of course.[29] On this basis, it is more probable
that 'the Son' is a shortened designation of 'the Son of God (the Father)'.
There are also exegetes who believe that Jesus really did say this, because
it is unthinkable that the first church attributed to Jesus, whom they
worshipped as divine, ignorance about the last day.[30] Yet it is very well
possible that the first Christians, even though they worshipped Jesus as
divine, regarded him subordinate to God the Father, so that he did not
have all of the knowledge of the Father at his disposal.[31] By this approach
too, Jesus could have made this statement. However this may be, this
verse in the Gospel of Mark is a confirmation of the view that Jesus was
'the Son', which apparently means 'the Son of God'.

When Jesus was captured and subsequently interrogated by the high
priest, he was asked, 'Are you the Messiah, the Son of the Blessed One?'
(14:61). 'The Blessed One' is a Jewish designation of God and because,
according to this account, the high priest uses this term here, it means he
is reacting to the rumour that Jesus as Messiah was also the Son of God.
In his answer, Jesus confirms this by saying, 'I am' (14:62), a statement

---

27 E.g., Joachim Gnilka (1999), *Das Evangelium nach Markus (Mk 8,27–16,20)* (5th edn).
    Zürich, Düsseldorf: Benzinger Verlag, Neukirchen-Vluyn: Neukirchener Verlag, p. 207.

28 E.g., Rudolf Pesch (1977), *Das Markusevangelium 2*. Freiburg: Herder, p. 310.

29 This absolute use of 'the Son' in relation to God the Father by Jesus also occurs in
    Matthew 11:27 and Luke 10:22. For this, see section 2.3.

30 Vincent Taylor (1959), *The Gospel According to St. Mark*. London: MacMillan &
    Co, p. 522; B. M. F. van Iersel (1961), *'Der Sohn' in den synoptischen Jesusworten:
    Christusbezeichnung der Gemeinde oder Selbstbezeichnung Jesu?*. Leiden: Brill, pp. 117–
    123; Meier, *A Marginal Jew* I, 169; Craig A. Evans (2001), *Mark 8:27–16:20*. Nashville
    TN: Word Books, p. 336. Cf. also section 1.2.

31 Compare for this 1 Corinthians 15:23–28, from which it is apparent that Christ is
    subordinate to God the Father and that the moment in which all enemies will be
    subjected to Christ and the end will come is not settled, but depends on the battle yet to
    be fought.

to which we will get back further on in this section and in the discussion of the Gospel of John.

Finally, it is recorded that a centurion of the Roman army, when he saw how Jesus on the cross breathed his last, exclaimed, 'Truly this man was God's Son!'(15:39). The expression used in Greek can also be translated as 'this man was a son of God' or 'the son of a god'. Yet, in the context of the Gospel of Mark, this statement is clearly intended as an allusion to all the other texts where Jesus was called the Son of God.

So we see that this gospel repeatedly presents Jesus as the Son of God. We will consider the background and meaning of this title in chapter 8. First, we will return to the title 'Son of Man' (literally: 'the son of the human being'), which Jesus regularly uses in this gospel to indicate himself. In various statements, he refers to himself in this way when he announces his suffering, dying and resurrection,[32] but he also says that the Son of Man has authority to forgive sins and that he is lord of the Sabbath (2:10, 28). Moreover, according to this gospel, Jesus says that the Son of Man will be ashamed of whoever is ashamed of him and his words when he comes in the glory of his Father with the holy angels (8:38). Just as in a few other verses (13:26, 14:62), Jesus speaks of his coming (in the sense of 'second coming') as the Son of Man from heaven. To be sure, it is possible simply to interpret the title 'Son of Man' as 'human being', as in Psalm 8:4, which reads, 'What is man, that thou art mindful of him? and the son of man, that thou visitest him?' (KJV).[33] Another possibility is to connect this designation with the heavenly figure of whom Daniel says, 'As I watched in the night visions, I saw one like a human being [the Son of man, KJV] coming with the clouds of heaven' (Daniel 7:13). In the Book of Parables, that is the Second vision of the first book of Enoch, this figure regularly appears as a heavenly being residing directly under God ('the Lord of the spirits'), and ruling in heaven from his throne.[34]

---

32 Mark 8:31; 9:9, 12, 31; 10:33, 45; 14:21, 41.

33 See, e.g., Hurtado, *Lord Jesus Christ*, pp. 290–306. Joseph A. Fitzmyer (1979), *A Wandering Aramean: Collected Aramaic Essays*. Missoula: Scholars Press, pp. 143–160 concludes that it is not apparent from contemporaneous Aramaic texts that at that time the term 'son of man' was a special title.

34 1 Enoch 46:3–4; 48:2; 62:5, 7, 9, 14; 63:11; 69:29; 70:1; 71:17 (in 60:10 and 71:14 Enoch is addressed as 'Son of Man'). The parables of the book of Enoch have only been passed down in Ethiopic (OTP 1). Given that no Aramaic fragments of this have been found in Qumran and on the basis of the alleged historical context, J. C. Hindley (1967–68), 'Towards a date for the Similitudes of Enoch: An Historical Approach', *New Testament Studies* 14, 551–565, argued that they have been written at the beginning of the second century CE. J. T. Milik (1976), *The Books of Enoch: Aramaic Fragments of Qumrân Cave 4*. Oxford: Clarendon Press, pp. 91–96, dated the Parables to around 270

Because in the Gospel of Mark Jesus refers to himself in similar terms as
the Son of Man from heaven, it is almost impossible not to connect these
statements to this heavenly figure from the first book of Enoch.[35] This
implies that the term Son of Man points to Jesus' heavenly identity.

After this examination of the designations Son of God and Son of
Man, we will once more go through the Gospel of Mark to point to a few
other texts which allude to Jesus' special origin and identity.

From the beginning of this gospel, a special light is shed upon Jesus.
Mark 1:2–3 holds a combined quote from Exodus 23:20, Malachi 3:1
and Isaiah 40:3, 'See, I am sending my messenger ahead of you, who will
prepare your way; the voice of one crying out in the wilderness: "Prepare
the way of the Lord, make his paths straight".' In the context of Exodus
and Malachi, it is God the LORD speaking here. In the Gospel of Mark,
these words have been so understood to mean that God sent his messenger
John the Baptist ahead of Jesus to prepare his way. While it is written
in Malachi 3:1, 'See, I am sending my messenger to prepare the way
before *me*' – and this 'me' refers to the LORD – Mark 1:2 reads, 'who will
prepare *your* way', which refers to Jesus. The same application to Jesus
of a text about the LORD is seen in the following quotation from Isaiah
40:3 in Mark 1:3. The 'voice' alludes to the voice of John the Baptist,
whose mission was to 'prepare the way of the Lord' and 'make his paths
straight'. Where Isaiah 40:3 speaks of 'the way of the LORD' and of 'the
paths of our God', these words, in the context of Mark, point to the way
and paths of Jesus. So, from the very beginning of this gospel, Jesus is
implicitly identified with God the LORD.[36]

CE or slightly later. If one of these datings is correct, then the term 'Son of Man' in these
Parables can not be used as an explanation for this title in the New Testament gospels.
Matthew Black (1985), *The Book of Enoch or I Enoch: A New English Edition*. Leiden:
Brill, pp. 181–189, however, states that the Parables do date back to before 70 CE, just as
E. Isaac, in James H. Charlesworth, ed. (1983), *The Old Testament Pseudepigrapha* 1.
London: Darton, Longman & Todd, p. 7. The translation 'Son of Man' conveys different
Ethiopic expressions. See the notes in the translation of Isaac in Charlesworth, ed., *The
Old Testament Pseudepigrapha* I, 34–50; also C. Colpe (1972), '*ho huios tou anthrôpou*'
B III 2a, in Gerhard Friedrich and Geoffrey W. Bromiley, eds, *Theological Dictionary of
the New Testament* 8. Grand Rapids MI: Eerdmans, pp. 423–427, and Black, *The Book
of Enoch or I Enoch*, pp. 206–207, who elucidates that all Ethiopic expressions stem
from the same original Hebrew or Aramaic term 'Son of Man'.

35 See Simon J. Gathercole (2006), *The Preexistent Son: Recovering the Christologies of
Matthew, Mark, and Luke*. Grand Rapids MI, Cambridge: Eerdmans, pp. 253–271.

36 See Rudolf Pesch (1976), *Das Markusevangelium* 1. Freiburg: Herder, pp. 77–78; Robert
A. Guelich (1989), *Mark 1–8:26*. Dallas TX: Word Books, p. 11; Joachim Gnilka (1998),
Das Evangelium nach Markus (Mk 1–8,26) (5th edn). Zürich, Düsseldorf: Benzinger
Verlag, Neukirchen-Vluyn: Neukirchener Verlag, pp. 44–45.

In Mark 1:8, John the Baptist states that Jesus will baptize with the Holy Spirit. For the prophets of the Old Testament, it is the LORD who will give his Spirit.[37] This means that Jesus will assume the role of the LORD.

Mark 2:1–12 tells of Jesus saying to a lame man laid in front of him, 'Son, your sins are forgiven' (2:5). The scribes who heard this, considered it blasphemy, because only God can forgive sins. Jesus, perceiving their objection, said to them, 'Which is easier, to say to the paralytic, "Your sins are forgiven", or to say, "Stand up and take your mat and walk?" But so that you may know that the Son of Man has authority on earth to forgive sins' – he said to the paralitic – 'I say to you, stand up, take your mat and go to your home' (2:9–11) – which the paralytic subsequently did. Since the traditional view of the scribes that only God can forgive sins[38] is not contradicted here, and Jesus as the Son of Man forgives the lame man his sins, it can be concluded that, according to this story, Jesus has divine authority and therefore acts on behalf of God.[39]

Mark 4:37–41 describes that Jesus is on a boat in the Sea of Galilee where he, to the amazement of his disciples, rebukes a heavy storm. Their question, 'Who then is this, that even the wind and the sea obey him?' (4:41) is not explicitly answered in this story. In the composition of this gospel, however, the answer is given by a possessed man in the land of the Gerasenes, who shortly thereafter addresses him as 'Jesus, Son of the Most High God' (5:7). From the perspective of the Old Testament, it is God (or the LORD) who stills turbulent waters.[40] Thus the evangelist suggests that Jesus is clothed with the power of God.

Mark 6:47–51 once more declares that Jesus is more powerful than the wind and the sea. The story reads that during the night he walked on the water towards his disciples, while they were rowing against the wind. In the Old Testament, it is God who tramples the waves.[41] Furthermore, two other allusions to the Old Testament suggest that Jesus is described as the LORD in this story. It was his intention 'to pass by' his disciples (6:48). In the Old Testament, it is said of the LORD that he passes by Moses and Elijah,[42] which refers to his appearing to them. Moreover, Jesus answers his disciples by saying, 'Take heart, it is I [*egô eimi*; literally: "I am"]; do not be afraid' (6:50). In the Old Testament, it is often the LORD who says in the same words, 'It is me (or I am with you), fear not.'[43] Especially in

---

37 Isaiah 44:3; Ezekiel 36:25–27; Joel 2:28–29.
38 E.g., Exodus 34:6–7; Psalm 103:3, 10–12; 130:3–4; Isaiah 43:25; 44:22; Daniel 9:9.
39 Cf. Gnilka, *Das Evangelium nach Markus (Mk 1–8,26)*, p. 101.
40 E.g., Psalm 65:7–8; 77:17; 89:10; 93:3–4; 107:29.
41 E.g., Job 9:8; Psalm 77:20, and the references of the previous note.
42 Exodus 33:19–22; 34:6; 1 Kings 19:11.
43 Genesis 26:24 LXX (LXX = Septuagint); 46:3 LXX; Isaiah 41:10 LXX; Jeremiah 1:8 LXX; 1:17 LXX; 26:28 LXX / 46:28 MT (Masoretic text); 49:11 LXX / 42:11 MT.

the Greek translation of the book of Isaiah, the words 'I am' are spoken several times by the LORD.[44] These words also recall the name of the LORD in Exodus 3:14, 'I am who I am,' reproduced in the Greek translation as 'I am the One Who Is.' As stated earlier, in our discussion of the Gospel of John we will further examine the meaning of the words 'I am' coming from Jesus' lips.

The story of Jesus' entry in Jerusalem (11:1–11) is also of importance. At first it is ambiguous if Jesus' statement about the colt, 'the Lord needs it' (11:3), refers to himself, to God or to the owner of the colt. However, when he rides into Jerusalem, he is greeted with the words of Psalm 118:26, which read, 'Hosanna! Blessed is the one who comes in the name of the Lord!' (11:9). This implies that this story closely associates him with the LORD.

The Gospel of Mark gives another concealed indication of Jesus' extraordinary origin, just before the end of its description of Jesus' public appearance (12:35–37). Jesus poses the question how the scribes could say that the Messiah is a son of David. David himself, inspired by the Holy Spirit, declared, 'The Lord said to my Lord, "Sit at my right hand, until I put your enemies under your feet"' (12:36; Psalm 110:1). Jesus then asks how it is possible that David called the Messiah Lord, while the Messiah is at the same time David's son. To these mysterious words neither reaction, nor explanation follows. Yet, the hidden purport is clear enough.[45] By now, the readers of this gospel know that Jesus is the Messiah.[46] It follows that he spoke about himself and about his future exaltation to God's right hand, in a concealed manner. In his view, David had already prophesized this. This teaching meant therefore, that Jesus, as Messiah, surpassed David so that David called him 'my Lord', even though Jesus was descended from David. The question is, however, how Jesus surpassed David. Did this – considered from David's point of view – relate only to the future, as Jesus' exaltation unto the right hand of God still lay in the future?[47] Or did Jesus – or the Gospel of Mark – suggest that David, when he composed the psalm, called the Messiah 'my Lord', because he acknowledged him as such, even though his exaltation was still to come? In that case, the Messiah precedes David in time and this gospel suggests in enigmatic language that the origin of Jesus

44 Isaiah 43:10, 25; 45:18–19, 22; 46:4; 48:12, 17; 51:12; 52:6.
45 Riemer Roukema (2006), 'De Messias aan Gods rechterhand', in G. C. den Hertog, S. Schoon, eds, *Messianisme en eindtijdverwachting bij joden en christenen*. Zoetermeer: Boekencentrum, pp. 92–107 (92–95).
46 See Mark 1:1; 8:29 and section 1.3.
47 Thus Joachim Jeremias (1971), *Neutestamentliche Theologie* I. Gütersloh: Gerd Mohn, p. 247.

as Messiah should not be looked for in his birth, but in days long gone.[48] In that case this passage would be an important but concealed testimony of Jesus' pre-existence. I indeed think that this text has to be explained in this way. For this point of view, it is of little importance whether Jesus himself really said this in these words. However, I do think that the exegetes who plead for the authenticity of this instruction could be right.[49]

If it is correct that in the Gospel of Mark Jesus is described as the LORD, who apparently already existed before he came to earth as a human being, then the texts speaking of Jesus' 'coming' deserve special attention. Thus the demons said to him in Mark 1:24, 'Have you come (*êlthes*) to destroy us?' It is possible to apply this 'coming' to Mark 1:14, where the same Greek verb (*êlthen*) is used to state that Jesus came to Galilee. It is also possible that Jesus' 'coming' refers to his previous heavenly existence, just as in other writings the angels say that they have come, for example to a human being on earth.[50] In addition, when Jesus says about the proclamation of his message, 'for that is what I came out to do (*exêlthon*)' (1:38), this can be interpreted in this sense, although a more down to earth explanation is not excluded.[51] The same goes for Jesus' sayings, 'I have come not to call the righteous, but the sinners' (2:17) and 'but the Son of Man came not to be served but to serve' (10:45).[52]

48 Thus, e.g., Oscar Cullmann (1957), *Die Christologie des Neuen Testaments*. Tübingen: J. C. B. Mohr, p. 133; Pierre Bonnard (1963), *L'Évangile selon Saint Matthieu*. Neuchâtel: Delachaux et Niestlé, pp. 330–331; Julius Schniewind (1968), *Das Evangelium nach Matthäus*. Göttingen: Vandenhoeck & Ruprecht, p. 223; William L. Lane (1974), *The Gospel According to Mark: The English Text with Introduction, Exposition and Notes*. London: Marshall, Morgan & Scott, p. 438; Joseph A. Fitzmyer (1985), *The Gospel According to Luke (X–XXIV)*. New York: Doubleday, p. 1312.

49 Roukema, 'De Messias aan Gods rechterhand', pp. 92–95; Taylor, *The Gospel According to St. Mark*, pp. 490–493; Ernst Lohmeyer (1967), *Das Evangelium des Markus* (17th edn). Göttingen: Vandenhoeck & Ruprecht, pp. 261–263; David M. Hay (1973), *Glory at the Right Hand: Psalm 110 in Early Christianity*. Nashville TN: Abingdon Press, pp. 110–111; Pesch, *Das Markusevangelium 2*, p. 254; Michel Gourgues (1978), *A la droite de Dieu: Résurrection de Jésus et actualisation du Psaume 110:1 dans le Nouveau Testament*. Paris: Gabalda, p. 142; Fitzmyer, *The Gospel According to Luke (X–XXIV)*, pp. 1309–1313.

50 Sevenster, *De Christologie van het Nieuwe Testament*, pp. 103–104; Gathercole, *The Preexistent Son*, pp. 53; 84; 101; 113–147; 150–152, etc. I consider James D. G. Dunn's criticism of Gathercole's interpretations exaggerated. (http://www.bookreviews.org/pdf/5607_6160.pdf, consulted 1 May 2007). Dunn however, would not even hear of Jesus' pre-existence in Paul (see the previous section), so his criticism was to be expected.

51 Thus Ernst Lohmeyer (1967), *Das Evangelium des Markus* (17th edn). Göttingen: Vandenhoeck & Ruprecht, p. 43; Walter Schmithals (1979), *Das Evangelium nach Markus Kapitel 1–9,1*. Gütersloh: Mohn, Würzburg: Echter Verlag, p. 134.

52 Sevenster, *De Christologie van het Nieuwe Testament*, p. 103; Gathercole, *The Preexistent Son*, pp. 154–158; 167–168.

In this discussion of the Gospel of Mark, I have not always examined
the question of whether a saying or act of Jesus is really authentic. For
many stories, this cannot be determined any more, and from a historical-
critical point of view it is often considered doubtful. For this investigation,
however, the answer to this question is not of vital importance. What
matters is how the author of the Gospel of Mark portrayed Jesus
'theologically'. We have seen that he traces Jesus' origin, in his capacity
of Messiah, to the time before David. Jesus is regularly called Son of
God and he calls himself the Son of Man. It is told that he forgives sins
with divine authority and that he rebukes the turbulent sea. A few Old
Testament quotations closely associate Jesus with the LORD. On a few
occasions he said, 'It is I,' which alludes to the name of the LORD. The
texts in which his 'coming' are mentioned, can be explained as references
to his heavenly origin. It is obvious that in this gospel, Jesus is not merely
characterized as a very special man, although he most certainly was.

2.3 The Gospel of Matthew

As has already been remarked in section 1.3, a large part of the Gospel
of Mark, often in a slightly different form, is echoed in the Gospel
of Matthew; it is generally accepted that the author of the Gospel of
Matthew assimilated the Gospel of Mark in his own book about Jesus.
The Gospel of Matthew is generally dated around 80–90 CE.[53] All sorts of
passages about Jesus' origin and identity examined in the previous section
are included in this gospel too. This means that here also, Jesus sees the
Holy Spirit descend upon him at his baptism and is called 'my beloved
Son' by a voice from heaven (3:16–17). Also elsewhere in this gospel he is
repeatedly described as the Son of God; sometimes, compared to the text
of Mark, this title has even been added to the story.[54] Jesus regularly calls
himself the Son of Man and speaks even more often than in the Gospel
of Mark about the purpose for which he has come.[55] In this gospel too,
Jesus teaches that the Messiah is David's Lord and therefore it suggests
that in time he precedes David (22:41–46).

---

53 Ulrich Luz (2002), *Das Evangelium nach Matthäus (Mt 1–7)* (5th edn). Düsseldorf,
    Zürich: Benzinger Verlag, Neukirchen-Vluyn: Neukirchener Verlag, pp. 103–104.
54 Thus in Matthew 14:33, where Jesus' disciples in the boat, after he has walked on the sea
    towards them, and the wind had died down, say, 'Truly you are the Son of God'; and in
    Matthew 16:16, where Peter says, 'You are the Messiah, the Son of the living God.'
55 Sayings on his 'coming' which are not written in Mark do appear in Matthew 5:17;
    10:34–35.

Using the Gospel of Mark as his starting point, Matthew has added other stories and sayings of Jesus. In the first place, it is striking that the Gospel of Matthew contains some stories about Jesus' origin, birth and earliest childhood. Over forty-two generations his genealogy is traced back to David and Abraham. Furthermore, it is mentioned that Joseph, penultimate on the list, was the husband of Mary who gave birth to Jesus, called the Christ (1:1–17). Directly following this, it is made clear why it is not written that Joseph fathered Jesus by Mary; an angel explains to Joseph that the child conceived in her is from the Holy Spirit. The evangelist sees in this the fulfilment of a prophecy of Isaiah (1:18–23; Isaiah 7:14). This implies that, according to this gospel, Jesus is conceived by the Holy Spirit and born of Mary while she was yet a virgin. This story of his miraculous birth testifies to the extraordinary intervention of God and therefore of Jesus' exceptional origin and identity. Although one might expect that someone who is said to be conceived by God's Holy Spirit is, for this reason, called 'Son of God', this explanation is not explicitly given in this gospel. Yet it is true that as a small child Jesus was already called 'my Son' by God, when it is told that he returns with his parents from Egypt to Israel. The evangelist regards this as a fulfilment of the prophecy: 'Out of Egypt I have called my Son' (2:15; Hosea 11:1).[56] Furthermore, the fact that Jesus was called Emmanuel, which means 'God with us' (1:23), testifies to his exceptional identity.

The Gospel of Matthew describes much more emphatically than the Gospel of Mark that Jesus came as the shepherd to look for the lost sheep of Israel and to have mercy on those who have no shepherd.[57] Young S. Chae makes a reasonable case for the evangelist seeing in this a fulfilment of the prophecy of Ezekiel that the LORD himself will search for his sheep and as a shepherd look for his flock (Ezekiel 34:11–16). In this gospel Jesus predicts that he, as the coming Son of Man, will separate the sheep from the goats (25:31–46). This image refers to Ezekiel 34:17–22, which reads that the LORD will judge between the sheep, the rams and the he-goats. Chae concludes that in Matthew Jesus not only obtains the characteristics of David, whom God, according to Ezekiel 34:23, will appoint over his flock, but that he is also described as shepherd in terms of the LORD himself.[58]

---

56 In Hosea 11:1 the people of Israel are originally meant by 'my son'.
57 Matthew 2:6; 9:36; 10:6, 16; 15:24; 25:31–46; 26:31; cf. Mark 6:34; 14:27.
58 Young S. Chae (2006), *Jesus as the Eschatological Davidic Shepherd: Studies in the Old Testament, Second Temple Judaism, and in the Gospel of Matthew*. Tübingen: J. C. B. Mohr, pp. 173; 205–233; 387–395. For the LORD as shepherd see also, e.g., Psalm 23:1-4; 74:1; 78:52; 79:13; 80:1; Isaiah 40:11; Jeremiah 23:1–5; 31:10; 50:19; Micah 2:12; 4:6–7.

Furthermore, Matthew has some passages in common with the Gospel of Luke, which do not, or not in the same form, appear in the Gospel of Mark. Exegetes presume that in those cases Matthew and Luke go back to an older source, named Q.[59] In this source also, Jesus is named 'the Son of God' and he speaks of himself as the Son of Man. In the story of Jesus' temptation in the wilderness, the devil says to him: 'If you are the Son of God ....'[60] In another passage Jesus praises God in the following words,

> I thank you, Father, Lord of heaven and earth,
> because you have hidden these things from the wise and the intelligent
> and have revealed them to infants;
> yes, Father, for such was your gracious will.
> All things have been handed over to me by my Father;
> and no one knows the Son except the Father,
> and no one knows the Father except the Son
> and anyone to whom the Son chooses to reveal him.[61]

In these words Jesus designates himself as 'the Son'. He indicates that he and God the Father know each other in a unique, intimate way and that only he as the Son is able to share the knowledge of God his Father with others.[62] Therefore, the high position Jesus occupies according to Q and according to the Gospel of Matthew (and also that of Luke) is evident.

A few remarkable sayings of Jesus, originating from Q, occur at the end of a scathing speech to the Pharisees. According to this gospel, Jesus first says here,

> Therefore I send you prophets, sages, and scribes,
> some of whom you will kill and crucify,
> and some you will flog in your synagogues
> and pursue from town to town. (23:34)

Here Jesus is speaking with divine authority, as it were, since according to this text he is responsible for sending prophets, sages and scribes to the people of Israel.[63] These and the following words (23:35–36) have

---

59 J. M. Robinson, P. Hoffmann, J. S. Kloppenborg, eds (2000), *The Critical Edition of Q: Synopsis including the Gospels of Matthew and Luke, Mark and Thomas with English, German, and French Translations of Q and Thomas*. Leuven: Peeters, Minneapolis: Fortress.

60 Matthew 4:3, 5; Luke 4:3, 9.

61 Matthew 11:25–27; cf. Luke 10:21–22.

62 Cf. the absolute use of 'the Son' in Matthew 24:36 and Mark 13:32 (see section 2.2).

63 Cf., e.g., Jeremiah 35:15; 2 Chronicles 24:19; 36:15–16, where it is the LORD who sends his prophets.

a parallel in Luke 11:49–51, but there Jesus states that God's Wisdom has spoken thus. In Matthew 23:34, the reference to the figure of God's Wisdom[64] is absent and Jesus speaks in his own name. In this way, the evangelist identifies him as the incarnation of God's Wisdom.

Subsequently, Jesus says:

> Jerusalem, Jerusalem, the city that kills the prophets and stones those who are sent to it! How often have I desired to gather your children together as a hen gathers her brood under her wings, and you were not willing. (23:37)

These words explicitly addressed to Jerusalem, are surprising in the context of this gospel, because it does not say that Jesus has been to Jerusalem previously. Yet he says to the city, 'How often have I desired to gather your children together.'[65] The evangelist, therefore, has Jesus say something that we can expect from the mouth of a prophet on behalf of God, who by the voice of his prophets has so often addressed Jerusalem. Jesus says this however – according to this gospel – not after the prophetic introduction, 'Thus says the Lord,' but in his own name. Therefore, he speaks as if he were the LORD, or at least the Wisdom of the LORD himself.[66]

---

64 See, e.g., Proverbs 1:20–33; 8:1–9:18; Ecclesiasticus 24:1–22; Enoch 42 and chapter 8 in this book; also Gathercole, *The Preexistent Son*, pp. 199–201.

65 More or less the same is true of the parallel in Luke 13:34; Jesus had only been to Jerusalem as a newborn baby and a twelve-year-old according to Luke (Luke 2:22–52). According to the Gospel of John, Jesus had been to Jerusalem more often during his public appearance (John 2:13; 5:1; 7:10; 12:12).

66 Ulrich Luz (1997), *Das Evangelium nach Matthäus (Mt 18–25)*. Zürich, Düsseldorf: Benzinger Verlag, Neukirchen-Vluyn: Neukirchener Verlag, p. 380, assumes that Matthew 23:37–39 originated from an early Christian prophet who spoke in the name of the exalted Lord Jesus. Sherman E. Johnson, George A. Buttrick (1951), 'The Gospel According to Matthew', in George A. Buttrick et al., eds, *The Interpreter's Bible* VII. New York, Nashville TN, pp. 229–625 (540) and M. Eugene Boring (1995), 'The Gospel of Matthew: Introduction, Commentary, and Reflections', in Leander E. Keck et al., eds, *The New Interpreter's Bible* VIII, Nashville TN, pp. 87–505 (438) refer here to Jesus as the incarnation of God's Wisdom. Gathercole, *The Preexistent Son*, pp. 210–221 also explains Matthew 23:37 as a reference to Jesus' attempts to bring together Jerusalem before he became a human being.

2.4 *The Gospel of Luke*

Like the Gospel of Matthew, the Gospel of Luke is also often dated about 80–90 CE.[67] Because this gospel has many passages in common with Mark and Matthew, it corresponds to a large degree with these gospels regarding Jesus' origin and identity. In this gospel too, Jesus is described as the Son of Man, as the Son of God and as the Messiah who is David's Lord (20:41–44).

Characteristic for the Gospel of Luke are, among other things, the stories about Jesus' birth. In contrast to the Gospel of Matthew, an angel here announces not to Joseph but to Mary that she is to conceive by the Holy Spirit. The angel, named Gabriel, instructs her to give her son the name Jesus. He announces that Jesus will be called the 'Son of the Most High' and 'Son of God', and that God will give him the throne of his father David. Jesus will reign over the house of Jacob for ever and there will be no end of his kingdom, says Gabriel according to Luke (1:26–34). To be sure, the view that Jesus is conceived by the Holy Spirit and born of the Virgin Mary is shared by the Gospel of Luke and the Gospel of Matthew, but we see that the stories are told very differently. In contrast with the Gospel of Matthew, the Gospel of Luke does show a relationship between Jesus' conception by the Holy Spirit and his designation as 'Son of God'. In this way the Gospel of Luke wants to point to Jesus' divine origin and identity.

This is also evident when the angel Gabriel tells ageing Zechariah about his son John (the Baptist), saying that he will prepare the way for the Lord (1:17). Later, Zechariah uses these words when he says of his newborn son, 'And you, child, will be called the prophet of the Most High; for you will go before the Lord to prepare his ways' (1:76). These words remind one of the prophecy in Malachi 3:1, where Malachi speaks in the name of the LORD of a messenger who will prepare the way for him. It is also reminiscent of the prophecy in Isaiah 40:3 which we have already discussed in our examination of the Gospel of Mark.[68] Considering that in the Gospel of Luke, John the Baptist is regarded as Jesus' forerunner,[69] these Old Testament prophecies about the way of the LORD are understood here too as the way of Jesus. Directly afterwards, Zechariah speaks of 'the tender mercy of our God, when the dawn from

---

67 Joseph A. Fitzmyer (1981), *The Gospel According to Luke (I–IX)*. New York: Doubleday, pp. 53–57; François Bovon (1989), *Das Evangelium nach Lukas (Lk 1,1–9,50)*. Zürich, Düsseldorf: Benzinger Verlag, Neukirchen-Vluyn: Neukirchener Verlag, p. 23.

68 In Luke 3:4 it reads, 'The voice of one crying out in the wilderness: "Prepare the way of the Lord, make his paths straight"'. See section 2.2.

69 See also Luke 3:1–7, which quotes Isaiah 40:3–5; Luke 7:27.

on high will break upon us' (1:78). The term translated here with 'dawn', *anatolê*, means on the one hand sunrise, but in the Septuagint it is also a designation for the messianic saviour, to be translated as 'offspring' or 'branch'.[70] With this term Zechariah points to Jesus, of whom he says that he comes 'from on high', therefore from heaven.[71]

Jesus' unique identity is confirmed when the angels announce to the shepherds at Bethlehem that a Saviour is born unto them who is called Christ the Lord (2:11). Since elsewhere in this gospel the name 'the Lord' is used for God,[72] here Jesus is again closely associated with God. In the continuation of the Gospel of Luke, Jesus is regularly called 'the Lord;[73] in this respect, this gospel differs from the Gospels of Mark and Matthew, where the explicit use of 'the Lord' meaning Jesus hardly ever occurs.[74]

In the account of the appearance of John the Baptist, Jesus' baptism is all but mentioned in passing. Here, all the emphasis is put on the Holy Spirit who descended upon Jesus as a dove and on the voice sounding from heaven (3:21–22). It is doubtful, however, what this voice said according to the original text of the Gospel of Luke. Most manuscripts read, 'You are my Son, the Beloved; with you I am well pleased' (3:22), which literally corresponds to Mark 1:11. Yet, various manuscripts dating from the second to the fifth centuries here read, 'You are my son, today I have begotten you.' These words come from Psalm 2:7, where they are spoken by the LORD to the king. When they are applied to Jesus, they suggest that he became God's Son on the day of his baptism and that he was not so before. As we will see in section 9.4, a persuasion existed in early Christianity holding that God the Father adopted Jesus as his own Son at his baptism, but this view has been rejected by the church. Some exegetes consider it probable that Luke 3:22 originally read, 'You are my Son, today I have begotten you.' They believe that copyists of the manuscripts have replaced these words with the text from the Gospel of Mark, which did not so much suggest that only at his baptism Jesus was begotten or adopted to be God's Son.[75] If Luke 3:22 indeed originally

---

70 Jeremiah 23:5; Zechariah 3:8; 6:12.

71 Fitzmyer, *The Gospel According to Luke (I–IX)*, pp. 387–388; Bovon, *Das Evangelium nach Lukas (Lk 1,1–9,50)*, pp. 109–110; Gathercole, *The Preexistent Son*, pp. 238–242.

72 See, e.g., Luke 1:6, 9, 11, 16, 17, 25, 28, 32, 38, 43, 45, 46, 58, 66, 68, 76; 2:9, 15, etc.

73 E.g., in Luke 7:13, 19; 10:1, 39, 41; 11:39; 12:42, etc.; see Fitzmyer, *The Gospel According to Luke (I–IX)*, pp. 200–204; C. Kavin Rowe (2006), *Early Narrative Christology: The Lord in the Gospel of Luke*. Berlin, New York: Walter de Gruyter.

74 Apart from the address 'Lord', which can also be understood as 'sir', the absolute use of 'the Lord' for Jesus in the other synoptic gospels might possibly occur in Mark 11:3 and Matthew 21:3; see also Matthew 24:42 and section 2.2.

75 Ehrman, *The Orthodox Corruption of Scripture*, pp. 62–67.

did contain the text from Psalm 2:7, this would emphasize the great importance the evangelist attached to this event, in which the Spirit of God descended upon Jesus. This does not alter the fact, that in this gospel God's involvement with Jesus as God's Son does not begin at his baptism, but at least at his conception in the Virgin Mary.

In a different way, the subsequent genealogy traces back Jesus' origin to God via seventy-seven forefathers. Joseph is named first, with the comment that Jesus was believed to be his son, and Adam is mentioned last as '(the son) of God' (3:23–38). This genealogy of Jesus stemming from God seems a confirmation of the previous stories, but actually does not tell anything extraordinary. In this way, it can after all be said of all of Jesus' forefathers that they stem from Adam and thus from God.

A statement of Jesus which only appears in the Gospel of Luke reads, 'I came to bring fire to the earth; and how I wish it were already kindled!' (12:49).[76] Apparently, it is suggested that this fire is thrown from heaven. This fire can point to punishment[77] or, which is more probable here, to Jesus' message and the Spirit.[78] This saying has been understood as pointing to Jesus' heavenly pre-existence, from where he came to hurl fire on the earth,[79] but an objection to this explanation is that it does not say that Jesus came from heaven with this fire in his hand.[80] Yet, this statement does suggest that Jesus came to hurl this fire from a high position.

Finally, a remarkable aspect of the Gospel of Luke is the recurrent mentioning of God looking after his people or – translated differently – visiting his people.[81] Adelbert Denaux connects this theme with texts from the Hellenistic world and from the Old Testament in which a god or the LORD looks for people.[82] He points out that in the Gospel of Luke

---

76 Other sayings in which Jesus discusses with what purpose he came can be found in Luke 5:32; 12:51; 19:10.

77 See, e.g., Genesis 19:24; 2 Kings 1:10–14; Luke 3:9, 17; 17:29; in Luke 9:54–55 Jesus rejects the suggestion of his disciples to command fire to come down from heaven and consume the inhospitable Samaritans.

78 Thus François Bovon (1996), *Das Evangelium nach Lukas (Lk 9,51–14,35)*. Zürich, Düsseldorf: Benzinger Verlag, Neukirchen-Vluyn: Neukirchener Verlag, pp. 346; 349–352; cf. Luke 3:16; Acts 2:3, 19.

79 Cf. Sevenster, *De Christologie van het Nieuwe Testament*, pp. 103–104; Gathercole, *The Preexistent Son*, pp. 161–163.

80 Thus correctly Theodor Zahn (1913), *Das Evangelium des Lucas*. Leipzig: Deichert, p. 514. According to him, the saying means that the fire would descend upon earth on Jesus' order or prayer, while he was on earth.

81 *Episkeptesthai* in Luke 1:68, 78 (where 'the dawn from on high' is the subject); 7:16; *episkopê* in Lucas 19:44.

82 In the Old Testament: Genesis 18–19; 21:1; 50:24–25; Exodus 4:31; 13:19; Psalm 8:5; 79:15 LXX/80:15 MT; Jeremiah 36:10 LXX/29:10 MT; Zephaniah 2:7; Zechariah 10:3.

Jesus, on his journey to Jerusalem, visits this city and thus humanity. According to Denaux this suggests that in Jesus, God comes to mankind, and this gospel thus points to Jesus' divine origin.[83]

2.5 *The Gospel of John*

In the synoptic gospels we saw that Jesus is described in different ways as the Son of God and as the Lord. In a more or less concealed manner, they refer to his heavenly origin and therefore his pre-existence with God. This exalted view of Jesus' origin and identity comes to light much more emphatically in the Gospel of John.[84] This gospel is usually dated to the end of the first century (90–100 CE), but there are also scholars who believe that it was written in the 60s of the first century.[85]

The introduction (often called prologue) of this gospel begins like this:

> In the beginning was the Word, and the Word was with God, and the Word was God. He was in the beginning with God. All things came into being through him, and without him not one thing came into being. (1:1–3)

John 1:14 says that the Word became flesh, meaning that this divine Word became a mortal human being. The non-suspecting reader could possibly ask himself who is this Word (*Logos* in Greek). A bit later on it is disclosed that it concerns Jesus Christ in his pre-existence, for the evangelist continues,

> And the Word became flesh and lived among us, and we have seen his glory, the glory as of a father's only son, full of grace and truth. (John[86] testified to him and cried out, 'This was he of whom I said, "He who comes after me ranks ahead of me because he was before me."') From

---

83 Adelbert Denaux (1999), 'The Theme of Divine Visits and Human (In)hospitality in Luke-Acts. Its Old Testament and Graeco-Roman Antecendents', in J. Verheyden, ed., *The Unity of Luke-Acts*. Leuven: Peeters, pp. 255–279 (276–279). See also Rowe, *Early Narrative Christology*, pp. 159–166.

84 See for this section: Riemer Roukema (2006), 'Jesus and the Divine Name in the Gospel of John', in George H. van Kooten, ed., *The Revelation of the Name YHWH to Moses: Perspectives from Judaism, the Pagan Graeco-Roman World, and Early Christianity*. Leiden: Brill, pp. 207–223.

85 Klaus Berger (1997), *Im Anfang war Johannes: Datierung und Theologie des vierten Evangeliums*. Stuttgart: Quell; P.L. Hofrichter, ed. (2002), *Für und wider die Priorität des Johannesevangeliums*. Hildesheim: Olms.

86 John the Baptist is meant here.

his fullness we have all received, grace upon grace. The law indeed
was given through Moses; grace and truth came through Jesus Christ.
No one has ever seen God. It is God the only Son, who is close to the
Father's heart, who has made him known. (John 1:14–18)[87]

It appears that, according to the evangelist, Jesus is the 'Word incarnate'
and the Son of God, who since the beginning of creation is with God the
Father and is himself also God. Just as Paul wrote earlier in 1 Corinthians
8:6, it is written here that everything originated by him (the Logos, Jesus
Christ). The evangelist does not write that the Logos was already called
Jesus during his pre-existence, but elsewhere in this gospel, Jesus alludes
to his origin prior to his life on earth. So he says, 'before Abraham was, I
am' (8:58). While according to the synoptic gospels, Jesus merely alludes
to his pre-existence in a concealed manner, according to the Fourth
Gospel, he refers to it without any reservation.

In this gospel, John the Baptist points right away to Jesus' heavenly
origin when he says that the one whom he announces was before him
(1:15, 30). The Fourth Gospel, as opposed to the synoptic gospels, does
not relate explicitly that Jesus was baptized. Therefore, no voice sounds
from heaven calling him 'my Son'. John the Baptist does testify, however,
that he saw the Holy Spirit descend upon Jesus and that he then called
him 'the Son of God' – at least, according to most manuscripts (1:34).[88]
As opposed to the synoptic gospels, in the Fourth Gospel Jesus' disciples
immediately acknowledge him as the Messiah and as the Son of God
(1:41, 49). This acknowledgement is confirmed in various passages in
this gospel.[89] Jesus also speaks here about himself as the Son of Man who
descended from heaven.[90]

Like the synoptic gospels, the Gospel of John suggests that Jesus is
the LORD of the Old Testament. John 1:14 says that the Word is full of
grace and truth, and John 1:17 says that grace and truth came through

---

87 The reading 'God the only Son' (*monogenês theos*; 1:18) appears in the oldest manuscripts
    and with a few early church fathers, but the variant reading 'the only Son' (*ho monogenês
    huios*) is much stronger attested. Ehrman, *The Orthodox Corruption of Scripture*, pp.
    78–82, argues that 'the only (or: unique) Son' is the original reading, which has been
    replaced by 'God the only Son' (or, as he translates it, 'the unique God') for dogmatic
    reasons. Probably he is right in this. – In older translations the term 'only' (*monogenês*)
    was translated as 'only-begotten'. For this, see section 9.1, note 7.
88 There are, however, also manuscripts which read in John 1:34: 'that he is the elect of
    God', and Ehrman, *The Orthodox Corruption of Scripture*, pp. 69–70, might be right
    in his argument that this has been the original reading, which has been replaced in most
    manuscripts by 'the Son of God'.
89 E.g., John 3:18; 4:25–26; 5:25; 10:36; 11:27; 17:3; 20:31.
90 John 3:13; cf. 1:51 [52]; 3:14; 6:27, 53, 62; 8:28; 9:35; 12:23, 34; 13:31.

Jesus Christ. In Exodus 34:6, the description 'full of grace and truth' (also translated as 'great in love and faithfulness') refers to the LORD when he appears to Moses on Mount Sinai. Anthony T. Hanson rightly deduces from this similarity in formulation that on occasions in Israel's history where God appears, in the view of the Gospel of John, not God (the Father) appears, but the Logos, i.e. the Word.[91] Further on we will see again that in the theology of this gospel the terms Logos and LORD refer to the same divine figure.

That the LORD has come in the person of Jesus is confirmed by a few Old Testament prophecies and images in which statements about the LORD are related to Jesus. Just as in the synoptic gospels, the prophecy from Isaiah 40:3 appears.[92] In John 1:23, John the Baptist quotes this text, 'I am the voice of one crying out in the wildernes, "Make straight the way of the Lord"'. In Isaiah 40:3, this text is about the way of God the LORD, but John the Baptist means that he wants to prepare the way for Jesus. 'The LORD' therefore refers to Jesus. Likewise, this gospel holds more allusions to Jesus' heavenly identity. In a similar way to Mark 1:8, John the Baptist says in John 1:33 that Jesus 'baptizes with the Holy Spirit'. We already saw that in the Old Testament it is the LORD who will pour out his Spirit.[93] In John 3:29, John the Baptist uses the image of the bride, the bridegroom and the friend of the bridegroom; he distinctly regards himself as the friend of the bridegroom. Thus he alludes to the Old Testament image of the LORD who as bridegroom marries his people, and he associates Jesus as bridegroom with the LORD.[94] Like the synoptic gospels, the Gospel of John tells of Jesus' entry into Jerusalem. According to the Fourth Gospel, the crowd greets him crying, 'Hosanna! Blessed is he who comes in the name of the Lord, the King of Israel' (12:13). To this quotation of Psalm 118:26, the title 'the King of Israel' has been added from Zephaniah 3:14–15. Andrew C. Brunson explains that in the person of Jesus, it is in fact Yahweh (the LORD) who visits his city.[95] A final example: in John 12:40, the evangelist quotes Isaiah 6:10

---

91 Anthony T. Hanson (1980), *New Testament Interpretation of Scripture*. London: SPCK, p. 103 = Hanson (1976), 'John i. 14–18 and Exodus xxxiv'. *New Testament Studies*, 23, 90–101 (p. 96); also in Hanson (1991) *The Prophetic Gospel: A Study of John and the Old Testament*. Edinburgh: T&T Clark, pp. 21–32; and Nils A. Dahl (1962), 'The Johannine Church and History', in W. Klassen, G. Snyder, eds, *Current Issues in New Testament Interpretation: Essays in Honor of Otto A. Piper*. New York: Harper, pp. 124–142 (132).

92 See sections 2.2 and 2.4; Mark 1:3; Matthew 3:3; Luke 1:17; 1:76; 3:4–6.

93 Isaiah 44:3; Ezekiel 36:25–27; Joel 2:28–29.

94 See Isaiah 54:4–8; 62:4–5; Jeremiah 2:2; 3:20; Ezekiel 16:8; 23:4; Hosea 2:19–20.

95 Andrew C. Brunson (2003), *Psalm 118 in the Gospel of John: An Intertextual Study on the New Exodus Pattern in the Theology of John*. Tübingen: J. C. B. Mohr, pp. 179;

which says that the people of Israel have a hardened heart and blinded
eyes, so that they cannot turn and be healed. Isaiah heard these harsh
words in the temple in Jerusalem, where he saw the LORD sitting upon
his throne and he himself was called to be a prophet (Isaiah 6:1–7). The
evangelist quotes these words because he believes they can be applied to
those contemporaries of Jesus who did not believe in him. Furthermore,
he declares in John 12:41 that Isaiah said these things 'because he saw
his glory'. This means that Isaiah saw Jesus' glory in the temple, i.e.,
Jesus Christ in his pre-existence.[96] Thus, in the view of this gospel, the
pre-existent Jesus Christ appeared as the LORD upon his throne to Isaiah
in the temple of Jerusalem. What is important here is the expression 'his
glory' (12:41). This term 'glory' (*doxa* in Greek) is also found in John
1:14, which says of the incarnate Word, 'we have beheld his glory, glory
as of the only Son from the Father'. This text about the glory of the Word
refers to the glory he had with God the Father and corresponds to the glory
of the LORD which Isaiah witnessed in the temple. This correspondence
again demonstrates that 'the Word' (the Logos) from the prologue to this
gospel is identical to the LORD (Yahweh) of the Old Testament. In both
cases it concerns the glory of Jesus Christ in his pre-existence. We can add
that, according to John 17:5 and 17:24, Jesus himself also mentions the
'glory' that he possessed with his Father before the world existed.

Furthermore, the Gospel of John points out with yet another Old
Testament motive that Jesus is the manifestation of the LORD. It contains
a large number of sayings of Jesus stating or beginning with 'I am'. In
our examination of the Gospel of Mark, we saw that Jesus said, 'It is
I' (or 'I am') in Mark 6:50 and 14:62, and that in the Old Testament
it is repeatedly the LORD who says this. In the Gospel of John, Jesus' 'I
am' sayings can be divided in two categories. First, there are sayings in
which he uses 'I am' in the absolute sense. To this category belongs John
6:20, where Jesus (as in Mark 6:50) says, 'It is I, do not be afraid.'[97] In
John 8:24, 8:28, 18:5–6 and 18:8, Jesus also says 'I am' in the absolute
sense, which is a strong reminder of the words of the LORD in the book of

---

223–239; 277–279. He refers, e.g. (p. 237) to Numbers 23:21; Psalm 146:10; Isaiah 6:5;
24:23; 33:22; 43:15; 52:7; Jeremiah 8:19; Micah 2:13; 4:7. See also Psalm 89:19; Isaiah
41:21; 44:6.

96 Thus Rudolf Bultmann, *Das Evangelium des Johannes*. Göttingen: Vandenhoeck &
Ruprecht 1953, p. 347; Rudolf Schnackenburg, *Johannesevangelium* 2, Freiburg:
Herder, p. 520; also M. J. J. Menken (1996), *Old Testament Quotations in the Fourth
Gospel: Studies in Textual Form*. Kampen: Kok Pharos, p. 119; G. Reim (2001), 'Wie
der Evangelist Johannes gemäß Joh 12,37ff. Jesaja 6 gelesen hat'. *Zeitschrift für die
neutestamentliche Wissenschaft*, 92, 33–46 (35–36).

97 Cf. Genesis 26:24 LXX; 46:3 LXX; Isaiah 41:10 LXX; Jeremiah 1:8 LXX; 1:17 LXX;
26:28 LXX/46:28 MT; 49:11 LXX/42:11 MT.

Isaiah[98] and of the explication of his name as 'I am who I am' in Exodus 3:14. In the second category after 'I am' follows what Jesus then states to be: for example, 'I am the light of the world' (8:12). In this way Jesus identifies himself with the light of the Word which, according to John 1:4–9, shines in the darkness to enlighten everyone. In the Old Testament the LORD is often represented as light.[99] Another example: in John 10:11, Jesus states, 'I am the good shepherd.' This points, among other things, to the prophecy we examined in the discussion of the Gospel of Matthew, Ezekiel 34, where the LORD is the good shepherd who will look after his people.[100] So, these texts affirm what we saw in the use of other Old Testament texts and motives, that Jesus is presented as the LORD.

There is yet another aspect of the Gospel of John that deserves our attention. A few times, Jesus speaks of the name of his Father. In John 5:43, he says, 'I have come in my Father's name,' and in John 10:25, 'The works that I do in my Father's name testify to me.' In John 12:28, Jesus prays, 'Father, glorify your name.' In John 17:6, he says, 'I have made your name known to those whom you gave me from the world,' and in 17:26, 'I made your name known to them, and I will make it known.' C. H. Dodd connects this revelation and glorification of God's name with Jesus' 'I am' statements and with the previously mentioned prophecies from the book of Isaiah, where these words sound as utterances of the LORD.[101] Jesus' revelation and glorification of God's name mean, therefore, that in his teaching and deeds he has shown who his Father really is. His extremely close bond with the Father can also be read in Jesus' saying, 'I and the Father are one' (10:30).

Finally, at the end of the gospel an important statement comes from the mouth of Jesus' disciple Thomas, when he says to the risen Jesus, 'My Lord and my God' (20:28). In this gospel, Jesus is often addressed as 'Lord', and in John 13:13, Jesus says that his disciples rightly call

---

98 Isaiah 43:10, 25; 45:18–19; 46:4; 48:12, 17; also 41:10; 43:10; 45:22; 52:6. See D. M. Ball (1996), *'I Am' in John's Gospel: Literary Function, Background and Theological Implications.* Sheffield: Sheffield Academic Press, and C. H. Williams (2000), *I am He: The Interpretation of 'Anî Hû in Jewish and Early Christian Literature.* Tübingen: J. C. B. Mohr, who repeatedly refers to Deuteronomy 32:39.

99 Exodus 13:21–22; Psalm 27:1; Isaiah 60:1, 19.

100 Ezekiel 34:12–22, 31; in 34:23 only, it is David, who is the good shepherd. See also the Old Testament texts mentioned in note 58.

101 C. H. Dodd (1963), *The Interpretation of the Fourth Gospel.* Cambridge: University Press, pp. 93–96; 417; as also Raymond E. Brown (1970), *The Gospel According to John (xiii–xxi).* Garden City NY: Doubleday, pp. 755–756; C. T. R. Hayward (1978), 'The Holy Name of the God of Moses and the Prologue of St John's Gospel'. *New Testament Studies,* 25, 16–32 (29: 'Jesus is God's name come in the flesh'); see also Jean Daniélou (1958), *Théologie du Judéo-Christianisme.* Paris: Desclée, pp. 199–216.

him 'Teacher and Lord'.[102] It is, however, indisputable that the phrase 'my Lord and my God' coming from the mouth of Thomas, has a much deeper meaning than the address 'Lord'. The title 'my God' refers to John 1:1, which reads, 'In the beginning was the Word, and the Word was with God, and the Word was God.' We saw that in this gospel the pre-existent Word, which is God, corresponds to the LORD of the Old Testament and that both names can be applied to Jesus. This correspondence is confirmed by Thomas calling Jesus 'my Lord and my God' in the same breath.

2.6 *Evaluation of the New Testament data*

Besides the 'undisputed' letters of Paul and the four gospels, the New Testament contains several other letters, a book of Acts and the Revelation of John, in which various authors have written about Jesus' origin and identity. Although these writings certainly have their own character, they barely offer new views on Jesus' origin and identity. Because we do not strive for completeness, we will pass over these New Testament writings.[103] Before examining various other early Christian writings and testimonies which are not included in the New Testament, we will first evaluate what Paul and the New Testament evangelists write about Jesus' origin and identity. We have seen that their writings share various views, even though not every element is presented to the same degree. In all of them, Jesus is regarded as the Son of God. With 'God', the God of the Old Testament is meant. It is of importance that Paul, as well as the four evangelists, regularly quote the Old Testament to support their views. It is remarkable that in the gospels Jesus is also described in terms of the LORD; this is the name of God originally read as Yahweh. Especially in the letters of Paul and in the Gospel of John, a subtle difference is made between God (the Father) and Jesus, who is the LORD in its Old Testament meaning. This points to a certain plurality in God. Furthermore, in the Gospel of John, it appears that the LORD of the Old Testament is equated to the Logos or Word. According to the letters of Paul (1 Corinthians 8:6) and according to the prologue of the Gospel of John (1:1–3), the Lord Jesus Christ or the Logos was involved in the creation of the world. From this, and from various other texts, it seems that Jesus was regarded as pre-existent; this

---

102 Jesus is addressed to as 'Lord' in, for example, John 4:11, 15, 19, 49, 5:7; 6:34, 68; 9:36, 38, etc.; 'Lord' can, however, sometimes be understood here as 'sir'. Texts in which Jesus is described as 'the Lord' are John 4:1 (according to important manuscripts); 6:23; 11:2; 20:2, 13, 18, 25; 21:7.
103 In section 9.4 (note 37) we will briefly refer to Acts 2:36 and 13:33, texts that have been interpreted in an adoptianistic sense.

means that he was with God long before he was born as a human being. In the synoptic gospels an allusion is made to his pre-existence, when Jesus states the purpose of his coming and in his discussion about Psalm 110:1. Furthermore, it can be deduced from the description of Jesus as Son of Man and as the LORD, that he did not only have a human origin.

These elevated views on the man Jesus of Nazareth can be regarded as *theological* interpretations of his identity. This is different from our being able to *historically* determine that Jesus was the pre-existent Son of God and is to be regarded as the manifestation or incarnation of the LORD. On a historical level, we can determine that Paul and the authors of the gospels thought of Jesus in this way, but that does not imply that they were right in their theological views. We could, however, try to determine that Jesus as a historical person had a strong awareness of his high calling and heavenly identity. Then we would leave aside the question of whether Jesus correctly considered himself the pre-existent Son of God. Even though, in my view, it is very well possible that the historical Jesus had such a strong awareness of his high calling and heavenly identity, it remains impossible to prove this conclusively. As already remarked in section 1.2, practice proves after all that opposite New Testament scholars who trace Jesus' divine awareness and identity back to himself, there are those who rather tend to discredit the New Testament testimonies. But even if one believes that the testimonies of the New Testament about Jesus as the LORD and as the pre-existent Son of God go back to his own life, it remains impossible to determine by historical means that he truly was so. In historiography, after all, one cannot make theological statements about God, and therefore one cannot make them about the Son of God either. Everyone who reads the New Testament may decide for him- or herself whether to believe in this high description of Jesus or not.

Does this interim evaluation clear the way for unrestrained subjectivity? I would not agree with this, for it is possible to show historically that the terms in which Jesus was described in the oldest writings about him were known in contemporaneous Judaism. We will examine this in chapter 8. Along this line can be demonstrated that, historically speaking, it is possible that these terms were applied to Jesus early on and perhaps in part go back to Jesus himself. But first we will go on with the discussion of documents and testimonies outside the New Testament.

2.7 *The Gospel of Thomas*

The first work to be considered is the Gospel of Thomas. This collection does not contain stories about Jesus' birth, nor about his baptism by John the Baptist. The compiler of this gospel assumes, however, that the readers know who John the Baptist is, as he mentions him once.[104] However, Jesus does say in a few sayings who he – according to the compiler of this gospel – is. In saying 61 he says, 'I am he who comes from the one who is an equal. I was given some who belong to my Father.' From this can be inferred that Jesus, according to this gospel, regarded God the Father as his equal and that he originated from God. In Gospel of Thomas 101, Jesus speaks of his 'true Mother' who gave him life; apparently, this stands in contrast to his earthly mother, but it is not clear here who is meant by his true Mother. According to the Jewish Christian Gospel according to the Hebrews, Jesus speaks about 'my Mother, the Holy Spirit'.[105] Therefore, it is very well possible that 'my true Mother' in Gospel of Thomas 101 is also to be understood as the Spirit.

In Gospel of Thomas 77, Jesus says,

> I am the light of the world which is above all things.
> I am everything.
> From me, everything came forth,
> and up to me, everything reached.
> Split the wood and I am there;
> lift up the stone and you will find me there.

This saying proclaims that everything originated from the pre-existent Jesus, and that he is present in everything. This reminds one of John 1:3, which says about the Logos that all things came into being through him, and without him not one thing came into being.[106] That Jesus is the light, also occurs in John 1:5–9 and 8:12.

In Gospel of Thomas 28, Jesus says, 'I stood in the midst of the world and I appeared to them in flesh.' These last words resemble 1 Timothy 3:16, where the 'mystery of faith' is thus expressed, 'He was revealed in flesh'; for 'in flesh' the same expression is used there as in Gospel of Thomas 28 (*en sarki*). This statement also reminds one of John 1:14, where it is written, 'the Word became flesh', and of 1 John 4:2, 'every spirit that confesses that Jesus Christ has come in the flesh is from God'. However, it is uncertain if in Gospel of Thomas 28 the same is intended as in the New Testament writings, namely that Jesus became a mortal human being, or that it is subtly saying that he, as a heavenly figure, did

---

104 Namely in Gospel of Thomas 46, 'Jesus said, from Adam to John the Baptist, no one among those born of women is more exalted than John the Baptist that the person's gaze should not be deferent. Yet I have said, "Whoever from among you will become a child, this person will know the kingdom and he will be more exalted than John."'
105 Elliott, *The Apocryphal New Testament*, p. 9.
106 See also 1 Corinthians 8:6.

appear in a mortal body, but without really becoming a mortal human being. The notion that Jesus only seemingly became a human being occurred more often at that time.[107] Some people believed that Jesus as a divine figure could not really become a human being, but appeared as a heavenly messenger or angel.

In the Gospel of Thomas, Jesus is regarded as 'the Son', even to the extent that the Father, the Son and the Holy Spirit are named parallel to one another:

> Jesus said,
> 'Whoever blasphemes against the Father will be forgiven,
> and whoever blasphemes against the Son will be forgiven.
> But whoever blasphemes against the Holy Spirit will not be forgiven,
> neither on earth nor in heaven.' (44)[108]

Regarding Jesus' origin, it is of importance that, according to this gospel, he does not join up with the Old Testament prophets. His disciples are alleged to say that Israel's prophets have spoken being inspired by Jesus – i.e., in his pre-existence (52).[109] According to this gospel, Jesus responded, 'You have left out the Living One who is in your presence and you have spoken about the dead.' 'The Living One' means Jesus himself,[110] and 'the dead' points to the prophets. This is completely different from that which Jesus, with an appeal to Moses, says about the Old Testament patriarchs in a discussion about the resurrection of the dead. According to Mark 12:27, he then states, 'He is not God of the dead, but of the living.'[111] In Gospel of Thomas 52, however, the Old Testament prophets and their books are disqualified as being irrelevant. Accordingly Jesus, in the Gospel of Thomas, makes virtually no reference to the Old Testament books and is critical about the Jews and their practices.[112] In the biblical

---

107   E.g., among the believers referred to by Ignatius of Antioch in *Trallians* 9:1; *Smyrnaeans* 1–2 (LCL 24); furthermore, in *Trimorphic Protennoia* (Nag Hammadi Codex XIII, 1), 47, 13–19. See also J.-É. Ménard (1975), *L'Évangile selon Thomas: Traduction et commentaire*. Leiden: Brill, pp. 122–123.

108   Cf. Matthew 12:32 and Luke 12:10, which only mention the Son of Man and the Holy Spirit; Mark 3:29 only mentions the Holy Spirit.

109   This view is found in, e.g., Luke 24:27, 44–46; Clement of Rome, *Corinthians* 17:1; Ignatius, *Magnesians* 8:2; 9:2; *Philadelphians* 5:2; 9:2 (LCL 24); Barnabas 5:6 (LCL 25). As we have seen before, whenever Jesus was considered as the LORD, it is all the more clear that the prophets were considered to be inspired by the pre-existent Jesus.

110   See the heading, 'These are the secret words that the Living Jesus spoke and that Didymus Judas Thomas wrote down.'

111   According to Luke 20:38 Jesus adds to this, 'for to him all of them are alive'.

112   Gospel of Thomas 46 and 85 refer to Adam, and Gospel of Thomas 66 alludes to Psalm 118:22, 'Show me the stone that the builders rejected. It is the cornerstone.' This

gospels as well, Jesus regularly criticizes his Jewish contemporaries, but there he also passes favourable judgements on them[113] and regularly points to Moses and the prophets in a positive sense.[114]

In section 1.3, we made mention already of the three secret words which Jesus, according to Gospel of Thomas 13, spoke to Thomas only. Bertil Gärtner supposes that these three words are 'I-am who I-am', which is the name of the LORD from Exodus 3:14. This means that Jesus would have made himself known as the LORD to Thomas only. Thomas said that if he were to pronounce these three words, his companions would stone him to death. According to Leviticus 24:16, death by stoning was the punishment for someone who blasphemed the name of the LORD, and among the Jews the pronunciation of the name of the LORD was regarded as blasphemy.[115] This interpretation is indeed possible and would fit in with the representation of Jesus as the LORD in the letters of Paul and in the New Testament gospels.[116] However, it seems inconsistent that if Jesus, according to the Gospel of Thomas, is the LORD, he at the same time rejects the Old Testament prophets who have spoken in the name of the LORD.

We can conclude that in the Gospel of Thomas Jesus is represented as the light and as the Son of God the Father who appeared on earth in a body. He is described as the one from whom everything came forth and is perhaps designated as the LORD. This roughly coincides with the New Testament testimonies. Deviating from this, however, is that in this

means that the Jews rejected Jesus; in this way the Jews are criticized on the basis of their own Scripture (as also in Mark 12:10). Other criticism on the Jews and their Old Testament customs can be found in Thomas 6; 14; 43; 53; 104. See Antti Marjanen (1998), 'Thomas and Jewish Religious Practices', in Risto Uro, ed., *Thomas at the Crossroads: Essays on the Gospel of Thomas*. Edinburgh: T&T Clark, pp. 163–182.

113   E.g., Mark 12:28–34, 41–44; 14:3–9.

114   E.g., Mark 7:6–13; 10:2–9; 12:35–37; Matthew 9:13; 12:7, 40.

115   Bertil Gärtner (1961), *The Theology of the Gospel of Thomas* (translated from Swedish by Eric J. Sharpe), London: Collins, p. 123; also Jarl E. Fossum (1995), *The Image of the Invisible God: Essays on the Influence of Jewish Mysticism on Early Christology*. Freiburg: Universitätsverlag, Göttingen: Vandenhoeck & Ruprecht, p. 116, who refers to Mishna, *Sanhedrin* 7:5. John 10:30–31 tells that Jesus is threatened to be lapidated after he said, 'The Father and I are one.'

116   Fossum, *The Image of the Invisible God*, p. 114, also refers to the Gospel of Philip (Nag Hammadi Codex II, 3), 54, 5–12 (12) and to Irenaeus, *Against Heresies* I, 21, 3 (SC 264). In other explanations of the three words attention is drawn to the words *kaulakau saulasau zeêsar* from Isaiah 28:10, which Hippolytus of Rome, *Refutation of all heresies* V, 8, 4 (PTS 25) quotes as 'three significant words' of the 'Gnostics', and to a threefold Iaô, another rendering of the name Yahweh, which Jesus expresses in *Pistis Sophia* 136 (GCS 45). See Bo Frid, Jesper Svartvik (2004), *Thomasevangeliet med Jesusorden från Oxyrhynchus* (2nd edn). Lund: Arcus, pp. 155–156.

gospel Jesus holds a very critical position towards the Old Testament prophets. With his 'true Mother', the Holy Spirit may be·meant.

2.8 *Cerinthus and the Ophites*

Round about the year 180 CE, the church father Irenaeus of Lyons briefly summarizes the ideas that Cerinthus from Asia Minor had about Jesus. Irenaeus was critical of Cerinthus, and therefore it is possible that he did not give an honest presentation of his views. The testimonies of Irenaeus, however, are roughly confirmed by the original, so-called 'gnostic' writings of Nag Hammadi. Hence we can cautiously use him as a source of information. Cerinthus probably came forward with his ideas around 100 CE.[117]

Irenaeus writes that, according to Cerinthus, Jesus was not born of the Virgin Mary, but was a son of Joseph and Mary. This implies that Cerinthus denies the traditions about Jesus' birth recorded in the Gospels of Matthew and Luke. Cerinthus believes that after Jesus' baptism, the Christ descended upon him; this Christ was a heavenly figure, originating from the highest Power, the unknown Father, whom he distinguishes from the lower Creator of the world. According to Cerinthus, even the Creator was ignorant of the existence of the highest God and it was Jesus who proclaimed this unknown Father.[118]

A related, but much more complex view, was adhered to by a faction described by Irenaeus which, based on other testimonies, is identified with the Ophites.[119] This name is derived from the Greek word *ophis*, 'snake'. This refers to the snake who, according to Genesis 3, tempted Adam and Eve to eat from the forbidden fruit, thus acquiring knowledge (*gnosis*) which the Creator did not want to give them. According to this faction, there was a most high Father or the First Man, secondly his Son, called the Son of Man, and thirdly the Holy Spirit or the first Woman. The First Man begat with his Son, by the first Woman, a third male figure, Christ, the Son of these three. When the heavenly light from the first Woman left the Father, descended into lower regions and assumed a body, this light, called Sophia or Wisdom, could no longer return. Sophia gave birth to a son, Yaldabaoth, who, together with six powers emanating from him, created other angelic powers and formed Adam and Eve. The Old

---

117 Gareth Lee Cockerill gives a survey of the sources on Cerinthus in: David N. Freedman, ed. (1992), *The Anchor Bible Dictionary* 1, New York: Doubleday, p. 885. See also Roukema, *Gnosis and Faith in Early Christianity*, pp. 126–127.
118 Irenaeus, *Against Heresies* I, 26, 1; cf. III, 11, 1 (SC 264; 211).
119 Cf. Roukema, *Gnosis and Faith in Early Christianity*, pp. 51–53.

Testament writings are inspired by Yaldabaoth and the six other powers, but Sophia also has regularly spoken through the prophets about the First Man, the eternal high heaven from which she originates, and about Christ who was to descend from this high heaven. When Sophia saw that things went completely wrong with the world and the people on it, she called to her Mother, the First Woman, for help. The First Woman asked the Father to send Christ to his sister Sophia to come to her aid. Sophia made John the Baptist announce that her heavenly brother was on his way and instituted the baptism of repentance. She also made Jesus willing to receive, as a vessel, the descending Christ. Jesus was born of the Virgin Mary and he was therefore wiser, purer and more righteous than all other human beings. In his descent Christ first clothed himself with Sophia, and subsequently descended upon Jesus. Although Irenaeus does not relate that, according to the Ophites, this occurred at Jesus' baptism, this probably was their view.[120] Subsequently, Jesus began to perform miracles, proclaim the unknown Father and make himself known as the Son of the First Man.[121]

Concentrating on the origin and identity of Jesus, both difference and affinity are to be found between Cerinthus and the Ophites. Cerinthus does not believe that Jesus was born from the Virgin Mary, while the Ophites included this element in their myth. They have in common that they both consider Christ as a heavenly, divine figure descending upon the man Jesus. This seems to be a correction of the synoptic gospels, which read that the Holy Spirit descended upon Jesus at his baptism. The idea that the Messiah is a pre-existent heavenly figure also occurs in the book of Enoch and in other Jewish texts.[122] The mythological frame which the Ophites give to this figure, however, is not to be found there. As is known, the Greek term *christos* is the translation of the Hebrew *mashiach* or, in Greek form, *messias*, 'anointed'. Jews expected an 'anointed' saviour from God,[123] and the first followers of Jesus believed that this saviour had come in his person. For this reason he was called 'Jesus the Messiah' or 'Jesus (the) Christ'.

In evaluation it can be said that in the Jewish context in which Jesus acted it was not initially suggested that the Christ descended upon Jesus, but that Jesus was the Christ. Peter expressed this in saying, 'You

120 This is also assumed by Daniel A. Bertrand (1973), *Le baptême de Jésus: Histoire de l'exégèse aux deux premiers siècles*. Tübingen: J. C. B. Mohr, p. 63.
121 Irenaeus, *Against Heresies* I, 30, 1–13 (SC 264).
122 1 Enoch 46; 48; 52:4; 62 (where the Messiah is also called Son of Man); 2 Baruch 29:3; 30:1 (OTP 1).
123 See, e.g., 1Q Rule of the Community (1QS) II, 11–12; 4QGenesis Pesher V; Psalms of Solomon 17:32; 18:7 (OTP 2).

are the Christ' (Mark 8:29). The view of Cerinthus and the Ophites therefore represents a different, secondary interpretation of the name 'Jesus Christ'. Furthermore, both Cerinthus and the Ophites believe that Jesus proclaimed the unknown Father and not the heavenly powers who inspired the Old Testament books. This is a new interpretation of the identity of Jesus' heavenly Father, which deviates from the presentation given in the biblical gospels.

2.9 The Gospel of Judas

In section 1.1, the Gospel of Judas was briefly mentioned. After long wanderings, it was published in 2006 and translated from the Coptic language.[124] A note by Irenaeus concerning the Gospel of Judas had already been known. He describes the ideas of a faction which felt related to people such as Cain, Esau, Korah and the inhabitants of Sodom. In the view of this faction, these figures had a bad reputation in the Old Testament because the Creator had turned against them.[125] Because this group regarded the Creator as an inferior God, they assumed that his opponents, like Cain, therefore must have originated from the good and highest God, and have a divine spark of light within them. On grounds of a similar reaction, this faction also had a positive opinion of Judas, who is unfavourably described in the biblical gospels because he delivered Jesus to his opponents. It was believed that Judas was the only disciple of Jesus who knew the truth and he was to execute 'the mystery of the betrayal'. Irenaeus supposes that the Gospel of Judas, which describes this mystery, originates from this faction.[126]

The recently published Gospel of Judas may indeed correspond with the writing mentioned by Irenaeus.[127] If this is true, it can be dated, at least in its original Greek text, before Irenaeus and thus about the middle of the second century. Judas is presented as the disciple of Jesus par excellence, although this does not mean that he has understood everything perfectly. The beginning of this narrative reads that when Jesus' disciples were

---

124 Rudolphe Kasser, Marvin Meyer, Gregor Wurst, eds, (2006), *The Gospel of Judas from Codex Tchacos*. Washington DC: National Geographic; Rudolphe Kasser, Gregor Wurst et al. (2007), *The Gospel of Judas together with the Letter of Philip, James, and a Book of Allogenes from Codex Tchacos: Critical Edition*. Washington DC: National Geographic.

125 Genesis 4; 18–19; 27; Numbers 16.

126 Irenaeus, *Against Heresies* I, 31, 1 (SC 264).

127 However, Simon Gathercole (2007), *The Gospel of Judas: Rewriting Early Christianity*. Oxford: Oxford University Press, pp. 114–131, throws some doubt on this assumption, although he does not fully reject it.

praying and giving thanks Jesus laughed about this because they did not do it of their own will, but because thus their God would be worshipped. His disciples said, apparently full of astonishment, 'Master, you are [...] the Son of our God!' Upon which Jesus asked them how they knew him and he remarked that no one of their kind of people will know him. When his disciples got angry with him, Jesus blamed their God who was in them. Only Judas appeared to be able to tell who Jesus was,

> I know who you are and where you have come from. You have come from the immortal aeon of Barbelo. And I am not worthy to utter the name of the one who has sent you.

Then Jesus initiated Judas into the mysteries of the kingdom (33–35). Afterwards, Jesus taught him about the creation of the heavenly world and about the origin of the rebellious angels, such as Yaldabaoth, who created mankind. He seems to remark, furthermore, that Seth is called the Christ,[128] and that with five other powers he reigned over the underworld and over chaos (47–52).

In this document, the difference between a higher and lower God again comes to light. Judas knows that Jesus originates from the high world of Barbelo. In other writings, Barbelo is the divine Mother, the partner of the highest God, who came forth from him.[129] That in this gospel Jesus is connected to the high world of Barbelo corresponds with his mockery of the worship of the inferior God of his Jewish disciples. For his identity it is of importance that he is continually designated by the name Jesus. At one point, it seems that Seth, the third son of Adam and Eve, whom certain gnostic groups regarded as their prototype, is identified with the Christ (52). It remains uncertain what the relationship between Jesus and the Christ is, according to this document.

128 Jacques van der Vliet (2006), 'Judas and the Stars: Philological Notes on the Newly Published Gospel of Judas (*GosJud*, Codex Gnosticus Maghâgha 3)'. *The Journal of Juristic Papyrology* 36, 137–152 (pp. 147–151), however, argues that the phrase, 'The first is [S]eth, who is called the Christ' (52, 4–6), is corrupt and that originally the name Athoth was meant.
129 See, e.g., the *Apocryphon of John* 12–22. Even though the name Barbelo is known from various gnostic sources, it is not certain what it means. For this, see Alastair H. B. Logan (1996), *Gnostic Truth and Christian Heresy: A Study of the History of Gnosticism*. Edinburgh: T&T Clark, pp. 98–100.

2.10 *Theodotus*

Other beliefs about Jesus can be found with Theodotus, who belonged to the eastern school of the 'gnostic' Valentinians.[130] Clement of Alexandria, who considered himself to belong to the 'catholic church', has studied and summarized a document of Theodotus (probably at the end of the second century) and from this it is somewhat possible to come to know his beliefs. It appears, however, that Theodotus also discussed the views of other Valentinians, but Clement does not always clearly indicate the transitions between the various lines of thought. Theodotus' work can be dated about 160–170 CE.

Similar to the authors of previously discussed texts, Theodotus distinguishes between the highest Father and God the Creator. According to Clement, the Valentinians generally believed that the Father is unknown, and that he wants to make himself known to the heavenly powers, the aeons. Theodotus apparently shares a Valentinian explanation of John 1:1–18, which holds that the Only Begotten or Son comes forth from the Father, and that the Father makes him known to the aeons. The Logos (the Word) was regarded as a heavenly figure who is included in the Only Begotten, but must be distinguished from him; this Logos was identified with the heavenly Christ. The demiurge or Creator is the image of the Only Begotten; for that reason his works are perishable.[131] Upon the origin and nature of the Creator, Theodotus – in Clement's rendering – does not elaborate. He also speaks about Sophia, the figure who has left the Father[132] and who was also mentioned by the Ophites.

The Saviour, Jesus Christ, who from the fullness (the *pleroma*) of the Father descended on earth, is identified with the Logos, but initially not entirely with the Only Begotten Son. In John 1:14 is written, after all, that his glory was *as* of the Only Begotten, from which is concluded that his glory must be distinguished from this (7, 3b). When the Logos or Saviour descended, Sophia, according to Theodotus, provided a piece of flesh (*sarkion*), namely a carnal body, also called 'spiritual seed' (1, 1). At Jesus' baptism, 'the Name' in the form of a dove descended upon Jesus; this Name is 'the Only Begotten Son'. Theodotus adds that

130 Roukema, *Gnosis and Faith in Early Christianity*, pp. 61–62; 129–130; 133–134; F. Sagnard (1970), *Clément d'Alexandrie: Extraits de Théodote* (SC 23). Paris: Cerf, pp. 28–49; Einar Thomassen (2006), *The Spiritual Seed: The Church of the "Valentinians"*. Leiden: Brill, pp. 28–38.

131 Clement of Alexandria, *Excerpts from Theodotus* 6–7 (SC 23); in other terms Irenaeus, *Against Heresies* I, 8, 5 (SC 264), attributes this interpretation of John 1:1–18 to the Valentinian Ptolemaeus.

132 This episode is not explicitly discoursed upon in the excerpts, but Clements does hint at it; *Excerpts from Theodotus* 23, 2; 30, 2; 31, 3; 32, 3.

through the descent of this Name, Jesus himself was also saved. Later on, he distinguishes between the visible side of Jesus, which he identifies with Sophia and with the 'Church (*ekklêsia*) of the special (spiritual) seeds', and Jesus' invisible side, namely 'the Name', which is 'the Only Begotten Son' (22, 6–7; 26, 1).

Besides these complex beliefs, Theodotus also discusses another view of the Father, the Creator and the other heavenly powers. In this view, God the Creator is the image of the Father and also becomes Father himself when he creates the psychic Christ, archangels and other angels (47, 1–3). Here, Jesus is the heavenly Saviour who initially dwelled in the *pleroma* of the highest Father. When Jesus 'emptied himself' (Philippians 2:7) and descended from the *pleroma* of his Father to the world of the Creator, he had the seed of Sophia in him. This seed was a small part of the Father, the divine spark which all spiritual people have in them without the Creator knowing of it. Upon arriving on earth, Jesus clothed himself with the invisible psychic Christ announced by the law and the prophets. To become visible, he was given a body of an invisible psychic substance which, thanks to a divine power, could still be observed. Thus is explained what the angel said to Mary in Luke 1:35, 'The Holy Spirit will come upon you' (that is the spiritual element), 'the power of the Most High will overshadow you' (that is the body for Jesus, originating from the Creator).[133] With slightly varying words, Irenaeus confirms this Valentinian vision on Jesus. He lists that in this belief 'our Lord' is composed of four parts: a spiritual element coming from Sophia, a psychic element, Christ, coming from the Creator, a most exceptional body, and the Saviour who descended upon him as a dove.[134] According to another passage, Christ, however, originated from a thought of Sophia and he is an image of the *pleroma*. He left his mother (Sophia) – apparently after she had moved away from the Father – went into the *pleroma*, united himself with the aeons called the 'Totalities', and also with the Paraclete (the Spirit).[135]

According to Theodotus and the other Valentinians, the purpose of Jesus' coming is that all of the spiritual seeds, or divine sparks which are sown into certain people, are again united.[136]

We see that these various Valentinian views are related, in certain respects, with those of the Ophites. The hierarchical distinction between the highest Father, Sophia and God the Creator is present in these different

---

133   *Excerpts from Theodotus* 3, 1–2; 35, 1; 59–60; cf. 1, 1; 2, 1.
134   Irenaeus, *Against Heresies*, I, 7, 2 (SC 264).
135   *Excerpts from Theodotus* 32, 2–33, 1.
136   *Excerpts from Theodotus* 1, 2; 3, 2; 26, 3; 35, 2; 38, 3; 42, 2; 49, 1; 53, 2–5; 56, 3.

outlooks. In general, it is believed that the Saviour proclaims the highest Father and not the God who, according to the Old Testament, created this world. The precise views on the Saviour, however, are divergent. For Theodotus, the Saviour, Jesus Christ, is the Logos who descends upon earth from the Father, has the spiritual element in him and receives the name Only Begotten Son at his baptism. According to other Valentinians, Jesus is clothed with the Christ of the Old Testament Creator and receives a body from the Creator on earth. According to this view, the Creator is unaware of the heavenly world above him,[137] but apparently does work along with the plan towards the intended salvation of the divine sparks. According to the Ophites, Christ originates from the Father, has clothed himself with Sophia and descended upon the man Jesus. Here, there is no assistance from Yaldabaoth and his companions, even though the Ophites acknowledged that the Old Testament books spoke of the heavenly Christ.

2.11 *The Tripartite Tractate*

One of the longest works of the Nag Hammadi Codices has no title, but has been called the *Tripartite Tractate* by the first publishers, because of the division of the manuscript. The author of the book is unknown, but given the similarities with other Valentinian works, it must originate from or be related to the school of Valentinus. It was probably written in the third century.[138]

The first part of the book begins with a description of the Father, who has not been engendered by any other power. He is eternal, without beginning and without end, he is good and perfect, and all of the names and words that are used to describe him fall short. He is unknowable, unapproachable, invisible, unutterable and so on (51–57). Subsequently, the first-born and only Son of the Father is introduced, who has existed since the beginning. Out of the love of the Father and the Son, the church (*ekklêsia*) arises, existing since the beginning and consisting of many people dating from before eternity (57–58). Further on the numerous aeons are described, which originated as thoughts of the Father and came forth from him as emanations, which, in turn, produced new aeons.

---

137 *Excerpts from Theodotus* 49, 1.
138 See Harold W. Attridge, Elaine H. Pagels (1985), 'The Tripartite Tractate: Introduction', in Harold W. Attridge, ed., *Nag Hammadi Codex I (The Jung Codex)*. Leiden: Brill, pp. 159–190 (178–190); Einar Thomassen, Louis Painchaud (1989), *Le Traité Tripartite (NH I, 5): Texte établi, introduit et commenté*. Québec: Laval, pp. 38–46; Thomassen, *The Spiritual Seed*, pp. 46–58; 166–187; 248–251.

Together they formed in three levels 'the Totalities' or 'the members of the All', also called the *pleroma* (60–74).

For these aeons too, the Father was unnameable and incomprehensible, but one of them, the Logos, made an attempt, out of love, to understand the Father. His intention was called good, but he became arrogant and, in doing so, ended up outside the *pleroma*. In shadows and images he began to create spiritual beings who did not know about the higher world and had a rebellious nature. From them, belligerent, quarrelsome, and unfaithful people later came forth. Yet it is emphatically made clear that this development, that was brought about by the Logos, should not be condemned, since it was predestined (74–80). The Logos himself, however, came to the insight that he should repent. With the help of the aeons that he had abandoned, he prayed to the Father. The memory of his origin and his prayers again brought forth all sorts of spiritual beings, who had longed for the Father and strived for unity and love (80–85). The Logos split in two; one part distanced itself from the rebellious beings he had created, and ascended to the *pleroma* of the Father. Together with the other aeons, he prayed for the other defective part that remained outside of the *pleroma*. From the unity of the aeons, 'the fruit' came forth which unveiled the face of the Father. This fruit was also called 'his beloved Son', who then gave perfection to the defective Logos. This Son is also called the Saviour, Beloved and Christ (85–87). It is not explained, however, what the relationship is between this Son and the first-born and only Son, who was introduced earlier, neither in which relationship he stands to the repentant Logos, nor how the two parts of the Logos relate to each other after the defective part received perfection. It has been assumed that the Son, who has redeemed the Logos, stands at a different level than the Son of the Father, but also that it essentially concerns manifestations of the same being.[139] However this may be, it is said of the Logos who remained outside of the *pleroma*, but had received perfection, that on the grounds of the authority he had received he began to set the world in order. Rebellious powers were appointed over the outermost darkness and the underworld (88–89). In his own *pleroma* he put a 'Synagogue of Salvation' for those powers who had joined him, also called 'Storehouse' (Matthew 3:12; 13:30), 'Bride', 'Kingdom', 'Joy of the Lord' (Matthew 25:21, 23) and 'Church' (*ekklêsia*). The Logos arranged everything by analogy and as an image of the higher *pleroma* (90–95). He created images which he placed in the pre-existent paradise and other pre-existent future groups of people such as the Right Ones

---

139   Thus Majella Franzmann (1996), *Jesus in the Nag Hammadi Writings*. Edinburgh: T&T Clark, pp. 36–37. Thomassen, *The Spiritual Seed*, pp. 182–186, concludes that there is no absolute distinction between the Son and the Saviour.

or psychics, who do have a soul (*psuchê*), but not a divine spark, and the Left ones or hylics, meaning 'the material ones'. Above the heavenly powers (*archontes*) of his creation, he appointed as their Lord a Ruler (*archôn*), who was an image of the Father. This Ruler was also called 'Father', as well as 'God', 'Creator', 'King' and 'Judge'. Here the God of the Old Testament is intended. The Logos made use of this God like a hand to make a beautiful and good world here below (cf. Genesis 1:31) and to utter prophecies. To those who obeyed him, he promised rest and healing, and for those who were disobedient, he determined punishments. This God also has his own paradise and kingdom and everything that is in the spiritual world preceding him. However, he does not know that he is being led by the Spirit of the Logos who makes him act the way he wants (96–101).

The short second part of this tractate describes, with a few allusions to Genesis 1–3, how the Logos and the Creator (called 'demiurge') create the human being in a paradise (104–108). Because we are pre-eminently interested in the views on the origin and identity of Jesus, we pass by this part of the tractate. The third part deals, among other things, with the Hebrew prophets who spoke in the name of the Saviour and announced his coming and his suffering. They did not know, however, where he came from, that he was eternal, unbegotten and essentially could not suffer. Yet they have, thanks to the inspiration given them, not only stated that the Saviour should come forth from them, but also that he descends particularly from the Logos from whom he received his carnal body. His Father is the invisible, unknowable, incomprehensible God, who has nevertheless shown himself in the Saviour to become known and understood (111–114). The Saviour was begotten without sin and born as a child with a body and a soul, but he could not suffer. His name is Jesus Christ (115–117). We can conclude that the first-born Son here manifested himself on the third level.

This analysis merely reflects a few lines of thought of this very complex work. It is remarkable that the role occupied by Sophia in similar documents, is here played by the Logos. In other writings it is Sophia who distances herself from the Father and brings forth a being who becomes the Creator of the world. In the *Tripartite Tractate*, it is the Logos, with good intentions for that matter, who ended up outside the *pleroma* and brings forth a material creation over which he appoints a Lord and Ruler. It is remarkable that this pattern of events is not lamented, but is regarded as predestined. The material creation is emphatically called 'good', which is inspired by Genesis 1:31. As was the case with the Valentinians whose ideas were described by Theodotus, this *Tripartite Tractate* also acknowledges that the Old Testament prophets announced

the Saviour. Yet, according to this view, Jesus did not proclaim the Lord
of the Old Testament, but his Father who stood far above it.

2.12 *Comparison of the New Testament and other writings*

Among the early Christian documents not included in the New Testament
and examined here, the Gospel of Thomas is the most closely related
to the New Testament testimonies. In the Gospel of Thomas Jesus is
introduced as the light from which everything came forth and as the
Son of the Father who appeared on earth in a mortal body. Perhaps, he
called himself 'I am who I am', which designates the name of the LORD.
According to this gospel, however, Jesus was very critical towards the
Old Testament prophets. It remains obscure who is intended with the
term 'true Mother'. Perhaps, this refers to the Holy Spirit.

With regard to the other, so-called 'gnostic', persons and documents,
it is striking that in different levels they distinguish between the highest
God the Father and the lower Creator, who inspired the Old Testament.
This contrast differs from the letters of Paul and the Gospel of John,
where a distinction is made between God the Father and Jesus as the
LORD. In the gnostic writings Jesus' origin and identity are connected,
in various ways, either with the highest God (Cerinthus, the Ophites, the
Gospel of Judas), or with the highest God and lower Creator (Theodotus,
other Valentinians, the *Tripartite Tractate*). Sometimes the Old Testament
prophets are acknowledged for having spoken about Jesus the Saviour,
but most authors agree that Jesus has revealed the highest God and that he
did not or not substantially link up with the Old Testament writings. The
diverse descriptions of the heavenly world mention, however, not only
these figures, but also Sophia and the Logos, who is distinguished from
the Son. Their mutual relationships differ in each author or document.
Cerinthus and the Ophites believed that Jesus was a special human
being upon whom, at his baptism, the heavenly Christ descended. In a
Valentinian vision considered by Theodotus, it is the other way around.
Jesus the Saviour descended from the *pleroma* of the highest God and
was clothed on earth with the psychic Christ, a figure emanating from
the lower God, the Creator. Theodotus himself seems to support another
view on Jesus Christ as the heavenly Logos and Saviour, for whom Sophia
had prepared a carnal body and upon whom the Name 'Only Begotten
Son' descended at his baptism. The author of the *Tripartite Tractate* has a
much more complex view of the different manifestations of the Son, who
is also called Saviour and Christ.

It is remarkable that the representation of the heavenly world and of
Jesus' origin and identity in the 'gnostic' beliefs as described in sections

2.8–11 are far more complex than Paul's views and those recorded in the biblical gospels. Stated in a different manner: despite the differences in formulation, the view on Jesus presented in the New Testament writings turned out to be less complicated than those presented in the 'gnostic' writings examined here. To be sure, it would also be possible to compare such gnostic writings from the second and third centuries with other documents from the same period known from 'catholic' Christianity. However, what matters in this case is to establish that in the 'gnostic' writings discussed here, a different theology comes forth than from the New Testament writings.

Does this mean, historically speaking, that the New Testament writings give a more adequate description of Jesus' origin and identity than the 'gnostic' ones? In section 2.6 the conclusion was drawn that, from a historical point of view, it cannot be determined that Jesus really was the LORD and the pre-existent Son of God. What can be determined, however, is that the reviewed 'gnostic' sources of the second and third centuries need more complex frameworks to describe who Jesus Christ was. For example, 'the Son' was distinguished from 'the Logos', while in John 1:1–18 both of these terms are apparently meant to describe the same figure. Gnostics also regarded Christ as a figure having a very different origin from Jesus upon whom he descended. According to certain Valentinians, Jesus Christ consisted of four parts, which were derived from different heavenly figures. While according to the biblical gospels, Jesus believed in God as he was described in the Old Testament books, gnostics believed that Jesus proclaimed a higher God, and distanced themselves from the God of the Old Testament.[140]

The latter is understandable. In the Old Testament God is sometimes described as ruthless and whimsical, while Jesus, according to the New Testament gospels, gave the impression that he proclaimed God in the first place as a loving, caring Father.[141] The conclusion that Jesus Christ therefore stood merely indirectly in relationship to the God of the Old Testament, or merely partly originated from him, can be understood. Yet, this understandable conclusion is not older and more original for that reason than the view given by the New Testament writings. From a historical point of view the 'gnostic' views can be explained as being later, secondary interpretations of less complicated ideas expressed in the New Testament writings.

---

140 For the gnostic interpretation of the Old Testament see Roukema, *Gnosis and Faith in Early Christianity*, pp. 105–125; 159–168.

141 Nevertheless, this is a biased image, because God can also be severe, according to the biblical gospels; see, e.g., Matthew 8:11–12; 11:21–24; 12:32; 22:11–13; John 3:36; 5:29.

CHAPTER 3

Jesus' Teaching

After discussing Jesus' origin and identity, we will continue with Jesus' public appearance according to the different traditions. According to the Gospels of Matthew, Mark and Luke, he travelled about Galilee and Judaea and sometimes beyond with his disciples, speaking about God's kingdom and the way of life belonging to it. The Gospel of John differs in its account of Jesus' appearance, as in it, Jesus' teaching is strongly focussed on faith in himself. According to these four gospels, Jesus also performed all sorts of miracles of healing. The synoptic gospels tell us that Jesus delivered people who were plagued by demons, but such narratives are not present in the Gospel of John. In the previous chapter a few of the miracles Jesus performed according to the New Testament gospels were mentioned in passing. These count as powerful testimonies of his divine identity. His miracles also function as a confirmation of the authority with which he gives his teaching. Remarkably enough, on the other hand, the accounts of the miracles play almost no role in the 'gnostic' testimonies. For this reason – and because this examination is limited – in the comparison of Jesus' public appearance in the various traditions, we will concentrate on the contents of his teaching.

Because some of the witnesses examined in chapter 2 barely look at Jesus' concrete teaching, they are not treated in this chapter. In the first place this concerns Paul, in whose letters relatively little is found explicitly referring to Jesus' teaching.[1] Neither does Theodotus, in the excerpts we have of his work, explicitly enter into this. Also in Irenaeus' account of the ideas of Cerinthus and the Ophites, it is barely recorded what Jesus' teaching contained, except – as already mentioned – that

---

1   See 1 Corinthians 7:10–11; 9:14; 11:23–25; perhaps 1 Thessalonians 4:15–17. Also Romans 12:9–21; 13:8–10 seems to be inspired by sayings of Jesus.

Jesus proclaimed the unknown Father. In this chapter, instead of these witnesses, the Gospel of Mary and a few other traditions are discussed. The question of whether Jesus also had a secret teaching apart from his public teaching is not treated in this chapter, but will be examined in chapter 7.

3.1 *The Gospel of Mark*

The oldest document that gives an impression of Jesus' teaching is the Gospel of Mark. In Mark 1:15–16 is written that Jesus began to preach in Galilee, 'The time is fulfilled, and the kingdom of God has come near; repent, and believe in the good news.' Jesus meant that God's dominion over Israel and the world was to dawn in the near future. He summoned his audience to prepare for this. Furthermore, Mark tells us that in Galilee Jesus taught in the synagogues, in homes and outdoors.[2] Because initially the exact content of Jesus' teaching is hardly mentioned, we can assume that he spoke about the coming of God's kingdom. This is confirmed in the fourth chapter which contains a few evocative parables about the coming of this kingdom. However, it appears that many of those who listened to Jesus did not understand his parables. He then tells his closest followers that the 'mystery of the kingdom' is only given to them (4:10–12). More attention will be given to this saying in chapter 7.

In a discussion with the Pharisees it appears that Jesus did not share their strict interpretation of the keeping of the Sabbath as a day of rest. He permits his disciples to pick ears of grain on this day. He appeals to David who once ate bread of the presence in the house of God and in doing so, strictly speaking, violated the Mosaic law (2:23–28). With an appeal to the prophet Isaiah, Jesus also criticizes the oral traditions of the Pharisees about ritual purity and he scorns the setting aside of offerings, so as not to spend them for the care of parents. Instead of this, he appeals to Moses' command, 'honour your father and your mother'; he then speaks of 'the word of God' (7:1–15; Exodus 20:12). In discussion with the Pharisees about divorce, he again recognizes the authority of Moses, who allowed divorce. Beyond this, however, he appeals to the first chapters of the book of Genesis, from which he concludes that God did not intend divorce (10:2–9). To a young man eager to share in the promise of eternal life, he preaches the commandments from the law of Moses, 'do not kill, do not commit adultery, do not steal, do not bear false witness, do not defraud, honour your father and mother' (10:17–19; Exodus 20:12–16).

---

2   Mark 1:21–28, 39; 2:1–2, 13; 3:32–34; 6:2, 6, etc.

When Jesus comes to the temple in Jerusalem, he is outraged about the trade which is being conducted in the outer temple square and he sweeps it clean. With a quote from Isaiah 56:7, he preaches to the bystanders, 'My house shall be called a house of prayer for all peoples.' His reproach, 'but you have made it a den of robbers' is also derived from the prophets (11:15–18; Jeremiah 7:11). In a discussion about the resurrection of the dead, Jesus appeals to the book of Exodus where God is called 'the God of Abraham, the God of Isaac, and the God of Jacob'. He concludes that God is not a God of the dead but of the living, which in his view testifies to the resurrection of the dead (12:26–27; Exodus 3:6). When asked about the most important commandment, Jesus quotes from the law of Moses the commandments to love God and your neighbour (12:28–31; Deuteronomy 6:4–5; Leviticus 19:18). From these conversations and incidents it appears that Jesus appealed basically to the law of Moses and to the prophets, even though his demands on his own followers exceeded these. He asked them to leave behind their possessions and families in order to follow him and, in doing so, have a share in God's kingdom (1:16–20; 8:34–38; 10:21–31). Jesus exhorted his twelve disciples that whoever desired to be the most important among them, must be willing to serve the others (9:33–35; 10:35–44).

In section 1.3, we saw that at a certain moment Peter states that Jesus is the Messiah or Christ (8:29). Because Jesus does not deny this, he apparently, according to this gospel, gave his disciples the impression that he acted as Messiah to announce the coming of God's kingdom. Characteristic of this gospel is that Jesus wanted the insight that he is the Messiah to be kept a secret (8:30). Mark tells us that after this confession, Jesus began to prepare his disciples that he would die a violent death by the hands of the high priests and scribes (8:31; 9:31; 10:32–34). According to Mark, Jesus said that he, as the Son of Man, would give his life 'as a ransom for many' (10:45). At Jesus' last supper with his disciples, a similar interpretation of his death appears, namely that this would be to the benefit of others. After drinking the wine, he announces that his blood will be 'poured out for many', to which he adds that after his death, he will drink it anew in the kingdom of God (14:24–25).

In a sermon which, according to Mark 13, Jesus gave to four of his disciples, he prepares them for the events which, in his view, will take place in the future. The evangelist apparently means that hereafter God's kingdom will dawn, but this is not stated in this exact term. Jesus names the destruction of the temple in Jerusalem, the coming of false prophets and messiahs, persecution, wars and cosmic disasters. At the end, Jesus will, at a time also unknown to himself (see sections 1.2; 2.2), come from heaven as the Son of Man in order to gather his elect, with the help of his angels. His speaking of the elect (13:20, 22, 27) does not point to a developed doctrine of election, but indicates the group of people who believe in Jesus and who take his teaching seriously. Still, this saying does implicate God's ultimate judgement of those who have rejected Jesus.[3]

This sermon confirms the impression that Jesus announced the end of this world and that he wanted to prepare his disciples for the great changes which were in the air. Jesus discloses himself here as an apocalyptic preacher who imparts a revelation about the end to a few of his closest followers. At the same time he warns, in the description of the Gospel of Mark, that the time of the cosmic changes is not fixed and that his followers therefore must remain vigilant (13:32–36).

3.2 *The Gospel of Matthew*

The Gospel of Matthew follows the same narrative line as the Gospel of Mark, but it contains far more extensive descriptions of the contents of Jesus' teaching about the kingdom of God (in Matthew usually called 'kingdom of heaven'). A few elements of this gospel will be examined. Just as in Mark, the Gospel of Matthew tells of Jesus announcing in Galilee the coming of God's kingdom (4:17). However, in contrast to Mark, Matthew adds a long sermon in which Jesus, on a mountain, explains what 'the good news (or, gospel) of the kingdom' (4:23) contains and how one should live in accordance with this (Matthew 5–7). A great part of this Sermon on the Mount is derived from the source Q, but Matthew has also gathered other material. Characteristic for this gospel is that Jesus says here,

> Do not think that I have come to abolish the law or the prophets; I have come not to abolish but to fulfill. For truly I tell you, until heaven and earth pass away, not one letter, not one stroke of a letter, will pass from the law until all is accomplished. Therefore, whoever breaks one of the least of these commandments, and teaches others to do the same, will be called least in the kingdom of heaven; but whoever does them and teaches them will be called great in the kingdom of heaven. For I tell you, unless your righteousness exceeds that of the scribes and Pharisees, you will never enter the kingdom of heaven. (5:17–20)

Here Jesus is described as a teacher who wants to remain faithful to the Mosaic law and to the prophets.[4] In the continuation of this text, he quotes a few of the commandments from the law of Moses, intensifying

---

3   See also Mark 8:38.
4   This is also found in Matthew 23:3.

them even to the commandment of loving your enemies (5:21–48).[5] Further on, Jesus twice quotes the prophet Hosea who said in the name of God, 'I desire steadfast love, and not sacrifice' (9:13; 12:7; Hosea 6:6). In stating this, Jesus means to say that charity towards other people is both more important than bringing the required sacrifices to the temple and, in a broader sense, than the scrupulous observation of the law of Moses. It is unavoidable that the evangelist has had a hand in the formulation of such sayings.[6] We will now limit our discussion of the Gospel of Matthew to the observation that Jesus here refers to the Mosaic law and the Old Testament prophets even more extensively than in the Gospel of Mark.

Just as in the Gospel of Mark, Jesus announces the coming of God's kingdom in the Gospel of Matthew. Even more clearly than in the Gospel of Mark, Jesus says here, in a text originating from Q, that he who loves his father, mother, son or daughter more than him is not worthy of him (10:37). Nevertheless, Jesus rejects divorce, except in the case of unchastity (5:31–32; 19:3–9). What is new, also originating from Q, is that Jesus says, 'but if it is by the Spirit of God that I cast out demons, then the kingdom of God has come to you' (12:28). This points out that, with the person of Jesus, the kingdom of God has already come, at least in part. This gospel hints at the fact that the actual coming of this kingdom may perhaps take more time than was initially expected. This is why a servant says in a parable, 'my master is delayed' (24:48). In the parable of the ten bridesmaids, the same verb is used to say that 'the bridegroom was delayed' (25:5). This gospel does maintain, however, the expectation of a toilsome time of the end and Jesus' ultimate coming from heaven which coincides with the coming of God's kingdom (24:3–25:46). The double, present and future nature of God's kingdom also comes to light in the famous beatitudes at the beginning of the Sermon on the Mount. There Jesus promises this kingdom to the poor in spirit, those who mourn, the meek, those who hunger and thirst for righteousness, the merciful, the pure in heart, the peacemakers and those who are persecuted for righteousness' sake (5:3–10). This promise counts for the present and for the future of God's kingdom. The drawback of this is that, in the Gospel of Matthew, Jesus speaks harsh words about the judgement that will befall those who did not believe in him and who did not live in accordance with his teachings.[7]

---

5   The Old Testament, however, also contains some testimonies of loving the enemy; e.g., 2 Kings 6:21–23; Proverbs 25:21–22.

6   See Peter J. Tomson (2001), *'If this be from Heaven...': Jesus and the New Testament Authors in their Relationship to Judaism*. Sheffield: Sheffield Academic Press, pp. 144–159; 286–289; 404–408.

7   Matthew 8:12; 11:16–24; 16:27; 21:43; 23:1–36; 24:45–51; 25:12, 26–30, 41–46.

3.3 *The Gospel of Luke*

Different from the Gospels of Mark and Matthew, the beginning of the
Gospel of Luke does not contain a programmatic text about the nearness
and the coming of God's kingdom. Yet, regarding the contents, the three
synoptic gospels do correspond to a large degree. In Luke 4:16–30 is
written that Jesus applied the following text from the prophet Isaiah to
himself in the synagogue of Nazareth,

> The Spirit of the Lord is upon me,
> because he has anointed me
> to bring good news to the poor.
> He has sent me to proclaim release to the captives
> and recovery of sight to the blind,
> to let the oppressed go free,
> to proclaim the year of the Lord's favour. (4:18–19; Isaiah 61:1–2)

This text suggests that with Jesus' coming a time of salvation would
dawn. Shortly afterwards Jesus says that he must preach 'the good news
of the kingdom of God' to other cities also (4:43). Whereas Matthew has
his Sermon on the Mount, Luke has a partially corresponding although
shorter speech which Jesus, according to his description, preached on a
plain (6:17–49). In the Gospel of Luke, Jesus has special attention for
the poor. This is apparent in the previously quoted passage from Isaiah,
and is confirmed when Jesus begins his beatitudes by saying, 'Blessed
are you who are poor, for yours is the kingdom of God' (6:20). Luke
has various other texts in this vein which do not all have a parallel in
Matthew and Mark.[8] The reverse of Jesus' attention for the poor in this
gospel is his criticism of the rich and their wealth.[9] Apart from that, Jesus
does not only positively refer to Moses and the prophets in the synagogue
of Nazareth, but also on various other occasions.[10]

Luke's description of what Jesus expects of his disciples goes even
further than in the Gospels of Mark and Matthew. Here Jesus says
that whoever would follow him must break off with his father, mother,
wife, children, brothers and sisters (14:26). Later on in this gospel Jesus
confirms that Peter and the other disciples have left everything behind,
including home, wife and family for the sake of the kingdom of God
(18:29).[11] It is striking that in this list the wife is also mentioned; from

8   Luke 14:13, 21; 16:20; 18:22; 19:8; 21:3.
9   Luke 6:24; 12:16–21; 14:12; 16:19–31; 18:23.
10 Luke 5:14; 7:27; 10:25–28; 11:29–32 16:31; 17:26–33; 18:20; 20:17, 37–38, 41–44;
    cf. 11:49–51.
11 Also compare Joanna, the wife of Herod's steward Chuza, and many other women who

this it appears that, according to this gospel, marriage is subordinate to following Jesus. Jesus' characterization of the people who were not prepared for his (second) coming also does not sound positive about marriage: he says that they are as people in the time of Noah – they were eating and drinking, and marrying and being given in marriage (17:27). In the second century the preference that disciples of Jesus remain unmarried was sometimes inferred by what, according to Luke, he said to the Sadducees in their discussion on the resurrection of the dead,

> Jesus said to them, 'Those who belong to this age marry and are given in marriage; but those who are considered worthy of a place in that age and in the resurrection from the dead neither marry nor are given in marriage.' (20:34–35)

This saying is certainly intended with regard to the future, but has also been applied to the present. The true disciple of Jesus would then already during his life on earth need to lead an unmarried, angelic life and no longer die.[12] Yet this explanation is not obvious and we can justly conclude that Jesus accepted people in this world as getting married and being given in marriage.[13] What is remarkable in this context is that Luke did not include Jesus' conversation about divorce which is recorded in Mark 10:2–9, while he included to a large extent the passages from the Gospel of Mark immediately preceding and following this text.[14] With regard to divorce, Luke only mentions that Jesus disapproves of a man repudiating his wife and marrying another, or of a man marrying a divorced woman; he calls this adultery (16:18; cf. 18:20).

Regarding the coming of God's kingdom Luke shares the view that this has already happened with Jesus; therefore Jesus says that if by the finger of God he casts out demons then the kingdom of God has come (11:20). This presence of God's kingdom is also brought up when the Pharisees ask him when this will dawn. Jesus then answers,

---

followed and served Jesus (Luke 8:1–3). In Luke 14:20 the argument, 'I have married a woman and thus I cannot come,' is seen as an inacceptable excuse to decline an invitation to the dinner (as an image of the kingdom of God).

12 Cf. John 11:26. This explanation of an anonymous person is mentioned, but declined, by Clement of Alexandria, *Stromateis* III, 87, 1–3 (GCS 52 [15]). Perhaps he alluded to Marcion, who appealed to this verse as an argument for an unmarried life, according to Tertullian, *Against Marcion* IV, 38, 8 (SC 456). Cf. T. Baarda (1969), 'Als engelen …', *Voorlopig*, 1, 238–241.

13 In this case, 'the children of this world' ('those who belong to this age') are meant as 'the people in their earthly existence' and they are not in contrast with 'the children of the light', as in Luke 16:8; see Fitzmyer, *The Gospel According to Luke X–XXIV*, pp. 1108; 1305.

14 Cf. Mark 8:27–10:1 and Luke 9:18–51; Mark 10:13–34 and Luke 18:15–34.

The kingdom of God is not coming with things that can be observed;
nor will they say, 'Look, here it is!' or 'There it is!' For, in fact, the
kingdom of God is among you. (17:20–21).

In Greek it is written that the kingdom of God is *entos humôn*. This can
indeed be translated as 'among you', as it is in the NRSV. It may also be
translated as 'within you' or 'inside of you', but I regard 'among you' as
the most probable translation, as it is not likely that Jesus or the evangelist
wanted to create the impression that God's kingdom was already present
in the Pharisees with whom he regularly collided.[15]

Although in Luke's description Jesus presents God's kingdom in his
own person, this gospel, just as those of Mark and Matthew, also contains
Jesus' announcements of the horrors preceding its ultimate coming (17:22–
37; 21:5–36). Here also, his announcement of the judgement upon those
not taking him seriously can be heard.[16]

In general, the Gospel of Luke offers many narratives from and
about Jesus which do not appear in the other gospels.[17] Yet, despite its
own emphasis, it does not give an essentially different image of Jesus'
teachings.

3.4 *The Gospel of John*

The Gospel of John, however, does give a different image of Jesus'
appearance. For example, the emphasis on the coming of God's kingdom
does not occur there. Jesus only mentions God's kingdom when he tells
Nicodemus, a Pharisee, 'no one can see the kingdom of God without being
born from above', and 'no one can enter the kingdom of God without
being born of water and Spirit' (3:3, 5). This 'seeing' and 'entering' can be
explained with regard to the present as well as to the future. Facing Pilate,
Jesus remarkably enough speaks of '*my* kingdom', which is not of this
world (18:36).

Instead of proclaiming the coming of God's kingdom, in this gospel
Jesus speaks of 'eternal life', intended for those who believe in him and

---

15 Luke 5:17–26, 30; 6:2; 7:30, 36–50; 11:37–44, etc. A favourable exception can be
found in Luke 13:31. For the translation of *entos humôn* see François Bovon (2001),
Das Evangelium nach Lukas (Lk 15,1–19,27). Düsseldorf, Zürich: Patmos Verlag,
Benzinger Verlag, Neukirchen-Vluyn: Neukirchener Verlag, pp. 164–168.
16 Luke 6:24–26; 9:26; 10:10–15; 11:37–52; 12:9–10; 12:45–48; 13:23–30; 19:27.
17 E.g., Luke 10:30–37; 12:13–21; 13:1–9; 14:15–24; 15:11–16:9; 16:19–31; 17:7–19;
18:1–14; 19:1–10.

in his Father.[18] These expressions can be heard from the lips of Jesus as well as in the comments of the evangelist.[19] One of Jesus' prayers holds the following words, 'And this is eternal life, that they may know you, the only true God, and Jesus Christ whom you have sent' (17:3). This shows that 'eternal life', according to this gospel, is not so much something of the future, but designates a situation which begins as soon as someone comes to know God and Jesus Christ. Present and future melting into one another is also apparent from what Jesus says to Martha,

> I am the resurrection and the life;
> those who believe in me, though they die, will live,
> and everyone who lives and believes in me will never die. (11:25–26)

Upon which she confesses him as the Christ and the Son of God (11:27). That present and future melt into one another does not alter the fact that, in spite of this, Jesus, in the Gospel of John, announces the future resurrection of the dead from their graves and the following judgement (5:24–29). That this resurrection is something intended for the future is also apparent from these words of Jesus,

> No one can come to me unless drawn by the Father who sent me;
> and I will raise that person up on the last day. (6:44)

More than the other gospels, the Gospel of John deals with Jesus' teachings about his own identity and about faith in him.[20] As was apparent in section 2.5, in this gospel Jesus presents himself as the one whom God the Father has sent from heaven to make his name known and to act in his name. His 'I am' statements suggest that he presents himself as the LORD himself. According to this gospel, he has also made himself known as the Messiah, the Son of Man and the Son of God.[21] He speaks of an evil 'ruler of this world', whose power, however, is drawing to an end.[22] On several occasions he announces his exaltation, meaning his crucifixion and his exaltation unto God.[23] When he is lifted up from the earth, he will draw

18 John 5:24; 6:40, 47; vgl. 6:53–54; 10:25–28. Other texts about 'eternal life' or 'life': John 4:14, 36; 6:27, 33, 35, 48, 68; 8:12; 10:10; 12:25, 50; cf. 8:51.
19 John 3:15–16, 36; 20:31.
20 John 5:46–47; 6:29, 35; 7:38; 9:35–38; 12:44–46; 14:1, 10–12; 16:27; 17:8, 20–21; in explanatory texts of the evangelist: John 1:12; 2:11; 3:18; 4:39–42; 6:64; 7:31, 39; 8:30; 10:42; 11:25–27, 42, 45; 12:11, 42; 19:35.
21 John 4:25–26; 9:35–37; 10:36; cf. 1:41; 5:18.
22 John 12:31; 14:30; 16:11.
23 John 6:62; 8:28; 12:32; 20:17; cf. 3:13–14, which may be a comment of the evangelist.

all people to himself, so Jesus says in John 12:32. He tells his disciples that he is 'the way, and the truth, and the life', meaning that they can go to God the Father via him (14:6). In various passages, however, Jesus speaks critically and harshly about those who do not believe in him.[24]

Just as in the synoptic gospels, following Jesus is an important theme in the Gospel of John too,[25] but here Jesus makes no radical appeals to potential followers to abandon their wives and other members of their families. It is characteristic that, according to this gospel, Jesus performs his first miracle at a wedding in Cana, where he changes a large quantity of water into wine (2:1–11). Even if this narrative can be interpreted symbolically as a sign of Jesus' glory and the abundance of the messianic age, then it still speaks positively about the wedding performed in Cana.

Just as in the synoptic gospels, according to John, Jesus regularly refers to the Old Testament. He quotes Moses, the prophets and the psalms,[26] and the evangelist also characterizes him against this background.[27] In this gospel Jesus says that salvation is from the Jews (4:22). This salvation comes from God, and in using this term 'salvation' Jesus implicitly indicates himself.

In this gospel Jesus gives an important part of his teachings to his disciples privately (John 13–16). These texts are not about the end of the world and the coming of God's kingdom, but about Jesus' lasting bond with his disciples (15:1–10), their mutual love (13:34–35; 15:12–13), the coming of the Spirit (14:16–17, 26; 15:26; 16:7–15) and the opposition that awaits them (15:18–16:4). Chapter 7 will examine further to what degree this teaching can be called 'secret'.

We can assume that, where Jesus' language in the Gospel of John differs from the synoptic gospels, this is mainly due to the evangelist. It is often assumed that this gospel reflects the situation of the community for which it was written. Despite the differences, in the other gospels similar remarkable words of Jesus are also found. In section 2.3 a Johannine-sounding text of Jesus was quoted, which originated from the source Q: 'All things have been handed over to me by my Father; and no one knows the Son except the Father, and no one knows the Father except the Son and anyone to whom the Son chooses to reveal him.'[28] In the other

---

24 John 8:23–24, 43–47; 12:47–48; 15:6; cf. John 3:18–20, 36; 12:37–40.
25 John 1:37–43; 8:12; 10:4–5, 27; 12:26; 13:36–37; 21:19–22.
26 John 1:51; 5:39; 6:45; 7:22–23, 38; 8:17, 44, 56; 10:34–35; 12:8; 13:18; 15:25; 17:12.
27 John 1:45; 2:22; 3:14; 7:42; 12:13–15; 12:37–41; 19:24, 36–37.
28 Matthew 11:27; with some minor variations also in Luke 10:22; cf. John 3:35; 10:15; 13:3; 14:7–11; 17:2, 25.

gospels too Jesus pronounces the significant words 'I am'.[29] The great
emphasis which Jesus places on his own origin and identity in the Gospel
of John, however, does not appear in the synoptic gospels.

3.5 Evaluation of the New Testament data

We saw that in the synoptic gospels the kingdom of God is the main theme
of Jesus' teachings. On the one hand he announces its coming, on the other
hand he makes known that it has already come in his person. He invites
people to follow him and to live according to his moral codes of love. In
order to sustain this, he regularly appeals to the Old Testament books. A
result of a life in imitation of him is that family ties become less important.
In the Gospel of Luke, moreover, Jesus says that whoever wants to be
his disciple must leave his wife behind. The image of Jesus as a radical,
apocalyptical preacher, preparing his audience for the coming of God's
kingdom arouses the impression of generally going back to himself.

In the synoptic gospels Jesus is held as the Christ and the Son of
God, but that he actually is so, is not preached there by himself. Despite
various similarities with the synoptic gospels, the Gospel of John is set in
a different tone. Here, Jesus' teachings do relate to faith in him as the one
sent by God, as the Christ and the Son of God. Except for his conversation
with Nicodemus, where Jesus speaks about the seeing and entering of the
kingdom of God, this is not a theme in his teachings; instead of this, in
this gospel Jesus speaks about eternal life. Having a part in eternal life
begins by knowing God and Jesus during one's life on earth. In this gospel
the expectation for the future seems to be especially concentrated on the
personal future of those who believe in Jesus, but he also speaks of the
common resurrection of the dead from their graves and the judgement
following. The Gospel of John speaks of an evil 'ruler of this world'
whose power, however, is drawing to an end. It does not contain radical
appeals demanding of Jesus' disciples that they abandon their wives or
families. Just as in the synoptic gospels, Jesus appeals regularly to the
books of the Old Testament. The command to love, however, is limited
to the circle of Jesus' disciples.

The Gospel of John clearly differs in style and content from the synoptic
gospels. Apparently, the language and views of the early Johannine
community have been incorporated in it. We may assume, however, that
the core, at least, of Jesus, who, with a high level of self-consciousness
and with reference to the Old Testament, spoke about his own mission in
the name of God, stems from himself.

---

29 Mark 6:50; 14:62 and parallels; see section 2.2.

3.6 *The Gospel of Thomas*

Just as in the previous chapter, the Gospel of Thomas is the first source outside of the Bible to be considered. The heading above this gospel states that it contains 'secret' (or 'hidden') words of Jesus. The readers are incited to search for the explanation, and they are promised that 'whoever finds the meaning of these words will not die' (1). Such a person 'will be a king ruling over everything' (2), which means that he will be exalted above this world. Various sayings correspond more or less with the passages from the synoptic gospels and are therefore less secretive than the heading presumes. But often the texts of the Gospel of Thomas differ from the synoptic gospels and the drift is completely different.

Corresponding with the synoptic gospels is, that in this gospel Jesus regularly speaks about the kingdom of God; although in fact, he often speaks of 'the kingdom' without further addition,[30] and sometimes with the addition 'of the Father' and 'of heaven'.[31] The third saying contains an ironic polemic with other teachers about the nature of this kingdom:

Jesus said,
If your leaders say to you, Look! the kingdom is in heaven,
then the birds of heaven will arrive first before you.
If they say to you, It is in the sea,
then the fish of the sea will arrive first before you.
Rather the kingdom is inside of you and outside of you.
[Whoever] knows [himself] will find it.[32]
When you know yourselves, then you will become known
and you will understand that you are the children of the Living Father.
But if you will not know yourselves,
you are impoverished and you are poverty. (3)

According to these words, 'the kingdom' is not far away spatially, therefore it is not in the heaven above the earth either. On the contrary, it is something within Jesus' disciples, yet at the same time outside of them.

---

30   Thomas 3; 22; 27; 46; 49; 82; 107; 109; 113; cf. 21. In the New Testament the absolute use of 'the kingdom' occurs in Matthew 8:12; 9:35; 13:19; 13:38; 24:14; Luke 12:32 (but see also 12:31); 22:29 (but see also 22:30); Acts 20:25.

31   'Of the Father': Thomas 57; 76; 96; 97; 98; 113; 'of heaven': 20; 54; 114. The lacunous Greek text of Thomas 3 in Papyrus Oxyrhynchus 654 originally read either the expression 'the kingdom of heaven' or 'the kingdom of God'. The Greek text of Thomas 27 in Papyrus Oxyrhynchus 1 reads 'the kingdom of God'.

32   This line has only been transmitted, and, moreover, in lacunose form, in the Greek manuscript Papyrus Oxyrhynchus 654 and not in the Coptic text.

In the Greek text of the Gospel of Thomas 3 *entos humôn* is written for 'inside of you' just as in Luke 17:21;[33] because 'inside' here is used in contrast with 'outside', and because Jesus speaks here to his disciples and not – as in Luke – to the Pharisees , the translation 'inside of you' is more obvious than in Luke 17:21. That the kingdom is also outside of them is perhaps explained in a saying at the end of this collection, where Jesus answers the question of his disciples about when the kingdom would come,

> It will not come by waiting.
> It will not be said, Look! Here it is! or Look! There it is!
> Rather, the kingdom of the Father is spread out over the earth,
> but people do not see it. (113)

Here, however, no explanation is given how the kingdom is spread out over the earth. Soon it will become apparent that the statement about the kingdom being 'outside of you' can also be interpreted as a reference to the supercelestial kingdom from where Jesus' disciples come.

According to Gospel of Thomas 3, this kingdom finds expression in self-knowledge. The appeal 'know thyself' was well known in the Greek world, and in Judaism and early Christianity the importance of self-knowledge is also acknowledged. This refers, among other things, to knowledge of the origin, the deepest identity and the destination of human beings.[34] Whoever has acquired this knowledge is known by God, according to this saying in the Gospel of Thomas, and knows that he belongs to the 'sons of the living Father'. (It is also possible to translate 'sons and daughters', but because according to Gospel of Thomas 114, Mary Magdalene must first become masculine prior to entering the kingdom of heaven, preference should be given in Gospel Thomas 3 to the translation 'sons'.) What is meant by this is that he who lacks self-knowledge, and does not know where he comes from or what his purpose in life is, finds himself in spiritual poverty. According to Gospel of Thomas 67, Jesus says, 'Whoever knows everything, but needs (to know) himself, is in need of everything.' A glance behind the scenes regarding the origin of the human being is probably afforded in the following saying:

> Jesus said,
> The old man will not hesitate to ask a little child seven days old

---

33 See section 3.3.
34 See Roukema, *Gnosis and Faith in Early Christianity*, pp. 57–63; also Song of Songs 1:8 LXX ('if you do not know yourself ...'); the Hermetic writing *Poimandres* 18 (*Corpus Hermeticum* I, 18; ed. Nock and Festugière).

about the place of life,
and he will live. (4)

Because a baby, or at the very least its soul or spirit,[35] has but just come from 'the place of life', an old man can learn something from such a child; the elderly person, after all, stands close to death and stands before the passage to this 'place of life'.[36] That this place of life can also be called 'the kingdom', is apparent from Gospel Thomas 49:

Jesus said,
Blessed are the solitary, the chosen ones,
because you will find the kingdom.
For you are from it.
You will return there again.

We see that 'the kingdom', according to this gospel, is not only present in and among Jesus' disciples and spread out over the earth, but that it is also a place or state where Jesus' chosen disciples come from.[37] As stated earlier, the phrase that the kingdom is 'outside of you' (3) can also be interpreted in this sense. Later we will examine where this kingdom is located according to this gospel.

From Gospel of Thomas 50, it is apparent that 'the kingdom' can also be called 'the light'. After the death of the body, when a soul wants to return to the light, it must answer a few critical questions posed to her by hostile heavenly powers, as is evident from similar texts of the same period.[38] About this Jesus remarks:

35 See Thomas 87 and 112 for the difference between soul and body in this gospel. The spirit in a human being is mentioned in Thomas 14; 29; 114.
36 See Margaretha Lelyveld (1987), *Les Logia de la vie dans l'Évangile selon Thomas: A la recherche d'une tradition et d'une rédaction*. Leiden: Brill, p. 28; Michael Fieger (1991), *Das Thomasevangelium: Einleitung, Kommentar und Systematik*. Münster: Aschendorff, pp. 30–32.
37 This is also expressed in Thomas 19, 'Whoever existed before being born is blessed'; this refers to the pre-existence of the human soul or spirit.
38 See Ménard, *L'Évangile selon Thomas*, pp. 152–153; April D. DeConick (2001), *Voices of the Mystics: Early Christian Discourse in the Gospels of John and Thomas and Other Ancient Christian Literature*. Sheffield: Sheffield Academic Press, p. 93; Jan Helderman (2004), 'Logion 50 des Thomasevangeliums', in Mat Immerzeel and Jacques van der Vliet, eds, *Coptic Studies on the Threshold of a New Millennium* I. Leuven: Peeters, pp. 759–768; Roukema, *Gnosis and Faith in Early Christianity*, pp. 49–50, with references to *First Revelation of James* (Nag Hammadi Codex V, 3) 33–34; Irenaeus, *Against Heresies* I, 21, 5 (SC 264); Epiphanius, *Panarion* 36, 3, 2; see also *Panarion* 26, 13, 2 (NHS 35); *Gospel of Mary* 15–17 (see section 3.8); Giovanni Pugliese Carratelli (2003), *Les lamelles d'or orphiques: Instructions pour le voyage d'outre-tombe des initiés grecs*. Paris: Les belles lettres, pp. 35; 61; 68; 83; 84; 95.

If they say to you, Where did you come from?,
say to them, We came from the light, –
the place where the light came into being on its own accord
and established [itself] and became manifest through their image.
If they say to you, Is it you?,
say, We are its sons,
and we are the chosen people of the living Father.
If they ask you, What is the sign of your Father in you?,
say to them: It is movement and rest. (50)

The words, 'It is movement and rest,' constitute the password necessary
to be admitted to the kingdom of light.

Just as in the biblical gospels,[39] Jesus says in the Gospel of Thomas
that for a human being to enter the kingdom, he must become like a child,
but the manner in which he uses this image is here differently coloured.
The following conversation testifies to this:

Jesus saw little babies nursing.
He said to his disciples,
These little ones are like those who enter the kingdom.
They said to him,
Will we enter the kingdom as little babies?
Jesus said to them,
When you make the two one,
and when you make the inside like the outside,
and the above like the below,
and when you make the male and the female into a single being,
with the result that the male is not male nor the female female,
when you make eyes in place of an eye,
and a hand in place of a hand,
and a foot in place of a foot,
and an image in place of an image,
then you will enter the kingdom. (22)

This saying means that an adult human being, who is masculine or
feminine, must attempt to regain the asexual state of a child.[40] Various
sayings in this gospel dealing with becoming one and with the solitary[41]

---

39 See, e.g., Matthew 18:3–4; 19:14; John 3:3–5.
40 See T. Baarda (1983), *Early Transmission of Words of Jesus: Thomas, Tatian and the
Text of the New Testament: A Collection of Studies*. Amsterdam: Free University Press,
pp. 261–288; also in Baarda (1982), '2 Clement and the Sayings of Jesus', in J. Delobel,
ed., *Logia: Les Paroles de Jésus – The Sayings of Jesus*. Leuven: Peeters, pp. 529–556.
41 Thomas 4; 11; 16; 23; 49; 75; 106.

also point to this. In this vein, the end of Gospel of Thomas 4, the previously quoted saying of an old man asking a little child about the place of life, reads,

> For many who are first will be last
> and they will become one.

Gospel of Thomas 11 ends with these words:

> When you are in the light, what will you become?
> On the day when you were one, you became two.
> When you become two, what will you become?

This alludes to the conviction that the human being was originally one, and was subsequently split in two. Behind this is a myth recorded by Plato. In it, the comedian Aristophanes narrates that at first there were three sexes: men, women and people who were male and female at the same time – androgynous, therefore. When these creatures attempted to force their way into heaven, Zeus split them in two as punishment, so that each man or woman henceforth is looking for his or her other half.[42] The Gospel of Thomas leaves aside that according to Plato's myth men can desire men and women can desire women; in saying 22 only the polarity between men and women is considered.[43] Thus the Gospel of Thomas alludes to the view that in the light, where they come from, people – or their souls – were androgynous. When the souls came to earth from the supercelestial light, they were given male or female bodies. In their childhood, people are not yet sexually active, but when they become adults, they must strive to become one again by uniting the masculine and feminine within themselves and to leave behind the sexual orientation to the other sex. Whoever has made this insight and this ascetic and celibate way of life his own, is ready to enter 'the kingdom'.

Against the background of Jesus' teachings in the New Testament gospels the question arises whether according to the Gospel of Thomas as well, this kingdom is something of the future and whether this gospel in

---

42 Plato, *Symposium* 189e–193e.
43 The Jew Philo of Alexandria (first half of the first century CE) also states in his work *On the Creation* 76 (LCL 226) that the human being, according to Genesis 1:26–27, in the invisible model of creation, was initially male and female in one and was later (Genesis 2:21–23) split into two sexes; see Roukema, *Gnosis and Faith in Early Christianity*, pp. 82–84. Also in the Hermetic writing *Poimandres* 15–18 (*Corpus Hermeticum* I, 15–18; probably from the first century CE; ed. Nock and Festugière) the separation of the originally androgynous human being is only concerned with the polarity between men and women.

general offers a vision of the future. In Gospel of Thomas 113, we already saw that Jesus evasively answered the question about the moment of the coming of this kingdom by pointing out that it is already spread out over the earth. In Gospel of Thomas 51, his disciples pose a similar question:

When will the dead rest,
and when will the new world come?

Jesus' answer to this resembles the text in Gospel of Thomas 113:

What you look for has come,
but you have not perceived it. (51)

Yet in this gospel, Jesus does say something about the future. The beginning of Gospel of Thomas 11 reads:

This heaven will pass away,
and the one above it will pass away.
And the dead are not alive,
and the living will not die.
In the days when you ate what is dead,
you made it something living.
When you are in the light, what will you become?

From this we can infer that the first and the second heavens will pass away, and that 'the light', in which Jesus' disciples will come, is above this; as is evident from various texts, in Judaism the third heaven was interpreted as the place of paradise.[44] At the same time, it becomes clear that the kingdom from which Jesus' disciples originate, according to Gospel of Thomas 49, and to where they will return, is also to be found – in the conception of this gospel – above the first and second heavens. This is the kingdom which, according to Gospel of Thomas 3, is outside Jesus' disciples on earth.

In the beginning of Gospel of Thomas 111, another saying about the future is recorded, 'The heavens and the earth will roll up in your

---

44 See Albert L. A. Hogeterp (2005), 'The *Gospel of Thomas* and the Historical Jesus: The Case of Eschatology', in Anthony Hilhorst and George H. van Kooten, eds, *The Wisdom of Egypt: Jewish, Early Christian, and Gnostic Essays in Honour of Gerard P. Luttikhuizen.* Leiden, Boston: Brill, pp. 381–396 (390); he refers to the Testament of Levi 2:7–10 (OTP 1); 2 Corinthians 12:2–4; Revelation of Paul 20–21. See also Riemer Roukema, 'Paul's Rapture to Paradise in Early Christian Literature', in the same book, pp. 267–283.

presence.'[45] So this gospel does seem to hold an apocalyptic view of the future.[46] However, in another conversation, Jesus relativizes this searching for the end,

> The disciples said to Jesus,
> Tell us how our end will come about?
> Jesus said,
> Have you discovered the beginning that you seek the end?
> Because where the beginning is, the end will be also.
> Whoever will stand in the beginning is blessed.
> This person will know the end, yet will not die. (18)

This shows that, according to this gospel, Jesus especially wanted to incite his disciples to search for their origin. He who has come to understand that he originates from the kingdom of light, is prepared to return to it at the end of his earthly life, and in this sense, not to die.

It can be deduced from Gospel of Thomas 21 that those who enter the kingdom after their earthly life lay down their bodies. To Mary's (probably Mary Magdalene's) question 'Who are your disciples like?' Jesus answers,

> They are like little children sojourning in a field that is not theirs.
> When the owners of the field come,
> they will say, Leave our field!
> In front of them, they strip naked to abandon it,
> returning their field to them. (21)

Jesus' disciples dwell as children on earth, which belongs to foreign powers. When these powers come to claim their earthly possessions, the children lay down their bodies and leave the earth to the lower powers to ascend to the kingdom of the Father.[47]

An important aspect of Jesus' teaching is that, when someone wants to become his disciple, the distinction from Jesus vanishes. Thus he says,

---

45 Cf. Isaiah 34:4; Hebrews 1:10–12; Revelation 6:14.
46 Hogeterp, 'The *Gospel of Thomas* and the Historical Jesus', p. 387, also refers to the Greek text of Thomas 5 for a reference to the resurrection, which reads, 'For there is nothing buried that [will not be raised].' Because the last words in the manuscript are lost and can only be completed as conjecture, I will not go into this saying any further. This line cannot be found in the Coptic text.
47 Cf. Thomas 37, 'His disciples said, When will you appear to us? Jesus said, When you strip naked without shame, take your garments, put them under your feet like little children, and trample on them, then you will see the Son of the Living One and you will not be afraid.'

Whoever drinks from my mouth will become as I am.
I myself will become that person,
and what is hidden will be revealed to him. (108)

Something similar is meant in Gospel of Thomas 24:

His disciples said,
Teach us about the place where you are,
because we must seek it.
He said to them,
Whoever has ears should listen.
There is light inside each person of light.
And it lights up the whole world.
If it does not shine, it is dark.

This means that the true disciple of Jesus has the light within himself and
no longer needs Jesus who, according to Gospel of Thomas 77, is the
light which is above all things.

To an important extent the Gospel of Thomas aims at acquiring
the true insight into the origin and destination of the human being. It
contains few concrete moral instructions as we find them in, for example,
the Sermon on the Mount. Contrary to the Sermon on the Mount in
the Gospel of Matthew, it is not necessary for Jesus' disciples to fast, to
pray and to give alms, according to the Gospel of Thomas; this is even
called sinful and harmful.[48] Jesus does, however, teach here 'to fast with
regard to the world' and 'to observe the Sabbath as a Sabbath', criticize
wealth and praise generosity and poverty.[49] Jesus' emphasis on loving
one's neighbour, which appears in the synoptic gospels, is expressed here
as 'love your brother like your soul, watch over him like the pupil of
your eye' (25). The limitation of the love for 'the brother' – apparently in

48 Thomas 6; 14; 104; cf. Matthew 6:1–18. In Thomas 104 Jesus also says, 'Rather, when
the bridegroom leaves the bridal chamber, then they should fast and pray,' but this
does not apply to Jesus' true disciples, for, according to Thomas 75, they have to enter
the bridal chamber (cf. Mark 2:18–20 and parallels). See R. Schippers and T. Baarda
(1960), *Het evangelie van Thomas: Apocriefe woorden van Jezus.* Kampen: Kok, p.
127.
49 Thomas 27; 54; 63; 64; 95; 110. In saying 27, 'to fast with regard to the world' refers to
keeping distance towards the material world, and 'to observe the Sabbath as a Sabbath'
may allude to a spiritual understanding of the Sabbath; thus Ménard, *L'Évangile selon
Thomas*, pp. 120–121. Interestingly, T. Baarda (1994), *Essays on the Diatessaron.*
Kampen: Kok Pharos, pp. 147–171, translates 'if you do not sabbatize with respect to
the Sabbath' and argues that 'Sabbath' refers to the Old Testament God, from whom
one should withdraw.

the spiritual sense[50] – corresponds with John 13:34–35, where Jesus also commands his disciples to love one another. In a similar way in Gospel of Thomas 48 Jesus recommends members of the same household to live in peace, 'If two people make peace with each other in the same house, they will say to the mountain, Go forth! and it will move.'

Just as in the synoptic gospels, according to Thomas, Jesus does not have a high regard for family ties:

> Whoever does not hate his father and mother
> cannot become a disciple of mine.
> And whoever does not hate his brothers and sisters
> and carry his cross as I do will not be worthy of me. (55)

He or she who does not want to be a disciple of Jesus, will end up badly:

> Gaze upon the Living One while you are alive,
> in case you die and (then) seek to see him,
> and you will not be able to see (him). (59)

Likewise, Jesus speaks about those who either do or do not have the knowledge of 'the kingdom' within them (cf. Gospel of Thomas 3):

> When you acquire within you that certain thing,
> what is within you will save you.
> If you do not have it within you,
> what you do not have within you will kill you. (70)

Summarizing Jesus' teachings according to this secret and mysterious Gospel of Thomas, we see that in a concealed way Jesus brings a mystical message, often in images and parables, in which he incites his disciples to acquire self-knowledge. This knowledge concerns their origin and ultimate destination. His disciples need to know that they originate from 'the light', also called 'the kingdom', and that they are destined to return there. In preparation of this return, they need to unite the masculine and the feminine within themselves and live as celibate 'solitary ones', in simplicity and in mutual love. In addition, the bond with Jesus goes beyond the affiliation with one's own family. Although this kingdom essentially is something supercelestial, thanks to Jesus' teachings it has

---

50 Cf. Thomas 99, 'Those here who do the will of my Father, they are my brothers and my mother. They are the people who will enter the kingdom of my Father.'

spread out over the earth and Jesus' disciples have it within themselves. Thanks to that which they have within themselves – also called 'the light' – they become equal to Jesus and are exalted above the world. As soon as the moment has come that they will return to the supercelestial kingdom of light, they leave their bodies behind on earth. From Jesus' teachings in this gospel it is apparent that, even though everything comes forth from him and everything reaches up to him,[51] the earth belongs to hostile powers who will come and claim their possessions. Such powers also pose critical questions to the souls or spirits of Jesus' disciples who want to ascend to the light where they originally came from. Regarding the future of the world, this gospel teaches that the heavens and the earth will be rolled up and that the (first) heaven and the heaven above it will pass by. It can be deduced that, according to this gospel, the imperishable kingdom of light is to be found above the second heaven.

In section 2.7 we saw that in the Gospel of Thomas Jesus barely refers to Old Testament books. This secret gospel does not reveal that Jesus comes forth from Judaism and that for his teachings he refers to the law of Moses and Israel's prophets. Yet, various sayings of Jesus still point to his Jewish surroundings when, for example, Adam, Israel's prophets, John the Baptist, the Sabbath, the Pharisees, and a Samaritan on his way to Judea are mentioned.[52]

3.7 *The Gospel of Judas*

In section 2.9 it was already mentioned that, according to the Gospel of Judas, Jesus gave special teachings to this disciple about the heavenly powers, the origin of rebellious angels and the secrets of the kingdom. The gospel begins with a reference to Jesus' public appearance:

> When he appeared on earth, he performed miracles and great wonders for the salvation of humanity. And some walked in the way of righteousness while others walked in their transgression.

From this short sketch of Jesus' appearance and its result, it appears that the author of this gospel assumes that his readers are familiar with these traditions. Afterwards, a closer look is taken at the smaller circle of Jesus' disciples:

---

51 Thomas 77; see section 2.7.
52 Thomas 27; 39; 46; 52; 60; 85; 102.

The twelve disciples were called, and he began to speak with them about the mysteries beyond the world and what would take place at the end.[53]

Jesus speaks of a great and holy generation to which he himself belongs. He says that 'the souls of every human generation will die', whereas to those who on earth belong to this holy generation applies that 'when (…) the spirit leaves them, their bodies will die, but their souls will be alive, and they will be taken up'.[54] Of this holy generation and its destination, however, Jesus' disciples, with the exception of Judas, have no notion whatsoever. His disciples told him that in a dream they had seen priests, who were in a large house in which many others were present, bringing offerings on an altar and thereby invoking his name. These priests led a sinful life. The description of this dream reminds one of the Jewish sacrifices in the temple. Jesus explains to his disciples, however, that they themselves were the priests, but that they were serving the wrong God, Saklas, i.e. 'the Fool', the God of the Old Testament. In this way they were leading the believers astray.[55] This dream has been interpreted as a reference to the celebration of the Eucharist in early catholic Christianity. In this celebration bread and wine were offered as a sacrifice to the Creator. If this interpretation is correct, the author of the Gospel of Judas might indirectly be criticizing the celebration of the Eucharist in the Christian church of his own time, i.e. the second century.[56] Another explanation is that this dream refers to the bishops of the second-century church, who encouraged their believers to undergo martyrdom. The author of the Gospel of Judas may have interpreted this in such a way that the bishops in fact offered people to their God.[57]

Since, besides Judas, the twelve disciples did not understand any of Jesus' teachings and continued to worship their own God, the gospel concentrates on Judas. He is told the names of various angelic powers, how they are organized and that Saklas will complete the span of time assigned for him. Considering that the manuscript is mangled in many places, the purpose of this teaching is not always clear.

In this document Judas is described as Jesus' most intimate disciple, but even Judas does not seem to belong to the holy generation, which implies that he is not fully redeemed. This gospel does not contain any

---

53 Gospel of Judas 33; translations adapted from Rodolphe Kasser et al., *The Gospel of Judas*, p. 185.
54 Gospel of Judas 43.
55 Gospel of Judas 38–41; 56.
56 E.g., Gathercole, *The Gospel of Judas: Rewriting Early Christianity*, p. 77.
57 Thus Elaine Pagels and Karen King (2007), *Reading Judas: The Gospel of Judas and the Shaping of Christianity*. London, New York: Allen Lane, pp. 43–50; 74–75.

concrete teaching for Jesus' twelve disciples apart from Judas, let alone for the people.

3.8 *The Gospel of Mary*

The Gospel of Mary is partially preserved in Coptic, in the so-called Gnostic Codex of Berlin (8502, 1). From the numbering of the pages it appears that more than half of the manuscript has been lost. Two mangled Greek fragments of this gospel have also been found. It is credited to Mary, meaning Mary Magdalene. She is described as a faithful disciple of Jesus, who understands him better than his male disciples Peter, Andrew and Levi, and encourages them to preach Jesus' message without fear. The document can be dated to the first half of the second century.[58]

Jesus – always called 'the Saviour' – speaks only at the beginning of the remaining text; in the other passages Mary speaks with a few male disciples. Because the first six pages have been lost and as these probably included words of Jesus, a large part of his teachings in this gospel are missing. It may have included a description of Jesus appearing to his disciples after his resurrection from the dead, which would imply that his instruction took place in this context.[59]

On the first preserved page, Jesus speaks about the end of the world, when matter will be dissolved to its original nature. In answer to Peter's question about the sin of the world, Jesus says,

> Sin does not exist, but you are the ones who sin when you do things which are like the nature of adultery: that is called sin. Because of this the Good One came into your midst, to those who belong to all natural phenomena, in order to restore Nature up to her root.[60]

With the term 'the Good One', Jesus means himself.[61] Although it is strange that, according to this gospel, Jesus says that there is no sin, he does acknowledge that his disciples do commit sin. The purpose of his coming is radically to restore the world which has gotten into confusion by 'what is opposite to Nature' (8–9). Whereupon Jesus says that his

---

58 See Esther A. de Boer (2004), *The Gospel of Mary: Beyond a Gnostic and a Biblical Mary Magdalene*. London, New York: T&T Clark, pp. 12–100.
59 This is suggested by Pheme Perkins (1980), *The Gnostic Dialogue: The Early Church and the Crisis of Gnosticism*. New York: Paulist Press, pp. 133–134.
60 Gospel of Mary 7; de Boer, *The Gospel of Mary*, p. 19.
61 In Platonic philosophy 'the first Good' was God, i.e. the first Intelligence (*nous*); thus Alcinous, *Didaskalikos* 27 (ed. Whittaker and Louis); this goes back to Plato, *Republic* 504d–509c; 517b–521b.

disciples should not be led astray by people who say 'look here' or 'look there',

> for the Son of Man is within you. Follow him! Those who seek him will find him. Go then and preach the gospel of the kingdom. Do not lay down any rule other than the one I appointed for you, and do not give a law like the lawgiver so that you are not imprisoned by it.[62]

After he has said this, Jesus leaves his disciples and his teaching has temporarily ended. Jesus' words about the Son of Man who is 'within you' remind one of the Gospel of Thomas 3, where Jesus says about 'the kingdom' that it is 'within' or 'inside of you', but also of the Gospel of John, where Jesus states that he will be in his disciples.[63] Given that the first pages have been lost, it cannot be deduced with absolute certainty what is meant here regarding the rules that Jesus himself formulated. It is possible that an allusion is made here to his commandment of love.[64] In his saying that his disciples should not give a law in the manner of the lawgiver, the term 'lawgiver' could either be pointing to God who gave his law to Israel, or to Moses.[65] In the first case Jesus would be criticizing the God of the Old Testament in this gospel, but if 'lawgiver' refers to Moses, then Jesus would be distancing himself from the Jewish law as the apostle Paul also did.[66] In reaction to the view that the Gospel of Mary is of a gnostic character, Esther de Boer has argued that Jesus' teaching about the world and man are represented here in concepts derived from Stoic philosophy. Thus she disputes that this gospel has a gnostic content.[67] It is indeed correct that in the preserved pages of this gospel Jesus' teachings do not contain a negative judgement of the creation of the material world and of the Creator.

After Mary has instructed and encouraged Jesus' male disciples, Peter asks her to tell which of the Saviour's words she remembers. She answers that she will tell what is hidden (or secret) for the others and describes a vision in which Jesus taught her about the ascension of the soul (10). On this journey, the soul confronts the powers named Darkness, Desire, Ignorance, Jealousy of Death, Kingdom of the Flesh, Foolish Learning and Hot Tempered Wisdom. These powers interrogate the

---

62 Gospel of Mary 8–9; de Boer, *The Gospel of Mary*, p. 19.
63 John 14:20; cf. 6:56; 15:4–7; 17:23.
64 Thus de Boer, *The Gospel of Mary*, pp. 24; 58; 90 (e.g., Mark 12:31, John 13:34–35).
65 W. Gutbrod (1969), 'nomos', in Gerhard Kittel, Geoffrey W. Bromiley, eds, *Theological Dictionary of the New Testament* 4. Grand Rapids MI: Eerdmans, p. 1089.
66 E.g., in Galatians 3:1–25; see de Boer, *The Gospel of Mary*, pp. 29–34.
67 De Boer, *The Gospel of Mary*, pp. 35–59.

soul wanting to ascend to heaven about where it came from. If the soul answers correctly, the powers have to allow her to pass through (15–17). Apparently, according to this gospel Mary experienced this vision after Jesus' resurrection.[68] Andrew and Peter reacted negatively towards this and could not believe that this teaching came from Jesus himself, because it contained other ideas than they knew from their Lord (17–18). This teaching about the ascension of the soul and the answers that it had to give to the severe angelic powers corresponds to various other testimonies from the same period,[69] but it is absent from the canonical gospels.

3.9 *The Tripartite Tractate*

Jesus is not quoted as speaking in the *Tripartite Tractate*, but some data from this work still deserve to be mentioned. By analogy with the pre-existent world (cf. section 2.11) there are three types of people, according to this document. There is a spiritual type who has a divine light and a divine spirit (that is, the divine spark) within himself, there is a psychic type who does not have this light and this spirit but who can be redeemed, and there is a hylic or material type who will perish (118–121). In a passage about the incarnation of the Saviour and the people related to him is written that he taught them about himself in an invisible manner (114–115). According to Einar Thomassen this refers to the spiritual instruction that the Saviour gave to the spiritual people.[70] The author of the *Tripartite Tractate* does not enter into details about this, but regarding the contents of this teaching, he surely had in mind the earlier explained origin of the Saviour and his unknowable Father in the highest heaven (section 2.11). It is striking that he later speaks about baptism administered on the basis of faith in the Father, the Son and the Holy Spirit and leading to salvation (127–128). In this respect, the author of this document and the group for which he wrote apparently do not differ from the practice of the 'catholic' church, which corresponds to the baptismal command according to Matthew 28:19.

---

68 De Boer, *The Gospel of Mary*, pp. 73–75.
69 Cf. p. 73, where we referred to Thomas 50; *First Revelation of James* 33–34; Irenaeus, *Against Heresies* I, 21, 5; Epiphanius, *Panarion* 26, 13, 2; 36, 3, 2; see also Riemer Roukema (2003), 'Les anges attendant les âmes des défunts: une comparaison entre Origène et quelques gnostiques', in L. Perrone, P. Bernardino and D. Marchini, eds, *Origeniana Octava: Origen and the Alexandrian Tradition*. Leuven: Peeters, pp. 367–374.
70 Painchaud, Thomassen, *Le traité tripartite (NH I, 5)*, 423. However, in his book *The Spiritual Seed*, p. 48, Thomassen writes that this sentence does not fit in this context and was probably added later.

3.10 *Other teachings of Jesus after his death and resurrection*

A large number of books considered to be 'gnostic' describe Jesus after his death appearing to his disciples as the living Saviour and going into discussion with them and giving supplementary teaching.[71] To be mentioned are, for example, the *Secret Book of John*,[72] the *Book of Thomas the Warrior*, the *Wisdom of Jesus Christ* and *Peter's Letter to Philip*.[73] We have already encountered this pattern in our discussion of the Gospel of Mary, which presumably must be situated after Jesus' resurrection.

In those conversations after his resurrection, Jesus reveals to his disciples matters about God the Father, the supercelestial spheres and the powers dwelling there, and about Sophia, who of her own free will, without consent from the Father, wanted to bring forth a heavenly being. This being, called Yaldabaoth or Saklas, became a deformity, however, who together with other angelic powers began to create the material world and mankind. Jesus speaks of his own coming as messenger of the Father – and therefore not of the Creator Yaldabaoth – and of the manner in which the true knowledge or gnosis will lead to spiritual salvation. Since Jesus allegedly gave these revelations after his life on earth, the authors of these writings made no pretensions that this teaching stems from the earthly Jesus. It is thus obvious to conclude that this teaching was put into his mouth as the resurrected Saviour. For this reason we will pay no further attention to it.[74] We must note, however, that the groups who believed in these revelations regarded them as secret teaching intended only for a limited circle of Jesus' followers; or, stated differently, in their eyes it contained esoteric knowledge into which most Christians were not initiated. The question of whether Jesus gave exclusive esoteric teaching to a few of his most faithful followers during his life deserves separate discussion. As mentioned earlier, chapter 7 is dedicated to this.

---

71 See Perkins, *The Gnostic Dialogue*.

72 In Nag Hammadi Codex II, 1; III, 1; IV, 1 and the Gnostic Codex of Berlin 8502, 2; see Roukema, *Gnosis and Faith in Early Christianity*, pp. 36–49 and Karen L. King (2006), *The Secret Revelation of John*. Harvard: University Press.

73 In, respectively, Nag Hammadi Codex II, 7; III, 4 (and the Gnostic Codex of Berlin 8502, 3); VIII, 2.

74 In the next chapter we will also consider the sayings in the canonical gospels and the Acts of the Apostles ascribed to Jesus after his resurrection as traditions, historically speaking, from the early church and not as words of the historical Jesus.

3.11 *Comparison of New Testament and other writings*

How do the New Testament writings, which we examined in section 3.5, relate to the other early Christian works treated in this chapter? The Gospel of Thomas corresponds to the New Testament gospels to a certain extent. It contains various sayings of Jesus which it shares, usually in a slightly different wording, with these gospels. The kingdom that Jesus announces in the Gospel of Thomas is on the one hand something of the inner man, even though it is also spread out over the earth; on the other hand, it can be localized in the supercelestial sphere of light. A new element is that the earth will be claimed by lower, hostile powers pretending to be its owners. Like the synoptic gospels, the Gospel of Thomas is critical about family ties, and goes even deeper in its plea for a celibate way of life. The reason for this plea differs from the synoptic gospels; according to the Gospel of Thomas, people were originally asexual and androgynous and need to return to that state during their life on earth. Behind various sayings in the Gospel of Thomas there is a larger story which is not the background of the New Testament gospels. This holds that the human being essentially originates from the supercelestial kingdom of light, was united with a body on earth, and is destined to return to its origin without the body. Knowledge of this – i.e. self-knowledge – is necessary to be saved along this way. An important difference from the New Testament gospels is also that the Gospel of Thomas does not positively relate to the Old Testament. The prophets of Israel are even called 'the dead' and are placed opposite the Living Jesus. Also, the reference to a secret teaching intended only for Thomas and not for the other disciples is unfamiliar to the New Testament gospels. These differences point out that the compiler or compilers of the Gospel of Thomas interpreted and supplemented Jesus' teaching in a certain direction. This direction can be characterized as 'gnostic'.[75]

Like the Gospel of Thomas, the Gospel of Judas does not contain teachings of Jesus to the people, although it does refer to them. It pretends to offer Jesus' secret teaching to Judas, in which Jesus introduces the highest God, as opposed to his other disciples who hold on to their traditional God. What matters to a human being is to belong to the holy generation. Salvation for human beings consists in the ascension of their souls.

75 Cf. Antti Marjanen (1998), 'Is *Thomas* a Gnostic Gospel?', in Risto Uro, ed., *Thomas at the Crossroads: Essays on the Gospel of Thomas*. Edinburgh: T&T Clark, pp. 107–139, where Marjanen, by the way, erroneously concludes that if the Gospel of Thomas can be considered gnostic, this also applies to the Gospel of John. The Gospel of John, after all, does not contain any references to the origin of the human soul from the supercelestial kingdom, to which it is supposed to return. For this, see also section 5.1, note 1.

The Gospel of Mary teaches that the Son of Man is in the inner self of Jesus' disciples. It contains, among other things, the description of a vision in which Mary Magdalene saw how the soul in its ascent on high had to confront evil powers. This points to a connection with the previously discussed gospels.

The *Tripartite Tractate* and other testimonies treated in chapter 2 demonstrate that the view that Jesus proclaimed an unknown, exalted God who cannot be identified with the Old Testament God regularly emerges there. This view is usually called 'gnostic'. In the Gospel of Thomas this aspect of Jesus' teaching did not explicitly emerge, but the fragments which indicate that the earth is claimed by inferior powers and that, in its ascent, the soul has to confront these powers, do correspond with the gnostic world view. The Gospel of Mary has been passed down in too fragmentary a state to give a definite answer about its gnostic character.

From the historical point of view it is, however, completely out of the question that Jesus preached a God who by far surpassed the God of Israel. Consequently, the teaching that salvation consists in the ascension of the soul to the highest heaven of this more exalted God cannot originate from Jesus himself either. As a Jew, Jesus stood on the foundation of the Jewish Scriptures – in general the present Old Testament – and believed in the God of Israel. In his teaching, he has reverted to and continued building upon the books of Moses and the prophets. It is remarkable – as shown in chapter 2 – that early followers of Jesus recognized him as the LORD and that they sometimes saw a difference between Jesus the LORD and God the Father whom he proclaimed. Yet, the image of this Father does not correspond to the exalted God whom Jesus proclaimed according to the gnostic writings. This idea originated from the difficulty that later Christians had with the image of God in the Old Testament. Therefore they concluded that they were dealing here with a lower deity, while Jesus was to have originated from the perfect highest God. This view represents *theology* of a later date, but has no historical base in the life of Jesus.

CHAPTER 4

Jesus' Death, Resurrection and Exaltation

According to numerous ancient testimonies, Jesus died on a cross and after three days was resurrected or rose again from the dead. It is professed in various terms that he has been exalted or ascended to heaven, where he has taken his place at the right hand of God the Father. In this chapter we will examine how in the diverse ancient testimonies record has been made of Jesus' death, resurrection and exaltation, and which meaning has been given to these events.

4.1 *The letters of Paul*

To the church in Corinth, Paul testifies that he has preached the gospel which he himself received,

> that Christ died for our sins in accordance with the Scriptures, and that he was buried, and that he was raised on the third day in accordance with the Scriptures, and that he appeared to Cephas, then to the twelve. (1 Corinthians 15:3–5)

Presumably, Paul himself adds to this ancient tradition,

> Then he appeared to more than five hundred brothers and sisters at one time, most of whom are still alive, though some have died. Then he appeared to James, then to all the apostles. (1 Corinthians 15:6–7)

We will first address the interpretation of Jesus' death. It has been declared that his death took place 'for our sins' and corresponds with that which is already written in the Scriptures. Paul testifies that he did not think up this view himself, but that it has been passed down to him; this means that he has received this tradition from the first Jewish Christians after he himself came to believe in Jesus as the Christ. In several passages in his letters, Paul comes back to Jesus' death. They read that Jesus has suffered death in place of sinners, and that whoever believes in his vicarious death is reconciled with God. Paul continually refers, however, to the redemptive effect of Jesus' death in short expressions with hardly any or no explanation at all, because he assumes that the churches to which he writes share his view on the meaning of Jesus' death.[1] Thus he writes in 1 Corinthians 1:18, without further explanation, 'For the message about the cross is foolishness to those who are perishing, but to us who are being saved it is the power of God.'[2] In a passage about a licentious church member in Corinth, he says with this man in mind, 'Clean out the old yeast so that you may be a new batch, as you really are unleavened. For our paschal lamb, Christ, has been sacrificed' (1 Corinthians 5:7). Paul does not come back to Christ as a paschal lamb, because he assumes that the Corinthians know and understand this image.[3] In the same letter he twice writes that his readers are 'bought with a price' (6:20; 7:22), namely through Christ, who died for them and thus, in his death, bought them for God. Because Paul presumes that the Corinthians understand the image, he does not clarify it.[4] Just a bit later, he briefly reminds them, without further explanation, of the meal in which Jesus called the bread 'my body for you' and designated the cup of wine as 'the new covenant in my blood' (11:24–25). For the believers at Corinth this was familiar language. In a very compact passage in the letter to the Romans, he writes that God has put forward Jesus as a 'a sacrifice of atonement ... by his blood'; those who believe in him, receive forgiveness of their sins (Romans 3:25–26). Again it is striking that Paul does not explain exactly how Jesus, through his blood, functions as a sacrifice of atonement.[5] Apparently, he was confident that this view was common knowledge in the church of Rome and that there was no need to explain or defend this. In his letter to the Galatians, Paul disputes the Jewish Christian idea that non-Jewish Christians need to maintain the law of Moses and that the men therefore had to be circumcised. From his reply it appears that

---

1   See, e.g., Romans 3:25–26; 4:25; 5:1–11; 8:32; 14:15; 1 Corinthians 1:18–2:2; 5:7; 8:11; 2 Corinthians 5:14–21; Galatians 2:20; 3:13.
2   See, e.g., Gordon D. Fee (1987), *The First Epistle to the Corinthians*. Grand Rapids MI: Eerdmans, pp. 68–69.
3   Fee, *The First Epistle to the Corinthians*, pp. 217–218.
4   Fee, *The First Epistle to the Corinthians*, pp. 263–265.
5   See Dunn, *Romans 1–8*, pp. 180–183.

the disagreement between Paul and his opponents did not concern the redemptive effect of Jesus' death – basically, they apparently agreed on this – but about the consequences which had to be drawn from this.[6]

His quoting in 1 Corinthians 15:3 that 'Christ died for our sins, *as written in the Scriptures*', signifies that the first Christians found various prophecies of Jesus' death in the Old Testament. We have already mentioned the paschal lamb (1 Corinthians 5:7). According to the book of Exodus, this lamb was slaughtered by the Israelites preceding their deliverance from Egypt; where the blood of this lamb was brushed on the door posts, the first-born sons would remain alive, while they would die in the houses of the Egyptians where this blood was absent (Exodus 12). The protection of this blood and the deliverance from Egypt were celebrated every year at the Jewish Passover, in which Christians saw images of the effects of Jesus' blood, namely salvation from the power of sin and death.[7] Another example of an Old Testament text which the first Christians explained in relation to Jesus is the prophecy of the suffering servant of the LORD in Isaiah 53. When Paul writes in Romans 4:25 that Jesus 'is put to death for our trespasses and raised for our justification', he alludes to the Greek version of Isaiah 53:12. Here is written of this servant that 'his soul was given over to death, and he was reckoned among the lawless, and he bore the sins of many, and because of their sins he was given over'.[8] From this allusion to Isaiah 53 and from various other references to this chapter in other early Christian texts, it is apparent that the meaning of Paul's quotation is that 'Christ died for our sins, as written in the Scriptures.'[9]

We will move on to the previously quoted testimony of Christ's resurrection. In 1 Corinthians 15, the chapter par excellence about the resurrection of the dead, Paul does not explain how Christ's resurrection took place. He does say, however, about those who believe in Christ that they will be raised a 'spiritual body' (15:44). This means that they will physically rise from the dead, but with a different body from the earthly one. Afterwards, he speaks of the risen Christ as the spiritual, heavenly man (15:45–49).[10] From this we can conclude that Paul believed the risen

6   Galatians 2:20; 3:1, 13; 5:1–6; 6:12, 14.
7   In 160–170 CE, Melito of Sardes elaborated on this theme in his *Homily on the Passion* (SC 123).
8   According to the New English Translation of the Septuagint.
9   E.g., Matthew 8:17; Luke 22:37; Acts 8:32–33; 1 Peter 2:24–25; 1 Clement 16; Barnabas 5:2. For Romans 4:25, see, e.g., Dunn, *Romans 1–8*, pp. 224–225.
10 Fee, *The First Epistle to the Corinthians*, pp. 785–795; Wolfgang Schrage (1991), *Der erste Brief an die Korinther (1Kor 15,1–16,24)*. Düsseldorf: Benzinger Verlag, Neukirchen-Vluyn: Neukirchener Verlag, p. 383.

Christ to have a spiritual, heavenly body. It is Paul's opinion that Christ's resurrection makes possible and anticipates the more general resurrection of the dead (15:20–24).

In his letters, Paul offers no specific explanation for the phrase, 'on the third day, as written in the Scriptures' (1 Corinthians 15:4). Even in his elaborate discussion of the resurrection in 1 Corinthians 15 he does not consider it necessary to quote verses from the Old Testament to prove that Jesus' resurrection was prophesized there.[11] In his extensive letter to the Romans he refers to Christ's resurrection only in passing, as something which does not need to be demonstrated further nor defended.[12] Neither does Paul refer to the enumeration of Christ's appearances (1 Corinthians 15:5–7) elsewhere in his letters.

In section 2.1 we quoted the hymn from Philippians 2:6–11, which dealt with Jesus' humiliation unto death at the cross, and his exaltation by God. However, Paul does not go into more detail about the whys and wherefores of Jesus' death and exaltation there. By quoting this hymn he wanted to incite the Christians at Philippi to follow in Jesus' footsteps, be humble towards one another and renounce self-interest (Philippians 2:1–5). It is, however, remarkable that Jesus' death is not interpreted as a sacrifice for forgiveness of sins here and that no mention is made of his resurrection on the third day. Instead of the latter, it is said that God has highly exalted him and given him the name that is above every name (Philippians 2:9). Apparently this hymn originates from another tradition with different phrasing, which Paul could still borrow without a problem.

In Romans 8:34, Paul speaks in different terms about Jesus' exaltation. Here he states that Christ, after his death and resurrection, 'is at the right hand of God', where he intercedes for us. In 1 Corinthians 15:23–28 he also points to Christ's position in heaven where he rules as king until all his enemies will be subjected to him.[13]

The result of Christ's exaltation is that he can be invoked in prayer and in praise. In the introduction of the first letter to the Corinthians, Paul not only addresses the church at Corinth, but he adds to this,

---

11 He does indeed allude a few times to Old Testament verses (Psalm 110:1; 8:7; Isaiah 22:13; Genesis 2:7, respectively), but these do not function as proofs of Christ's resurrection. This is also true for the explicit quotation in 1 Corinthians 15:54–55 (compiled from Isaiah 25:8 and Hosea 13:14).

12 Romans 1:4; 4:24–25; 6:4–10; 7:4; 8:11, 34; 10:9; 14:9. See also 2 Corinthians 4:14; 5:15; Galatians 1:1; Philippians 3:10; 1 Thessalonians 1:10; 4:14.

13 Also from (among others) Romans 10:6; 1 Corinthians 15:47–49; 2 Corinthians 5:1–10; 1 Thessalonians 1:10; 4:16–17 it is apparent that Christ, according to Paul, is in heaven after his resurrection.

'together with all those who in every place call on the name of our Lord Jesus Christ, both their Lord and ours' (1:2).[14] In Romans 10:12–14, Paul mentions calling upon the name of the Lord, by whom he means Jesus, by quoting Joel 3:5, which concerns calling upon God the LORD. In 1 Corinthians 16:22 Paul quotes the Aramaic exclamation *maranatha*, which means either 'our Lord, come!' (*marana tha*) or 'our Lord has come' (*maran atha*). Of the two possibilities probably the first should be chosen, which means that this prayer is closely related to the Greek invocation in Revelation 22:20, 'come, Lord Jesus'.[15] From these texts it is apparent that, according to Paul, the believers could call upon the exalted Lord Jesus just as they called upon God the Father.

From this survey we can conclude that, in Paul's view, the death and resurrection of Jesus have a redemptive effect for those who believe in Jesus. Because Jesus died 'for us', all who believe in him are delivered from punishment for sins and from eternal death. Jesus' resurrection is the guarantee that those also who believe in him will be raised from the dead. As long as Jesus is still in heaven, he can be called upon there, which indicates his divine status. This was the gospel that Paul had learned from those who came to believe in Jesus before him and that he preached on his journeys and in his letters.

4.2 The Gospel of Mark

The Gospel of Mark tells rather quickly that Jesus encountered adversaries who plotted his death (3:6). After Peter recognizes him as the Christ, Jesus begins to announce that he, as the Son of Man, is to endure much suffering as a result of all the opposition and is to be put to death, but that he is to rise again after three days (8:31). Two more such announcements of his death and resurrection follow (9:31; 10:33–34). In this gospel, Jesus' interpretation of his forthcoming death is that he has come as the Son of Man 'to give his life as a ransom for many' (10:45). With these words Jesus answers the rhetorical question he raised in Mark 8:37, 'for what can a man give in return for his life?' The implied answer must be, 'nothing'. For this reason Jesus declares that he is prepared to give his life

---

14 To be sure, the quoted formulation can have been inserted later to make clear that this letter must be more widely read than by the church at Corinth only. However, it is more probable that Paul reminds the church of Corinth that it belongs to a much broader movement of people who were 'called to be saints'. See Fee, *The First Epistle to the Corinthians*, pp. 33–34; Schrage, *Der erste Brief an die Korinther (1Kor 1,1–6,11)*, pp. 104–105.

15 See Fee, *The First Epistle to the Corinthians*, pp. 838–839; Schrage, *Der erste Brief an die Korinther (1Kor 15,1–16,24)*, pp. 472–473.

for many. In section 1.2 we saw that, historically speaking, it is not certain that Jesus indeed said this in these words; it is possible – although in my opinion not in the least certain – that this saying stems from the early Christians. The same uncertainties apply to Jesus' announcements of his own death and resurrection. The fact that this announcement appears three times in the Gospel of Mark (and the other two synoptic gospels) in different variations leads James Dunn to conclude, however, that this saying probably does come from Jesus himself. Jesus would then have anticipated that his mission would not be embraced in Jerusalem and he wanted to explain to his disciples why he still had to go there.[16] Jesus' parable of the tenants also testifies to his presumption that he would suffer a violent death, since he tells that the son in this story was killed (12:1–8).

In this gospel Jesus also gives an interpretation of his death while he is participating in the last supper which he shares with his disciples. He says of the bread, 'Take; this is my body,' and of the cup of wine: 'This is my blood of the covenant, which is poured out for many' (14:22–24). This means that through his death Jesus would inaugurate a new covenant with God; the wording corresponds to Exodus 24:8 where Moses' inauguration of the covenant with Israel was thus described, 'See the blood of the covenant that the LORD has made with you in accordance with all these words.' That Jesus' blood would be poured out for many means that his death would bring about reconciliation with God for many.[17] Whether Jesus literally said this in such a way cannot be determined today from the historical perspective, but the possibility that he counted on the fact that his approaching death would have a redeeming effect is certainly not ruled out.[18] According to Mark, Jesus ends this interpretation of his death by proclaiming that he will not drink wine again until the day he will drink it new in God's kingdom (14:25).[19] This implies that he expected to enter this kingdom after his death. After the meal Jesus quotes the following oracle as a prophecy of his death and the confusion of his disciples, 'I will strike the shepherd, and the sheep will be scattered' (14:27; Zechariah 13:7).

Before Jesus prepared himself in prayer for his approaching death in Gethsemane, he submitted himself to that which he experienced as the will of God his Father (14:32–36). From Mark's account of Jesus'

16 Dunn, *Jesus Remembered*, pp. 798–802.
17 Gnilka, *Das Evangelium nach Markus (8,27–16,20)*, pp. 245–246. Among other texts, he refers to Isaiah 53:11–12.
18 Dunn, *Jesus Remembered*, 815–818; cf. Tomson, *'If this be from heaven'*, pp. 164–165.
19 Gnilka, *Das Evangelium nach Markus (8,27–16,20)*, pp. 246–247.

arrest, interrogation, mockery and flogging (14:43–15:20), we will note only the preference of the people that Jesus should be crucified instead of the bandit Barabbas (15:6–15). We will pick up the thread with the report that Simon of Cyrene was forced by Roman soldiers to carry Jesus' cross to Golgotha, apparently because Jesus himself had grown too weak (15:21–22). At Golgotha Jesus was crucified between two criminals at the third hour of the day (about nine o'clock in the morning); the inscription on his cross was, 'The king of the Jews'. Bystanders mocked him as 'the Christ, the king of Israel'. At the ninth hour of the day he called out with the words of Psalm 22:2, 'My God, my God, why have you forsaken me?' After this, Jesus uttered a loud cry and died (15:26–37). Considering some other ancient views, it must be noted that it is beyond doubt that according to Mark's description Jesus really did die. According to this gospel, his death took place on a Friday (15:42), the day which preceded the Sabbath, during the Jewish Passover (14:1,12).

Women who had followed and served Jesus from Galilee, stood at his cross and were witnesses to his death (15:40–41). Pilate allowed one Joseph of Arimathea to have Jesus' body. He buried it in a grave which was hewn out of a rock and rolled a stone against the entrance (15:42–46). After the Sabbath, at dawn on Sunday morning, when three women, among them Mary Magdalene, went to the grave, the stone had been rolled away. A young man, dressed in a white robe, told them that Jesus was raised and that they should tell this to his disciples; they should go to Galilee, where they would see him. The women were so frightened by this news that they dared not say anything to anyone (16:1–8). This is Mark's account of Jesus' resurrection from the dead, with which he remarkably enough concludes his gospel. The passage that follows this ending in most manuscripts and translations does not belong to the original text of this gospel.

We see that, according to the Gospel of Mark, Jesus did not die for nothing. By his death, he would save people – apparently from sin, punishment and perdition – and a new covenant with God would be established. Mark's testimony that Jesus is raised from the dead and that his disciples would see him again is a confirmation of Jesus' own announcements. The statement of the young man, that Jesus was raised, means that it was God who raised him from the dead. Remarkably enough, it is not further explained exactly how salvation by the ransom of Jesus' life exactly works. It is striking, however, that Mark and Paul use similar terms to indicate the significance of Jesus' death. If we count the Friday, Sabbath and Sunday inclusively as three days, then Mark's testimony of Jesus' raising corresponds to Paul's tradition of Christ's resurrection on the third day.

4.3 *The Gospel of Matthew*

In the Gospel of Matthew most sayings and stories about Jesus' death agree to a large degree with the Gospel of Mark. Jesus announces his death and resurrection on the third day at various times and he speaks about his death as a 'ransom for many'.[20] When at the Last Supper he says of the cup, 'For this is my blood of the covenant, which is poured out for many,' an explanation is added, 'for the forgiveness of sins' (26:28). More often than Mark, Matthew quotes Old Testament texts that foretold, in his view, Jesus' suffering and death.[21] In the Gospel of Matthew, a macabre addition to Mark's report states that the people present said to Pilate, 'His blood be on us and our children' (27:25), which expresses their acceptance of the responsibility of Jesus' death.[22] According to another addition of Matthew, many deceased saints came out of their graves alive and after his resurrection appeared in Jerusalem (27:52–53). This clearly legendary report apparently anticipates the ultimate resurrection of the dead and means that this will take place thanks to Jesus' death and resurrection.[23]

The account of Jesus' resurrection is more elaborate in the Gospel of Matthew than in Mark. Report is made of an earthquake, of an angel descending from heaven to proclaim Jesus' resurrection to two women, and of his appearance to these women. This gospel says that the women told about Jesus' resurrection (28:1–10). It ends with the appearance of Jesus to his eleven remaining disciples (Judas had by now taken his own life, 27:5) on a mountain in Galilee. According to this gospel, Jesus then says, 'All authority in heaven and on earth has been given to me' (28:18) and 'I am with you always, to the end of the age' (28:20). This means that after his resurrection he was clothed with divine authority and reminds the readers that he was already called 'God with us' in Matthew 1:23.[24] The emphatically pronounced words 'I am' are also a reminder of the name of God. Jesus commands the disciples present to make disciples of all nations and 'to baptize them in the name of the Father and the Son and the Holy Spirit' (28:19). This formula certainly corresponds to

---

20 Matthew 16:21; 17:22–23; 20:17–19, 28; 26:2; cf. 12:40; 21:37–39.

21 Matthew 26:31; 27:9–10, 35, 43, 46.

22 The evangelist was probably thinking here of the destruction of Jerusalem by the Romans in 70 CE, and not of the atrocities which have stricken the Jewish people in the long history since. See Ulrich Luz (2002), *Das Evangelium nach Matthäus (Mt 26–28)*. Düsseldorf, Zürich: Benzinger Verlag, Neukirchen-Vluyn: Neukirchener Verlag, pp. 281; 285–288.

23 Joachim Gnilka (1988), *Das Matthäusevangelium* 2. Freiburg: Herder, pp. 476–478.

24 See also Chae, *Jesus as the Eschatological Davidic Shepherd*, pp. 340–369; 383.

the liturgical practice of the church for which Matthew wrote.[25] Thus, Jesus as 'the Son' is placed on the same level as God the Father and the Holy Spirit. Although this text does not formulate a balanced theology of God's trinity, it does point in that direction.

4.4 *The Gospel of Luke and the Acts of the Apostles*

In the Gospel of Luke, Jesus announces his own death and resurrection more than once, but the statement that Jesus would give his life as ransom for many, as recorded in Mark and Matthew, is absent.[26] Only at Jesus' last supper is reference made to the redemptive effect of Jesus' death, when he tells his disciples that the bread is his body 'given for you'; likewise, Jesus also says of the cup of wine, 'This cup that is poured out for you is the new covenant in my blood' (22:19–20). The repeated 'for you' indicates that Jesus would die vicariously for his disciples. A striking difference between Luke and the gospels of Mark and Matthew is that Jesus does not say at his dying, 'My God, my God, why have you forsaken me?,' but 'Father, into your hands I commend my spirit' (23:46; Psalm 31:6). The confidence that he would be with God directly after his death is apparent from what he promises to one of the two criminals just prior to his death: 'today, you will be with me in paradise' (23:43).

In Luke, Jesus' resurrection is announced to three women by two men in dazzling clothes. When the women tell the apostles of this, the latter do not believe it at first (23:55–24:11). The Gospel of Luke ends with some appearances of Jesus to his disciples, in which he states that the suffering and resurrection of the Messiah were already described in the books of Moses and the prophets. Whoever is baptized in his name receives forgiveness of sins (24:26–27, 44–47). On the one hand, it is told that the risen Jesus suddenly disappears and reappears, so that his disciples once imagined they were seeing a ghost (24:31, 36–37). This indicates that, according to this description, Jesus no longer had a body of flesh and blood. On the other hand, the evangelist emphasizes that

---

25 Luz, *Das Evangelium nach Matthäus (Mt 26–28)*, pp. 452–453; cf. *Didache* 7:1, 3 (LCL 24). There is an opinion that this baptismal formula was added later to Matthew 28:19, but in that case, the shorter text should be found in the church fathers and in manuscripts more often than demonstrated so far. See Huub van de Sandt and David Flusser (2002), *The Didache: Its Jewish Sources and Its Place in Early Judaism and Christianity*. Assen, pp. 286–289, who prefer the originality of the shorter text. Luz, *Das Evangelium nach Matthäus (Mt 26–28)*, p. 431, rejects this idea and writes that it is barely supported any more. Ehrman, *The Orthodox Corruption of Scripture*, therefore does not deal with this text.

26 Luke 9:22; 9:44; 18:31–33; cf. 22:24–27.

Jesus' body was made up of flesh and bones and that he ate a broiled fish in front of his disciples (24:39–43). At the end, the gospel mentions that Jesus – apparently on the evening of the day of his resurrection[27] – ascended to heaven.

The book of the Acts of the Apostles, written by the same author, also reports that Jesus ascended to heaven and furthermore, that he appeared to his disciples over forty days.[28] Without going into details about this, Luke recounts that in those days Jesus proclaimed the coming of the Holy Spirit and spoke about the kingdom of God (1:1–8). In the book of Acts, Jesus' death and resurrection are proclaimed as the way by which people can receive forgiveness of sins. His resurrection counts as God's rehabilitation of the life of his Son. Many Old Testament texts are quoted as testimonies of these events.[29] The redemptive effect of Jesus' death is, however, expressed only implicitly and in passing.[30]

When Stephen is stoned to death as the first martyr for his faith in Jesus, he testifies according to Acts 7:56 that he sees the heavens opened and the Son of Man standing at the right hand of God. He dies with the words 'Lord Jesus, receive my spirit' and 'Lord, do not hold this sin against them' on his lips (7:59–60).

All in all it is clear that, according to Luke, Jesus' death and resurrection have a redemptive effect. He emphasizes that Jesus' death and resurrection are rooted in the books of Moses and the prophets, i.e. the Old Testament. A remarkable feature of his gospel is that after Jesus' resurrection his body is described as spiritual, and yet able to adopt a material form. After his resurrection, according to Luke and Acts, Jesus was taken up into heaven at God's right hand. There he could be called upon as the heavenly Lord.

4.5 *The Gospel of John*

The beginning of the Gospel of John immediately refers to Jesus' death and its effects, when John the Baptist is told to point to Jesus as 'the lamb of God, who takes away the sin of the world' (1:29, 36). It is not explained

---

27 Thus, e.g., Fitzmyer, *The Gospel According to Luke (X–XXIV)*, p. 1588.
28 An interesting interpretation of the relationship between Jesus' ascension and his appearances is given by Henk Jan de Jonge (2006), 'De hemelvaart van Jezus op de dag van zijn opstanding: Handelingen 1 en Lucas 24'. *Met Andere Woorden* 25, 3, 3–13.
29 E.g., Acts 2:22–36; 3:12–26; 4:8–12, 24–28; 8:32–35; 10:34–43; 13:23–41.
30 See Acts 20:28, where Paul says that God has obtained his church with the blood of his own Son. In Acts 8:32–33 Philip indeed quotes from Isaiah 53, but not the passages which say that the servant of the Lord died for the sins of his people.

here how Jesus, as the lamb of God, takes away the sin of the world, and it is difficult to discover whether this statement refers to a particular Old Testament text in which a lamb appears.[31] A reference to Jesus as paschal lamb is found in John 19:36 which, after the description of his death, quotes from Scripture 'none of his bones shall be broken'.[32] The paschal lamb did not serve, however, as a means of making atonement, but in the case of Jesus, different images may have flowed into each other and been given a new meaning. We probably must also think of the servant of the Lord who 'bears our sins', 'who bore the sin of many' and 'like a lamb that is led to the slaughter and like a sheep that before its shearers is silent, so he did not open his mouth'.[33] Be that as it may, at the beginning of the Gospel of John it is declared that Jesus was destined to take away the sin of the world as the lamb of God, meaning that he would bring about reconciliation between God and man. Apparently, he could not do this in any other way than by dying.

Jesus himself announces that he will die a violent death, although he uses different words from those in the synoptic gospels. We have already seen that Jesus announces his exaltation several times, by which he refers to his crucifixion and to his exaltation unto God, through which he will draw all people to himself.[34] Jesus says in this gospel that he lays down his life for the sheep and that he has power to take it up again (10:11–18).[35] That he dies vicariously for others is unconsciously confirmed by the high priest Caiaphas with the words, 'You do not understand that it is better for you to have one man die for the people than to have the whole nation destroyed.' The evangelist added to this that Jesus was about to die not only for his own nation, but also that he would gather into one the dispersed children of God (11:50–52).

Jesus' way to the cross and his death are elaborately described in this gospel too, although the report differs in various details from the synoptic gospels. From chapter 13 on, Jesus finds himself in the private circle of his disciples to share a last supper with them and to prepare them for his death. The conversations that took place at that time have already been discussed briefly in section 3.4. Just as in the synoptic gospels, it is stated

---

31 Cf. Exodus 12:3–13; 29:38–46; Leviticus 16:5–28; Isaiah 53:4, 7. See, e.g., Rudolf Schnackenburg (1979), *Das Johannesevangelium* 1 (4th edn). Freiburg: Herder, pp. 285–289. We must not assume, however, that John the Baptist actually did, at that moment, pronounce these words in such a way; they testify to the theology of the evangelist.
32 See Exodus 12:10 (LXX), 46; Numbers 9:12.
33 Isaiah 53:4 (LXX), 7, 12.
34 See section 3.4; John 8:28; 12:32; cf. 3:13–14.
35 See also Jesus' general saying in John 15:13, 'No one has greater love than this, to lay down one's life for one's friends.'

that Jesus' death occurred on a Friday (19:14). In this gospel, Jesus dies with the words 'it is finished' on his lips (19:30).

It is Mary Magdalene who, early on Sunday morning – on the third day therefore – is the first to discover that the tomb is empty. She reports this to Peter and another disciple, who make certain that the tomb is indeed empty (20:1–8). The evangelist adds to this that they had not yet understood from the Scripture that Jesus must rise from the dead. In these words he confirms the idea that Jesus' resurrection was announced in the Old Testament (20:9).[36] Furthermore, the risen Jesus appears to Mary Magdalene. He tells her that she may not hold on to him, and that he will ascend to his Father. Mary testifies of this appearance to the other disciples (20:11–18). The gospel ends with some other appearances of Jesus to his disciples. It is recorded that he gives them the Holy Spirit and authority to forgive or to retain sins (20:19–23). Special attention is given to Thomas, who does not believe in Jesus' resurrection at first, but becomes convinced of it after an appearance of Jesus and then recognizes him as Lord and God (20:24–29). A final chapter, probably added later, describes how Peter subtly receives forgiveness from the risen Jesus for the fact that, during Jesus' trial, he pretended not to know him. Peter receives the task to tend Jesus' sheep; thus the author confirms that a leading position was assigned to Peter in the early church (21:1–19).

We have already encountered an interpretation of Jesus' resurrection in section 3.4, where we quoted Jesus' saying that he is the resurrection and the life, and that those who believe in him will live, even though they die (11:25–26). Here a connection is made between Jesus' resurrection and the resurrection of the believers.

Although this gospel more than once suggests that the body with which Jesus appeared after his resurrection was physically present, it nevertheless also suggests that this body actually had another, spiritual form. After all Mary Magdalene may not hold on to Jesus (20:17), it is not reported that Thomas actually put his hands in the wounds of Jesus' body (20:27–29), and when Jesus offers his disciples fish and bread, it is not written – as in Luke – that he also ate of it himself (21:9–13).

In the Gospel of John too it turns out, just as in the synoptic gospels, that Jesus' death and resurrection are of principal importance. These events are related to the taking away and forgiving of sin. Jesus' death has a salutary effect on the nation and on the dispersed children of God. After his resurrection, Jesus restores the broken and disrupted relationship with his disciples and gives them tasks to perform on his behalf.

---

36 Cf. John 2:22.

4.6 *Evaluation of the New Testament data*

Despite the differences between the New Testament writings we have discussed, it turns out that with regard to Jesus' death and resurrection there are also important similarities. In view of the early Christian writings that we will presently examine, it will prove to be relevant to establish that, according to the New Testament gospels, Jesus suffered and died physically as a human being. It is also clear that the first Christians found references to and prophecies of Jesus' suffering, death and resurrection in the Old Testament.

With different emphases and in diverse images and expressions it is said that Jesus died vicariously for man and thus brought about God's forgiveness of their sins. In this way he established a new covenant with God. There is hardly any explanation, however, as to why the consequence of the sacrifice of his life is that God forgives sin and thereby saves those who believe in this from punishment and perdition. Apparently, the authors assume that the readers already understand the metaphors and Old Testament references.[37]

The testimonies we have discussed are in agreement about Jesus' resurrection having taken place on the third day and about his appearance to his disciples in a different, more spiritual body. This means that death no longer has power over him. Only Luke testifies to the expectation that directly after his death Jesus will be in paradise, and therefore with God. Again it is only Luke who writes that the risen Jesus had flesh and bones and could eat again. There is no precise description of how one imagined that Jesus has been raised or had risen from the dead; the evangelists confine themselves to the accounts of an empty grave. From their testimonies the conviction is apparent that by raising Jesus from the dead, God has rehabilitated his Son, and therefore his message as well. Paul considers Christ's resurrection as the anticipation of the resurrection of those who believe in him. In Matthew, a similar idea emerges from the record of the resurrection of deceased saints. In his own way, John also makes a link between Jesus as the resurrection and the life and eternal life he gives to those who believe in him. In the gospels of Matthew, Luke and John, the communication between Jesus and his disciples is restored through his resurrection. In these gospels and in Acts, Jesus' disciples are given the task of acting in his name and propagating his message. Apart from this – according to the New Testament gospels and Acts – the teachings that Jesus gave to his disciples after his resurrection barely add anything to that which had already been mentioned before his death.

---

37 In the New Testament, only the letter to the Hebrews contains an elaborate explanation of Christ's sacrifice for the sins of mankind.

According to various testimonies, after his resurrection Jesus ascended to God in heaven. In Paul and in Acts, it appears that believers can call upon Jesus in heaven, which points to his heavenly and divine status.

Jesus' death can be regarded as a historical fact, but in my view it exceeds the competence of historians to defend Jesus' resurrection from the dead and his ascension to heaven as historical facts.[38] In daily life it happens, after all, that people are violently killed, but not that they regain life after their death, and ascend to heaven. Therefore, it is not recorded that Jesus, after his death, appeared publicly alive and well so that friend and foe alike could be convinced of his resurrection. It is only asserted that at intervals Jesus appeared again to his own disciples. It is indeed presumed that – regarded historically – his resurrection was initially imagined as a resurrection in heaven, from where he, from the third day after his death, appeared to his disciples now and again. Whatever historians may say about this, the fact that his disciples did go on to spread his message after the humiliating death of their master suggests that they had experienced something very special. After all, without such special experiences one would have expected that the movement that Jesus incited would have come to nothing after his death. Yet the conviction that Jesus was raised from the dead and exalted unto God the Father cannot be proved historically – because this exceeds the boundaries of historiography – but can only be affirmed in faith.[39]

When we turn to the interpretation of Jesus' death and resurrection, historically speaking we have still less to say about whether they have served to bring about God's forgiveness of the sins of mankind. We saw that, at a historical level, it is even difficult to determine how Jesus himself has interpreted his imminent death. It can be historically determined however, that, according to important ancient testimonies, Jesus' death and resurrection served to allow for the relationship between Jesus and his disciples, and thus also between God and mankind, to be restored.

38 See H. J. de Jonge (1989), 'Ontstaan en ontwikkeling van het geloof in Jezus' opstanding', in F. O. van Gennep et al., *Waarlijk opgestaan! Een discussie over de opstanding van Jezus Christus*. Baarn: Ten Have, pp. 31–50; Robin Lane Fox (1986), *Pagans and Christians*, London: Penguin Books, pp. 375–380.

39 See Klaus Berger (2002), *Sind die Berichte des Neuen Testaments wahr? Ein Weg zum Verstehen der Bibel*. Gütersloh: Gütersloher Verlagshaus, pp. 80–81; 159–164; he argues for the authenticity of the mystical experience of those to whom Jesus appeared after his death.

4.7 *The Gospel of Thomas*

We will continue with a few other early Christian testimonies; again, we will begin with the Gospel of Thomas. It is remarkable that this gospel barely refers to Jesus' death. Perhaps an allusion is made to his death on the cross by the following saying, 'Whoever (...) does not carry his cross as I do will not be worthy of me.'[40] What is meant by this carrying of the cross is, however, not further explained here.[41] Another allusion is found in the parable of the tenants of the vineyard, where the tenants kill the son of the owner (65). It is obvious that Jesus himself is meant by the son. However, this gospel does not explicitly describe that Jesus died[42] nor that he was raised from the dead and ascended to heaven. Still, Jesus is called 'the Living one' more than once.[43] This term refers, on the one hand, to Jesus during his earthly life, but at the same time suggests that he is also 'the Living one' for later readers, although he is no longer physically in their midst. Likewise, the risen Jesus is called 'the Living one' in Luke 24:5, and he makes himself known with this designation in Revelation 1:18 (although Jesus' name is not mentioned there). As Gospel of Thomas 50 can be explained as a conversation between the hostile heavenly powers and the human souls who want to ascend to the kingdom of light, we may assume that according to this gospel, the soul of Jesus also ascended in this manner.

The heading announces that the Gospel of Thomas contains the secret words of the Living Jesus, and not that it is about his death, resurrection and exaltation. That Jesus' death and resurrection largely remain unmentioned in this gospel can therefore only be concluded from the perspective of the New Testament gospels. Yet we can assume that for the compiler or compilers of this gospel, the report of Jesus' suffering, death, resurrection and exaltation and therefore also what he said in this context were not vital for obtaining the secret knowledge which would lead to spiritual salvation.

---

40 Thomas 55; cf. Matthew 16:24; Mark 8:34; Luke 9:23; John 19:17.
41 A Valentinian explanation of (roughly) this statement will be dealt with in section 4.10.
42 De Conick, *The Original Gospel of Thomas in Translation*, pp. 277–278, suggests that the lacunae in Thomas 101 can be completed in this way, 'For my [birth] mother [gave death], while my true [mother] gave life to me'; see also Nordsieck, *Thomasevangelium*, p. 351. Because this reconstruction is not certain, I will not pay attention to this saying.
43 Thomas *heading*; 52; 59; 111 (?). The Father is also called 'the Living one', in Thomas 3; 37; 50; perhaps 111.

4.8 *Cerinthus and the Ophites*

According to the description of Irenaeus, Cerinthus does make mention of the suffering of the man Jesus, but he adds that Christ then flew away from him. The Christ who descended upon Jesus from heaven at his baptism, was himself spiritual and could therefore not suffer. According to Cerinthus, however, the man Jesus was raised again after his suffering (and death, although Irenaeus does not explicitly mention this).[44] Cerinthus' idea that the heavenly Christ could not suffer corresponds to the Greek philosophy of his time, which held that God could not suffer and could not undergo death.[45] Because Cerinthus deems the heavenly Christ spiritual and divine, he assumes that Christ also could not suffer and that only the earthly man Jesus has suffered.

As mentioned in section 2.8, the Ophites' view of Jesus was related to Cerinthus' representation. This is also apparent in their view concerning Jesus' death and resurrection. They taught that when Jesus performed his miracles and proclaimed the unknown Father this aroused the anger of his Father and his powers, that is to say of the Old Testament God Yaldabaoth and his angels. They therefore tried to kill Jesus, but when the preparations for this were made, the heavenly Christ withdrew from Jesus together with Sophia, and he returned to the high heaven from which he came. So only Jesus died on the cross, without Christ. However, from heaven Christ raised Jesus in a psychic and spiritual body which was free of material elements. Therefore, after his resurrection, Jesus' disciples did not recognize him at first. Subsequently, they mistakenly thought that he was resurrected in his material body. Jesus' disciples had not understood that during his life Jesus had been united with the heavenly Christ. However, after his resurrection he remained on earth again for eighteen months to give clarification about this to a few. Subsequently, Jesus ascended to heaven and placed himself at the right hand of his father Yaldabaoth. When the people who got to know him have put aside their carnal body, Jesus receives their souls there, without Yaldabaoth knowing anything of it. The more holy souls Jesus receives there, the more the power of Yaldabaoth decreases. According to the Ophites – in Irenaeus' description – the end of the age consists of all of these souls ultimately being gathered up in the imperishable high heaven.[46]

---

44 Irenaeus, *Against Heresies* I, 26, 1 (SC 264).
45 See Michel Spanneut (1994), '*Apatheia* ancienne, *apatheia* chrétienne: Ière partie: L'*apatheia* ancienne', in Wolfgang Haase, ed., *Aufstieg und Niedergang der Römischen Welt* II, 36, 7, Berlin, New York: Walter de Gruyter, pp. 4641–4717 (4645–4648; 4707–4708).
46 Irenaeus, *Against Heresies* I, 30, 13–14 (SC 264).

4.9 *The Gospel of Judas*

The Gospel of Judas ends with Judas handing Jesus over to the Jewish scribes (58). What happened after this is not recorded in this document. Apparently, the author assumes that the story of Jesus' suffering and death on the cross are well known. Jesus proclaims that Judas will surpass all of his other disciples, who worship the Old Testament God. He motivates this by saying, 'For you will sacrifice the man who bears me' (56). This probably means that Jesus' outer man or his body will indeed be killed through Judas' doing, but that therefore his inner or heavenly essence will be able to return to its origin.[47] After he has made known the true gnosis to his special disciple Judas, Jesus is indeed ready to return to his heavenly father. No mention is made of his resurrection from the dead, nor of appearances after his death. With this conception of Jesus' death and the relatively positive role Judas played in it, the author of this gospel criticizes the church of his time, which regarded Judas as a devilish traitor[48] and saw in Jesus' death and resurrection the source of salvation for humanity.

That the author of the Gospel of Judas rejected the belief in salvation through Jesus' death and resurrection can also be concluded from the dream of his disciples which was described in section 3.7. In this dream, Jesus' disciples served as priests at an altar (37–39). We concluded that, by narrating this dream and Jesus' explanation of it (39–41), the author of the Gospel of Judas either criticized the view of the Eucharist or the view of martyrdom in the church of his own time, the second century. The Eucharist testifies to Christ's redemptive sacrifice and resurrection, and martyrs counted on receiving forgiveness of their sins and ascending directly to heaven if they died for their belief in Jesus' death and resurrection. Whatever explanation of the dream may be the most appropriate, in both ways belief in the redemption through Jesus' death and resurrection is implicitly dismissed in the Gospel of Judas.

4.10 *Theodotus*

We briefly discussed what the Valentinian Theodotus had to say about Jesus' origin and identity in section 2.10. It was also stated there that,

---

47 Thus, e.g., Gathercole, *The Gospel of Judas*, p. 106; April D. DeConick (2007), *The Thirteenth Apostle: What the Gospel of Judas Really Says*. London, New York: Continuum, p. 147.

48 E.g., Mark 3:19; John 6:70–71; 17:12. The view that in this gospel Judas plays a relatively positive role has been criticized, however, by April DeConick, *The Thirteenth Apostle*, who considers Judas a demon working for a demon (p. 146).

according to Theodotus and the other Valentinians, the purpose of Jesus' coming was that all of the spiritual seeds, i.e. the divine sparks, which were sown into certain people should again be united. In the previous chapter Theodotus was absent, because Clement's excerpts of his work only deal with Jesus' teachings indirectly. A little more is said of Jesus' death and resurrection, but unfortunately the texts about this are extremely concise and therefore enigmatic.[49]

For his view on Jesus' death, Theodotus quotes the words Jesus says on the cross in the Gospel of Luke, 'Father, into your hands I commend my spirit' (Luke 23:46). Theodotus identifies this spirit on the one hand with the heavenly Sophia and, on the other hand, with the spiritual seeds which the chosen have within themselves thanks to Sophia. Thus Jesus entrusts Sophia and the spiritual seeds (or divine sparks) to his heavenly Father.[50] Probably the highest Father in the *pleroma* is intended here. In a later passage Theodotus quotes Jesus' announcement, 'The Son of Man must be mocked, scourged and crucified,' and comments that Jesus turns out to be speaking about someone else, namely the one who can suffer.[51] According to Theodotus – or according to the Valentinian view which he reflects – Jesus referred to the psychic Christ, i.e. the earthly body with which the heavenly Jesus clothed himself when he came to earth.[52] In this view, only the psychic, earthly Christ (and therefore not the heavenly Jesus) is crucified. Theodotus then mentions another explanation of the words, 'Father, in thy hands I commend my spirit'; thus the psychic Christ again entrusted his (earthly) soul to the Father and Creator (i.e. the inferior demiurge).[53]

In another section Theodotus gives an allegorical explanation of the cross. In his view, this symbolizes the boundary between the lower material world and the *pleroma*, the heaven of the highest Father, and it divides the unbelievers from the believers. When Jesus carried the cross on his shoulders, it symbolized that he carried the spiritual seeds found within the true believers into the *pleroma*. In this connection Theodotus quotes the verse which we encountered in a somewhat different form in the Gospel of Thomas, 'Whoever does not carry his cross and does not follow me, is not my brother.'[54] This saying is explained thus: Christ 'carried the body of Jesus, which was of the same substance as the church'.[55] 'The church' here means the community of true believers or

---

49 See the analysis by Thomassen, *The Spiritual Seed*, pp. 62–76.
50 Clement of Alexandria, *Excerpts from Theodotus* 1, 1–2 (SC 23).
51 *Excerpts from Theodotus* 61, 4; cf. Mark 8:31; Luke 18:32; Matthew 20:19.
52 *Excerpts from Theodotus* 59, 2–3 and section 2.10.
53 *Excerpts from Theodotus* 62.
54 Cf. Matthew 16:24; Mark 8:34; Luke 9:23; 14:27; Thomas 55.
55 *Excerpts from Theodotus* 42.

the Valentinian gnostics, who are saved by Jesus' bearing of the cross. To this is added that the 'Right ones' (the non-gnostic believers) do know the names of Jesus and of Christ, but they do not know the power of the symbol of the cross.[56]

Theodotus quotes as saying of Jesus, 'on the third day I will go before you to Galilee'.[57] He explains that Jesus will raise the soul which is invisibly delivered, and restore it in the place to which he leads the way. This means that the Saviour precedes the spiritual seeds (the divine sparks which the Valentians have within themselves) to the *pleroma*.[58] After this, Theodotus remarks that Jesus died when the Spirit who had descended upon him at his baptism withdrew from him on the cross. Death did not overpower Jesus, but was itself conquered by a trick when Jesus' body died and he, as Saviour, annulled death. The victory over death was apparent when the Saviour raised his mortal body which he had freed of earthly passions.[59] How this resurrection took place is not explained. Apart from this, in Clement's excerpts Theodotus only mentions Jesus' resurrection indirectly.[60]

Clement's notes from the writings of Theodotus are often difficult to understand and do not always show a clear consistency. Yet it can be deduced that, according to the Valentinian view described here, differentiation must be made between the heavenly Jesus, who is the Saviour, and the earthly, psychic Christ proclaimed in the Old Testament and coming forth from the Creator. This division between Jesus and Christ is different from that put forward by Cerinthus and the Ophites. According to them, Jesus was an earthly figure and Christ came from heaven. According to the Valentinians, when the earthly Christ was crucified, Jesus the Saviour led the divine particles or sparks, which were found in the true believers, back to the heavenly *pleroma*. In this view, salvation means that those spiritual particles of the highest God, which were joined to material bodies on earth, are again brought back to the *pleroma* from which they originated. The heavenly Jesus came as Saviour to get that process started. The crucifixion of the psychic Christ, by which Jesus was clothed on earth, serves this purpose.

The idea that people have a spark within themselves which originates from God, is derived from Platonic philosophy, where souls are associated

---

56 *Excerpts from Theodotus* 43, 1; cf. 47, 2; 1 Corinthians 1:18 and Irenaeus, *Against Heresies* I, 3, 5 (SC 264).

57 Cf. Matthew 26:32; Mark 15:28, where, however, 'on the third day' is missing.

58 *Excerpts from Theodotus* 61, 5; thus Sagnard, *Clément d'Alexandrie: Extraits de Théodote* (SC 23), p. 181.

59 *Excerpts from Theodotus* 61, 6–7.

60 *Excerpts from Theodotus* 3, 2; 23, 2.

with stars. According to Michel Tardieu, the image of the soul as a spark was, however, concretely found for the first time in testimonies about gnostics; the first testimony he names is Irenaeus' report about Satornilus of Antioch, who lived at the beginning of the second century. According to Satornilus, the highest God has given the spark of life to man, who was created by lower angels but could not walk yet, in order to set him upright; after death the spark is destined to return to his origin. This originally Platonic image reappears in various texts of and about gnostics and also in the church fathers.[61]

4.11 *The Tripartite Tractate*

In section 2.11, attention was given to Jesus' origin and identity in the *Tripartite Tractate* of Nag Hammadi. There we saw that, according to this document, Hebrew prophets had announced the coming and suffering of the Saviour, born as a child with a body and a soul, although he actually could not suffer. Considering that this book is rather voluminous and contains elaborate discussions of the way in which humanity will be saved and restored, it is surprising how concisely and mysteriously reference is made to Jesus' death and resurrection. The author states that the Saviour not only underwent the death of those he wanted to save, but also their smallness, by being born as a child with body and soul. It is not clear whether this was aimed at non-gnostic 'catholic' Christians, who believed that Jesus died for them to redeem them, or at the gnostics.[62] Later the author refers to Jesus' death and resurrection when he writes about the 'Right ones' or psychic people, who do have a soul but lack the divine

---

61 About Satornilus see Irenaeus, *Against Heresies* I, 24, 1 (SC 264); see Michel Tardieu (1975), 'ΨΥΧΑΙΟΣ ΣΠΙΝΘΗΡ: Histoire d'une métaphore dans la tradition platonicienne jusqu'à Eckhart', *Revue des Études Augustiniennes* 21, 225–255 (227–229). Tardieu believes (pp. 252–253) that Plato, *Republic* 621b stands at the origin of this tradition. This states that the sleeping souls were suddenly lifted up as flashing stars to the place where they would be reborn. Apart from this reference, one must also think of Plato, *Timaeus* 41c–42d, which reads that the demiurge made just as many souls as there were stars, and subsequently sowed them in people who were formed by the young gods. Whoever has lived well will return to the star assigned to him. The view that a 'spark of knowledge' has been sown into human beings can also be found in Philo of Alexandria, *Who is the Heir* 308–309 (LCL 261).

62 *Tripartite Tractate* 114, 31–115, 11. In Painchaud, Thomassen, *Le traité tripartite (NH I, 5)*, pp. 423–424 Thomassen prefers the interpretation with regard to the non-gnostic believers, but in his later book *The Spiritual Seed*, pp. 46–58 (the chapter about 'The Soteriology of *The Tripartite Tractate*') he declares that the Saviour came for the sake of the gnostics ('spirituals') (p. 51). He sighs, 'Understanding these soteriological ideas is not easy' (p. 50).

spark within themselves, but are nevertheless called to salvation. This clearly concerns the non-gnostic believers of the 'catholic' church. They are saved because they abandoned their gods and believed in Jesus Christ, the Son of the unknown and invisible God (according to John 1:12, 18). It is written that, when he lay dead in the tomb, the angels thought that he lived and they received life from the one who had died.[63] If the term angels refers to the messengers of Jesus' resurrection according to the New Testament gospels,[64] then it is strange that they are said to receive life through Jesus' death. Therefore, it is more probable that the term refers instead to the spiritual, gnostic believers, as opposed to psychic, non-gnostic Christians.[65] However this may be, the most important thing is that, in this voluminous book about creation and salvation, these are the only references to Jesus' death and new life, and his resurrection on the third day is not explicitly mentioned. The author most likely conceived of Jesus ascending to his Father in the highest heaven after his death. From the very brief records of Jesus' death and life after death, we can conclude that this element of the tradition was of minor importance for the author.

4.12 *A tradition about Simon of Cyrene*

Although we have generally not discussed individual elements from 'gnostic' writings and testimonies, we will make an exception for an interesting interpretation which, according to Irenaeus, originates from Basilides. Basilides lived in the first half of the second century in Alexandria.[66] Irenaeus attributes the following view to him, although it is possible that in fact it originates from Basilides' disciples.[67] According to this account a struggle arose between the God of the Jews and other heavenly rulers about the power on earth. Therefore, the highest and unnameable God sent his first-born Son Christ to earth, where he was called Jesus. He appeared there as man, but did not have to suffer, as Simon of Cyrene was forced to carry his cross and in doing so underwent a metamorphosis.

---

63 *Tripartite Tractate* 121, 25–37; 133, 16–134, 1.
64 Thus Franzmann, *Jesus in the Nag Hammadi Writings*, p. 157; see Matthew 28:2, 5; Luke 24:23; John 20:12.
65 Thus Thomassen, *Le Traité Tripartite (NH I, 5)*, p. 450, who refers to *Tripartite Tractate* 125, 15–18.
66 See, e.g., Roukema, *Gnosis and Faith in Early Christianity*, pp. 127–129.
67 Winrich A. Löhr (1996), *Basilides und seine Schule: Eine Studie zur Theologie- und Kirchengeschichte des zweiten Jahrhunderts*. Tübingen: J. C. B. Mohr, pp. 255–273.

So Simon was crucified instead of Jesus. Jesus had assumed the facial features of Simon and mocked the heavenly rulers, who were not aware that they were being tricked.[68]

Another reference to Simon of Cyrene is found in the *Second Treatise of the Great Seth*. Here, Christ states in a revelation in which he looks back on his earthly life,

> Though they punished me, I did not die in actuality but only in appearance (...). I suffered only in their eyes and their thought (...). The death they think I suffered they suffered in their error and blindness. They nailed their man to their death. Their thoughts did not perceive me, since they were deaf and blind. By doing these things they pronounce judgment against themselves. As for me, they saw me and punished me, but someone else, their father, drank the gall and the vinegar; it was not I. They were striking me with a scourge, but someone else, Simon, bore the cross on his shoulder. Someone else wore the crown of thorns. And I was on high, poking fun at all the excesses of the rulers and the fruit of their error and conceit. I was laughing at their ignorance.[69]

Although this text does not explicitly mention that Simon of Cyrene was crucified instead of Jesus, it is denied that Christ suffered under this torture. His earthly body ('their man') was crucified, but Christ himself had then already withdrawn from it.

From these texts it is apparent that it was deemed unfitting that Jesus Christ, who came from the highest and unnameable Father, should really suffer and die. The Gospel of Mark, for that matter, could be read in a way that appears to give some support for Basilides' assertion that not Jesus but Simon of Cyrene was crucified. After Simon of Cyrene was introduced there, it is written that they brought 'him' to Golgotha and crucified 'him' there (Mark 15:21–24). Read in context, it becomes clear that 'him' refers to Jesus, because previously it is written, 'Then they led him out to crucify him' (Mark 15:20), and this is unmistakably about

---

68 Irenaeus, *Against Heresies* I, 24, 4 (SC 264); for Simon of Cyrene see Mark 15:21.
69 Nag Hammadi Codex VII, 2, 55, 16 – 56, 19; translation Marvin Meyer, in Marvin Meyer, ed. (2007), *The Nag Hammadi Scriptures*. New York: HarperOne, p. 480. Cf. Louis Painchaud (1982), *Le deuxième traité du Grand Seth (NH VII, 2)*. Québec: Laval, pp. 38–41; 102–106 and Gregory Riley (1996), 'Second Treatise of the Great Seth', in Birger Pearson, ed., *Nag Hammadi Codex VII*. Leiden: Brill, pp. 129–199 (137–138; 162–167). Painchaud and Riley understand 'their man' as the earthly body of Jesus. Painchaud understands 'their father' as a later addition which refers to Simon, considering that he is called the father of Alexander and Rufus in Mark 15:21; Riley explains 'their father' as a reference to the demiurge Yaldabaoth.

Jesus. In the transition from Mark 15:21 to 15:22, the evangelist has neglected to indicate, however, that he did not mean Simon, but Jesus who was brought to Golgotha. In this way, this gnostic exegesis could be invented.[70]

4.13 *Comparison of the New Testament and other writings*

Considering the gnostic testimonies that we examined, it is not superfluous to re-emphasize that in the writings of the New Testament, it is beyond doubt that Jesus Christ really did die on the cross. No distinction is made there between an earthly and a heavenly figure of which the first did and the second did not experience death. The New Testament writings also give a theological view on Jesus' death, namely that he died vicariously for humanity and that his death is the cause of God's forgiveness of the sins committed by mankind. Jesus' resurrection is understood as the evidence that he has conquered death and as the anticipation of the resurrection or eternal life for those who believe in him. In comparison to this, it is striking that in the other early Christian writings which we examined, Jesus' death and resurrection are either mentioned only in passing in a very different interpretative context, or not mentioned at all. The Gospel of Thomas has virtually nothing to say about this, and the elaborate *Tripartite Tractate* very little. In the Gospel of Judas, the fact that Judas delivered Jesus to the Jewish scribes, is explained as the sacrifice of his body. As a result of his death, Jesus' heavenly core would be released from his body. The Gospel of Judas does not refer to Jesus' resurrection at all. Cerinthus and the Ophites make a distinction between Jesus and Christ. According to them, Jesus was the earthly man upon whom the heavenly Christ descended at his baptism. Just before Jesus' crucifixion, the Christ withdrew from him, since the Christ, as a divine figure, could not suffer and die. In this point of view, Jesus was raised from the dead by the heavenly Christ. According to the Ophites, Jesus, taken up into the heaven of Yaldabaoth, will ensure that the souls of those who believe in him be led on to the heaven of the highest God. In this way, Jesus' death brings about salvation of those who believe in him. The Valentinian Theodotus, however, explained the names of Jesus and Christ just the other way around. He states that the earthly, psychic Christ has clothed himself with the heavenly Jesus, the Saviour. When the psychic Christ died, he entrusted his earthly soul to the Creator. According to another Valentinian view, however, Jesus entrusted the divine sparks to the highest

---

70 Cf. Klaus Koschorke (1978), *Die Polemik der Gnostiker gegen das kirchliche Christentum*. Leiden: Brill, p. 24.

God by laying his spirit in the hand of the Father. Moreover, Theodotus explains the cross allegorically as the division between the material world and the heaven of the highest God. In the Valentinian views represented by him, the purpose of Christ's death on the cross is apparently that in this way Jesus, as the Saviour, could lead back the divine sparks found within the gnostics to the heaven of the highest God. According to a tradition associated with the name of Basilides, not Jesus, but Simon of Cyrene was crucified. A rather awkward formulation in the Gospel of Mark may have provoked this far-fetched interpretation. Again, the reason for this view must be sought in the conviction that a heavenly, divine figure could not really die. According to the *Second Treatise of the Great Seth*, Jesus Christ was crucified only in name and did not suffer physically; for the enduring of physical suffering this treatise also alludes to Simon of Cyrene.

How should we then evaluate the gnostic views on Jesus' death and (if applicable) his resurrection and exaltation? First, we will examine the texts which entirely ignore the redemptive effect for mankind; of the writings that were treated here, this includes the Gospel of Thomas and the Gospel of Judas. This absence of references to the redemptive effect raises the question if this can refer to an old tradition which has been eclipsed by, among others, the theology of Paul and the canonical gospels.

With regard to the Gospel of Thomas, this is surely possible. It is conceivable that this gospel originally arose from a smaller collection of sayings credited to Jesus, which were later adapted and supplemented in a 'gnostic' sense.[71] If the compiler or compilers omitted references to Jesus' death and resurrection because they rejected the belief in the redemptive effect that other Christians acknowledged, this might testify to an implicit polemic against the other point of view. This may possibly be based on an early view on Jesus, which originated from Jewish believers who did not attribute the redemptive effect to his death and resurrection, which is put forward in the New Testament writings.[72] There is, however, not a shred of evidence for the belief that the 'gnostic' view on salvation, which appears in the now known compilation of the Gospel of Thomas,[73] goes

---

71 DeConick, *The Original Gospel of Thomas in Translation*, tries to distinguish between the 'kernel sayings' and the 'accretions', but she opposes the view that the complete Gospel of Thomas is a 'gnostic' collection (pp. 3–7).
72 See chapter 6.
73 See sections 3.6 and 3.11. This concerns, e.g., the origin of the androgynous souls from the kingdom of light and their way back, along the heavenly powers, to this supercelestial kingdom.

back to earliest Jewish Christianity (let alone to Jesus himself). This view is related, after all, to Christian-gnostic testimonies which originated at the end of the first and in the second centuries.

Although the Gospel of Judas contains an entirely different secret teaching of Jesus than the Gospel of Thomas, it does correspond to it as far as its scanty reference to Jesus' death is concerned. Insofar as Jesus' death leads to salvation, this concerns only himself, as he is saved from his earthly body in order to return to the highest God. In general, the Gospel of Judas is strongly opposed to the beliefs of the contemporaneous church. This is apparent, among other things, in its implicit criticism either of the martyrdom or of the Eucharist, both of which, in the view of the church, referred to salvation by Jesus' death and resurrection. Against this, the Gospel of Judas puts forward another, gnostic view on the salvation of the soul.[74] As the Gospel of Judas reacts to the church which had come to exist by that time, and reflects various gnostic ideas of the second century, it is very implausible that it preserves an independent ancient tradition about Jesus' death.

Secondly, some gnostic writings refer to the belief of 'catholic' Christians that Jesus had died for them, without any polemical arguments against this view. This is the case in the *Tripartite Tractate*. Here, an entirely different position is taken than in the gospels just named with regard to this theme. The brief report that Jesus, who lay in the grave, lived again and that the 'angels' (the spiritual Christians?) received life through him who had died resembles the belief of the 'catholic' church. Yet it is not reported that Jesus' resurrection took place on the third day; that he lives again can also mean that, after the death of his body, he was directly taken up to his Father in heaven. These elements, however, have not been given a prominent place in this elaborate work.

Thirdly, we have seen that Jesus' death and resurrection are indeed explained as 'redemptive' in various gnostic testimonies, but in an entirely different way than was usual within the church. The Ophites believed that, thanks to the crucifixion and resurrection from the dead of the earthly Jesus, the souls of those who have come to know him will be led on to the heaven of the highest God. The Valentinians believed in their own way that, because Jesus carried the cross or because of the fact that on the cross he laid his spirit in the hands of the Father, the divine sparks of the true believers were again brought back to this highest heaven. In this way, a redemptive value was indeed granted to Jesus' death, but the content of this salvation fits in more closely with the Hellenistic world.

74 See also section 3.7.

There we can find, after all, the Platonic image of the divine sparks spread out in people, which would return to their heavenly origin. This interpretation is clearly intended as an alternative for the 'catholic' view of salvation and is therefore of a later date.

Fourthly, it may be remarked that the idea that Jesus on his way to the cross and during the crucifixion did not really suffer is inspired by the Greek idea that God, or a divine figure, cannot suffer. The belief that Simon of Cyrene was crucified instead of Jesus is apparently a later interpretation of the Gospel of Mark and therefore cannot date back to an old tradition.

In conclusion, it is clear on the one hand that the gnostic views on the meaning of Jesus' death and – if applicable – resurrection differ sharply. On the other hand we have seen that the texts which we have discussed usually react to the beliefs of the church and, in a few cases, are engaged in a polemic against them. This means that their views are secondary compared to the beliefs of the church. Gnostics tried to offer an alternative to them, which they considered more credible.

This evaluation does not imply that the view on Jesus' death and resurrection which we have found in Paul and in the canonical gospels – with some differences of emphasis and expression – is the only legitimate one. Historically speaking, we may conclude, however, that the idea that Jesus died for the sins of mankind and that his resurrection is an anticipation of the resurrection of the dead has good credentials and appears earlier than the gnostic views.

Insofar as gnostics did not pay attention to the redemptive effect of Jesus' death and resurrection, it can be concluded that they found this view theologically incredible or even reprehensible. It is understandable that this theological rejection of the faith of the early church can count on understanding and sympathy in the present age. Modern or postmodern people generally have little or no understanding of the tradition according to which Jesus was given by God to offer his life vicariously for others and thus realize reconciliation with him. Christians may also experience a certain distance towards this traditional belief. The fact that in certain gnostic writings this element of the Christian faith is absent makes them all the more interesting for many people. From an historical perspective, however, this belief proves to go back to a very ancient tradition, even though its theological correctness can never be demonstrated historically. A historian can only describe theological statements and cannot pass judgement on them as a historian. Still, the traditional view on the liberating effect of Jesus' death and resurrection can be endorsed in faith.

CHAPTER 5

Interim Conclusions and New Questions

5.1 *Interim conclusions*

From the preceding chapters it has become apparent that in early Christianity very different views on Jesus were held. We concentrated on the letters of Paul, the canonical gospels, the book of Acts (although to a limited degree), a number of gospels which can be called gnostic or are at least related to gnosticism, and a few other gnostic writings and testimonies. From our discussions we will now draw a few conclusions.

In the New Testament writings, Jesus is presented as a real human being, who at the same time is regarded as the Christ and the Son of God. He acts with divine authority and is even regularly described in terms of the LORD, Yahweh. This means that he already existed before he was born as a human being. Explicitly or implicitly it is testified that from the very beginning he was pre-existent with God in heaven. In his earthly existence he lives trusting upon his heavenly Father, the God of Israel, and he regularly refers to the Old Testament. He proclaims the coming of God's kingdom and calls for a life in love towards God and neighbour. He exhorts those who want to follow him to subordinate their family ties to this. In the Gospel of John, Jesus proclaims himself as the one sent by God as the Christ and the Son of God more emphatically than in the synoptic gospels. Whoever will come to know God in him partakes of eternal life, which already begins during earthly life, according to the Fourth Gospel. Concerning Jesus' death, all of the canonical gospels testify that this was announced in the Old Testament scriptures and corresponds to God's purpose. It is asserted through various images and expressions that Jesus died vicariously for mankind and thus, by his death, brought about God's forgiveness of their sins. In this way a new covenant with

114

God is established. In the Gospel of John, this is expressed in such a way that Jesus, through his exaltation, will draw all people unto himself. Both Paul and the canonical gospels testify that on the third day of his death, Jesus was raised or rose from the dead. It is also stated that when he reappeared to his closest disciples, he spoke with them and commanded them to spread his message. From then on his place is in heaven, at God's right hand. From the New Testament writings can be deduced that God, by raising Jesus from the dead, rehabilitated him and that his resurrection anticipates the general resurrection of the dead. In his resurrection Jesus has, so it can be inferred, essentially overcome the power of death. In his exalted status he can be invoked by people on earth, which points to the divine status attributed to him.

The other, for the most part gnostic, testimonies partly correspond to the New Testament writings, but also often tell a different tale. Regarding Jesus' origin, the Gospel of Thomas is the most closely related to the New Testament witnesses. Jesus is represented as the light which is above all things and from which everything came forth, and as the pre-existent Son of the Father, who appeared in a mortal body. In the Gospel of Thomas, however, Israel and the Old Testament are not of any importance and Jesus speaks critically about Israel's prophets as 'the dead'. Although his teaching in the Gospel of Thomas is partly related to the synoptic gospels, there are also sayings which differ markedly from these. They refer, for example, to the androgynous origin of human beings in the supercelestial kingdom and their destination to return to it. The appeal to a celibate life is intoned even more emphatically than in the synoptic gospels and is motivated differently, namely on the basis of the androgynous origin and destination of the human being. The 'kingdom' in the Gospel of Thomas is on the one hand something supercelestial, on the other hand something inner, within Jesus' disciples – although he also states that it is something that is spread out over the earth. When Jesus speaks about the owners who come to claim the earth, this indicates that the earth will fall victim to inferior powers. He who then rids himself of his body and ascends with his soul, past the hostile powers, to the Father, is delivered from earthly existence. With regard to salvation, Jesus' death is of no importance and is barely mentioned anyway; of his resurrection no mention is made whatsoever. To take part in salvation, self-knowledge is most important, meaning knowledge of one's origin and destination. So the Gospel of Thomas turns out, in comparison with the synoptic gospels, to offer an alternative image of Jesus and his teaching, which sometimes shows some affinity to the Gospel of John. There, after all, Jesus is called the way to the Father and states that, in his exaltation, he will draw all people to himself. Jesus there speaks of an evil ruler of this world, although, contrary to the Gospel of Thomas, the Fourth Gospel adds that

the power of that ruler draws to an end. Another difference is that the
Gospel of John does not teach that human beings, before their birth on
earth, originated from that supercelestial kingdom.[1]

The idea that the human being is originally created androgynous and
needs to retrieve the original male–female unity is derived from Platonism.
From this is apparent that this is a later Hellenistic interpretation of,
or addition to, Jesus' instruction. That the Gospel of Thomas does
not attribute any redemptive meaning to Jesus' death (let alone to his
resurrection) may, however, stem from an early Jewish Christian tradition.
We will return to this in the following chapter.

Various gnostic testimonies make a distinction in Jesus Christ between
his human appearance and the divine, pre-existent figure which descended
upon him. The divine figure – called Jesus or Christ – is regarded as
descending from the heaven of the unnameable God, who surpassed the
God of the Old Testament. This is true for Cerinthus, the Ophites, the
Gospel of Judas, Theodotus and the *Tripartite Tractate*. Sometimes a
distinction is made between even more pre-existent heavenly figures, such
as the Logos and Sophia, who together brought about the person of Jesus
Christ on earth. It is clear that these views are in part derived from the
New Testament writings and consequently testify to later developments.
In early catholic Christianity, it was believed that Jesus was the promised
Christ and the Son of God – of God as he was described in the Old
Testament – and that in him God's Logos or the LORD himself appeared.
Gnostics, however, needed another, in their opinion more profound, view
on the union of the human and the divine in Jesus Christ. Because the
many variants of gnostic teaching are reactions to the faith of the church,
their views are obviously secondary and do not go back to the oldest
traditions about Jesus, let alone to Jesus himself.

Historical considerations rule out the possibility that Jesus really
came to proclaim a different, higher God. This idea was prompted by

---

1   John 1:9 can be translated in this way, 'He was the true light that enlightens everyone
who comes into the world.' This was how Origen understood this verse in, e.g., *First
Principles* I, 2, 6 (TF 24); *Homilies on Exodus* 13, 4 (SC 321); *Commentary on John*
XX, 288 (SC 290), and thus it has been translated in the Vulgate. In this interpretation,
this verse can be understood as if it concerns the human being who comes into the world
from pre-existence. However, because the Gospel of John takes no further notice of the
pre-existence of human souls, it would be far-fetched to explain this ambiguous verse
in that way. Preferable is, e.g., the NSRV, 'The true light, which enlightens everyone,
was coming into the world.' See Hermann L. Strack and Paul Billerbeck (1974),
Kommentar zum Neuen Testament aus Talmud und Midrasch II (6th edn). München:
Beck'sche Verlangsbuchhandlung, p. 358; Schnackenburg, *Das Johannesevangelium* 1,
pp. 230–231.

the difficulty that certain Christians had with the rough demeanour and speech of the Old Testament God. In the Old Testament it is told that the LORD kills people or has them killed in his name.[2] He is described as a jealous God who punishes the next generation for the sins of the fathers.[3] Philosophically educated Christians from the beginning of the Christian era therefore came to the conclusion that he must be an inferior God. They felt that Jesus proclaimed the highest God, who corresponded more to the way in which educated believers conceived of God. We can conclude that the introduction of an unknown, unnameable God who stands much higher than the God of the Old Testament arises from a rejection of the church's insistence on maintaining the Old Testament as Holy Scripture.[4] Since the New Testament writings describe Jesus as a Jew, whose teaching is linked to the Old Testament and the God of Israel, it is evident that in historical respect this is a more reliable description of his preaching and beliefs about God than can be found in the gnostic testimonies. Even when New Testament authors describe Jesus in terms of the LORD and furthermore refer to God the Father, this Father cannot be identified with the gnostic image of the high God.

According to various gnostic testimonies, salvation signifies that the divine particles – the seeds or sparks – which have been sown into the people who will acquire true knowledge (*gnosis*), are led back to the high heaven from which they originate. This type of salvation is also connected with Jesus' death and his resurrection. It fits in with Platonic philosophy and can therefore be regarded as a Hellenistic interpretation of the message that is found in the New Testament gospels. In this interpretation, however, Jesus' message has undergone a radical change. In the synoptic gospels Jesus proclaims, as the Christ and the Son of God, that the kingdom of God is at hand and that it has already come in his person. In the Gospel of John, Jesus points even more emphatically at himself as the Christ and the Son of God. Here he calls himself the way to the Father and states that he gives true, eternal life to those who know him and believe in him. The idea that people have a divine particle within themselves which needs to be delivered out of the earthly body does not appear in the New Testament gospels, in the letters of Paul, or in the other New Testament writings. Because this element is derived from Platonism and does not appear in the earliest sources about Jesus, we can conclude that it was originally not a part of his teaching.

---

2   E.g., Genesis 7:23; 19:24–25; Numbers 16:31–35; 1 Samuel 15:2–8, 33.
3   Exodus 20:5; Deuteronomy 5:9.
4   See Roukema, *Gnosis and Faith in Early Christianity*, pp. 105–120; 159–163.

The New Testament writings agree that Jesus, who is called the Christ and the Son of God, died on a cross. No attempts have been made there to obscure his cruel death. According to various gnostic testimonies, however, the divine figure in Jesus Christ – sometimes called Christ, at other times Jesus – did not die, but withdrew himself from his body before his death. Thus only his human form died. Some sources even propose that the man who was crucified was actually Simon of Cyrene. Apparently, these views too are later interpretations of the beliefs of the early church. The view that the divine figure withdrew himself from the body is a gnostic interpretation of the New Testament texts which tell that Jesus prior to his death 'breathed his last', which has been understood as the divine element leaving him.[5] In the New Testament gospels, however, it is nowhere suggested that the divine element in Jesus did not suffer. This view originated from the Greek belief that God, or a divine figure, cannot suffer and therefore cannot undergo death.

We have already remarked that the absence of the belief that Jesus died for humanity to bring about forgiveness of sins can go back to an ancient Jewish Christian tradition. Apart from this, it can continually be substantiated that the New Testament writings offer an older view on Jesus' person, message and death than the gnostic testimonies. Whoever feels attracted to one of the gnostic points of view thereby exhibits a *theological* preference. In historical respect it must be said, however, that the typically gnostic points of view are less ancient and less original than those which can be read in the New Testament.

5.2 *New questions*

According to these conclusions, the New Testament writings are relatively trustworthy with regard to Jesus' person and meaning in comparison to the various secondary gnostic interpretations. However, these conclusions raise new questions. It is clear after all, that the New Testament also contains *theological* interpretations of Jesus' life and death – to say nothing of his resurrection, exaltation and ascension to heaven. We already remarked that a historian can never determine that Jesus Christ is the Son of God, or that in him the LORD himself appeared on earth. Neither can it be proved historically that Jesus died for the sins of humanity and that God, on grounds of the death of his Son, forgives people their sins. This is the belief of the early Christians, who thus gave their theological interpretation of historical events. Here we can pose

---

5   In Matthew 27:50 and John 19:30, the Greek term for 'his last' is *to pneuma*, 'the spirit'. Mark 15:37 and Luke 23:46 read *exepneusen*.

the following question: are not the early Christian views which can be found in the New Testament secondary with regard to Jesus himself as well? Stated differently, have not the New Testament authors, with their accounts, also distanced themselves from the man from Nazareth? This question is pressing considering that there proved to be Jewish followers of Jesus who had a much simpler view of their master. These Jewish Christian groups will be discussed in chapter 6.

At the other end of the early Christian spectrum, the question arises of whether the New Testament gospels are complete and whether Jesus did not have a separate, secret teaching which is not included there. Jesus even seems explicitly to refer to a secret teaching which he gave to a small circle of his disciples, in contrast to that which he gave to the larger crowd. Accordingly, the authors of various gnostic writings claimed to report Jesus' secret words. Concerning a number of gnostic themes we have already drawn the conclusion that they do not stem from Jesus. Yet it does merit further investigation as to whether the New Testament gospels allow for the possibility that Jesus had a secret teaching, and whether the claims of other writings and authors are plausible in this respect. Chapter 7 is devoted to this question.

With regard to the testimony of the New Testament, we have established that whoever says that Jesus is the Son of God and that in him the LORD himself has appeared is making theological statements. This raises the question of whether these statements are out of place, arbitrary and unverifiable. Or can it be proved with historical arguments that, in the context of that time, it at least cannot be excluded that Jesus' first followers already regarded him as the Son of God and the LORD? To answer these questions, we will discuss some contemporaneous Jewish conceptions of God in chapter 8.

Finally, the question of Jesus and 'dogma' comes up for discussion. So far, we have compared New Testament and gnostic (or gnostic-related) testimonies to each other. The gnostic testimonies originate from the second and third centuries. In those centuries, Christians of the 'catholic' church also spoke and wrote about Jesus. At the time, various views were developed on the relationship between God the Father and Jesus Christ the Son. In 325 CE, the bishops who were gathered at the council of Nicaea declared that Jesus Christ is the eternal Son of God, and that he is consubstantial with the Father. This statement, which is contained in the Nicene Creed, led them to the dogma of God's trinity. According to this dogma the one God reveals himself as, and consists of, the Father, the Son and the Holy Spirit. But is this not likewise a secondary, later interpretation of Jesus' person? In any case, in the church of the first centuries other views on Jesus were also formulated that were eventually rejected. How credible therefore is the theological, dogmatic development of the church of the first centuries? Because the gnostic views on Jesus' person and actions were regularly inspired by Hellenistic interpretations, we may conclude that the continuity between Jesus and gnosis is weak. But what about the continuity between Jesus and the dogma formulated about him in Nicaea? How can this exceptional man from Nazareth be part of the divine trinity? We will examine this in chapter 9. But first our attention will be focussed upon Jewish Christianity.

CHAPTER 6

Jewish Christianity

In the previous chapters we examined how Jesus is described in a number of New Testament writings and in a number of gnostic works. We there found all sorts of different traditions and views, which went back to different authors and the communities to which they belonged. However, during that time many more groups with different views on Jesus existed. There were Jewish Christians who strongly held on to their Jewish identity and kept themselves apart from the 'catholic' church, which also admitted non-Jewish believers. There were also non-Jewish Christians who believed in Jesus in a way strongly related to Jewish Christianity. Although our interest especially lies in the continuity or discontinuity between Jesus, the gnosis of the gnostics, and the dogma of the council of Nicaea, we will also pay attention to the so-called 'Jewish Christian' beliefs about Jesus from the beginning of Christianity. On the one hand, we are doing this to find out to what extent these Jewish Christians preserved ancient traditions about Jesus. On the other hand, this theme is of importance, because as we will see in chapter 9, there have continually been Christians in the 'catholic' church who were inspired by Jewish Christian views.

We use the term 'Jewish Christian' here for a few specific groups from early Christianity. As a matter of fact, earliest Christianity as a whole arose from Judaism. Therefore some scholars used the term 'Jewish Christian' for all of those forms of Christianity in which Jewish patterns clearly remained visible.[1] In this chapter, however, those Jewish Christian texts are treated which come forth from groups which existed separately alongside the early 'catholic' church, because they held on to their Jewish origin more strongly.

---

1   Thus Daniélou, *Théologie du judéo-christianisme*.

121

6.1 *Testimonies of church fathers about Jewish Christians*

In the dialogue between Justin Martyr and the Jew Trypho (dating from about 150 CE), mention is made of Jews who believe in Jesus as the Christ and, at the same time, hold on to keeping the Mosaic law. Justin can approve of this as long as they do not try to persuade the non-Jewish Christians to live according to the law of Moses as well. The latter implied, for example, that they had to keep the Sabbath and that men had to be circumcised. Justin indicates that the Jews who believed in Christ, partly did and partly did not associate with non-Jewish Christians.[2] Other authors confirm that in the first centuries there were Jewish Christians who more or less agreed with the Christians from other nations. However, facts about them have to be gleaned from various scattered sources.[3]

Irenaeus is the first to mention the Ebionites about 180 CE. Their name is derived from the Hebrew *ebyōn*, which means 'poor' and refers, among other things, to Jesus' beatitude, 'blessed are the poor'.[4] Irenaeus writes that they only use the Gospel of Matthew. They accuse Paul of turning away from the law of Moses, while they honour the Jewish traditions, such as circumcision. They believe that Joseph is Jesus' father and so they deny that Jesus was born of the Virgin Mary.[5] In this respect, their text of the Gospel of Matthew apparently deviated from the prevailing version which does describe that Mary became pregnant by the Holy Spirit (Matthew 1:20–25). Origen of Alexandria reports that there were two types of Ebionites. According to him there was one group that did and another that did not believe that Jesus was born of the Virgin Mary.[6] The fact that there were Ebionites who had another gospel than Matthew's is confirmed by what Epiphanius of Salamis quotes from it. According to this gospel, a voice from heaven said to Jesus after his baptism, 'You are my Son, the Beloved; with you I am well pleased. Today I have begotten you.'

---

2 Justin, *Dialogue with Trypho* 47, 1–4 (ed. Goodspeed).
3 Sources from the church fathers have been compiled by A. F. J. Klijn and G. J. Reinink (1973), *Patristic Evidence for Jewish-Christian Sects*. Leiden: Brill. See also William L. Petersen (2001), 'Constructing the Matrix of Judaic Christianity from Texts', in Simon C. Mimouni and F. Stanley Jones, eds, *Le judéo-christianisme dans tous ses états: Actes du colloque de Jérusalem 6–10 juillet 1998*. Paris: Cerf, pp. 126–144.
4 Cf. Matthew 5:3 and Luke 6:20. Paul's characterization of the first church in Jerusalem as 'the poor' in Romans 15:26 and Galatians 2:10 may also be considered. See also Richard Bauckham (2003), 'The Origin of the Ebionites', in Peter J. Tomson and Doris Lambers-Petry, eds, *The Image of Judaeo-Christians in Ancient Jewish and Christian Literature*. Tübingen: J. C. B. Mohr, pp. 162–181 (178–180).
5 *Against Heresies* I, 26, 2; III, 11, 7; 21, 1; V, 1, 3 (SC 264; 211; 153). The belief that Joseph was Jesus' father they shared with Cerinthus, discussed in section 2.8. See also Origen, *Against Celsus* V, 65 (SC 147).
6 *Against Celsus* V, 61; cf. V, 65.

Subsequently, the voice spoke to John the Baptist, 'This is my Son, the Beloved, with him I am well pleased'.[7] These three sayings are compiled from the three synoptic gospels. This implies that this account cannot be older than the synoptic gospels.[8] Furthermore, this text demonstrates that the Ebionites believed that Jesus is God's beloved Son. Eusebius says, however, that in their view Jesus was 'a plain and ordinary man who had achieved righteousness merely by the progress of his character'.[9] We may conclude that, according to the Ebionites, Jesus became God's special beloved Son only at his baptism. Origen says that the Ebionites did accept Jesus as the Christ, but that their faith aside from that was poor. He does not deal with the question of how they believed in Jesus as God's Son, but he does state that, according to them, Jesus had only come for the Israelites.[10] Eusebius knows that the Ebionites who do believe in Jesus' virgin birth nevertheless do not acknowledge his pre-existence as Logos and Wisdom.[11] According to Epiphanius, the Ebionites descend from Christians who, during the siege of Jerusalem in 69–70 CE, fled from the city to Pella, on the other side of the river Jordan.[12]

Jerome reports in 404 CE that in all of the synagogues of the eastern part of the Roman Empire, the Jewish sect (*haeresis*) of the Nazarenes (or Nazoreans) is represented. This name is used in Acts 24:5 for the Jewish Christians and refers to the designation of Jesus as the Nazorean.[13] Jerome says of the Nazarenes that they 'believe that Christ is the Son of God, born of the Virgin Mary, and (...) that it is he who suffered under Pontius Pilate and is resurrected, in whom we also believe'. Because they want to be Jews as well as Christians, they are, according to Jerome, neither.[14] He probably exaggerates when he writes that such Nazarenes

---

7 *Panarion* 30, 13, 7 (NHS 35). Quoted are Mark 1:11; Luke 3:22 (see section 2.4) and Matthew 3:17. For Epiphanius' description of the Ebionites see Joseph Verheyden (2003), 'Epiphanius on the Ebionites', in Tomson and Lambers-Petry, eds, *The Image of Judaeo-Christians*, pp. 182–208.

8 Daniel A. Bertrand (1980), 'L'Evangile des Ebionites: une harmonie évangélique antérieure au *Diatessaron*', *New Testament Studies* 26, pp. 548–563, argues that this passage stems from a gospel harmony from 100–150 CE.

9 *Church History* III, 27, 1–2 (LCL 153); cf. Justin, *Dialogue with Trypho* 48, 4 (ed. Goodspeed).

10 *Against Celsus* II, 1 (SC 132); *First Principles* IV, 3, 8 (TF 24), with reference to Matthew 15:24.

11 *Church History* III, 27, 3 (LCL 153).

12 *Panarion* 30, 2, 7 (NHS 35). For the flight to Pella see Eusebius, *Church History* III, 5, 2–3.

13 E.g., Matthew 2:23; 26:71; Acts 2:22; 3:6.

14 *Epistles* 112, 13 (ed. Labourt); see Simon C. Mimouni (1998), *Le judéo-christianisme ancien: Essais historiques*. Paris: Cerf, pp. 139–152.

are present in all of the Jewish synagogues in the east. We can infer from his remarks, however, that in his view the belief of these Jewish Christians corresponds to the faith of the catholic Church, but that they did not belong to it. Epiphanius, who as bishop of Salamis on Cyprus came from Palestine, calls them Nazorenes and he localizes them (about 375 CE) here and there in Syria. He states that they also originated from the church which, during the time of the Roman siege in 69–70 CE, fled from Jerusalem to Pella across the river Jordan. He reports, contrary to what Jerome suggests, that the Nazoreans were hated by those Jews who did not believe in Jesus.[15]

Jerome writes what happened according to a Hebrew Jewish Christian gospel when Jesus came up out of the water of the river Jordan. He tells that the whole fountain of the Holy Spirit then descended upon Jesus and said to him, 'My Son, in all the prophets I expected that you might come and that I might rest on you, for you are my rest, you are my first-born Son, who reigns in eternity.'[16] We see that the voice from heaven, which we know from the synoptic gospels,[17] is interpreted in this gospel as the voice of the Holy Spirit. 'Spirit' is a feminine word in Hebrew (*ru'ah*); it follows that the Spirit calls Jesus her Son. This is similar to the Gospel of the Hebrews, which is quoted by Origen, where Jesus calls the Holy Spirit 'my Mother'.[18] That Jesus at his baptism was addressed elaborately by the Spirit seems to be a later and therefore secondary interpretation of the voice which, according to the older synoptic gospels, called him 'my beloved Son'; this voice is evidently supposed to come from God the Father.

Because no integral writings of groups such as the Ebionites and the Nazoreans have been preserved, our information about them depends

---

15 *Panarion* 29, 7; Eusebius, *Church History* III, 5, 2–3. Some scholars think that the Nazoreans only arose as a group in the fourth century, as no mention of their existence was made before that time. See S. C. Mimouni (1998), 'Les Nazoréens: Recherche étymologique et historique', *Revue Biblique*, 105, 208–262; Klijn and Reinink, *Patristic Evidence*, 44–52. Bargil Pixner (2001), 'Nazoreans on Mount Zion (Jerusalem)', in Mimouni and Jones, eds, *Le judéo-christianisme dans tous ses états*, pp. 289–316, however, maintains the view that there have always been Nazoreans through the first centuries.

16 *Commentary on Isaiah* 11, 1–3 (CCSL 73; translation inspired by Elliott, *The Apocryphal New Testament*, p. 10). Jerome attributes this passage to the Hebrew Gospel of the Nazaraeans, but it is often thought that it corresponds with the Gospel of the Hebrews, to be mentioned later. See Mimouni, *Le judéo-christianisme ancien*, pp. 207–222.

17 Matthew 3:17; Mark 1:11; Luke 3:22.

18 *Commentary on John* II, 87 (SC 120); *Homilies on Jeremiah* 15, 4 (SC 238). Cf. Gospel of Thomas 101.

on such fragmentary and critical testimonies of the church fathers.[19] Although their information is often biased, we can conclude from it that these Jewish Christians often did not agree with the high, divine view of Jesus and his pre-existence that can be found in the New Testament writings and that is confirmed in later dogmatic development.

6.2 *The Pseudo-Clementine writings*

For our knowledge of Jewish Christianity it is of the utmost importance that two fairly elaborate writings that deal with this have been well preserved. They are two novels from the fourth century which are attributed to Clement of Rome. As Clement lived in the first century, it is obvious that these novels were not actually written by him. One of the books was preserved in Greek and is known by the somewhat inappropriate title *Homiliai*, 'Homilies'. The Greek text of the other book is lost, but it has been handed down in a Latin translation of Rufinus of Aquileia from the beginning of the fifth century. The title of this work is *Recognitiones*, 'Recognitions'. Because both books have many passages in common, it has been deduced that an older, 'Jewish Christian' document underlies both these works. This older document originates from northern Syria and was written between 222 and at the very latest 325 CE.[20] In this document individual traditions can be distinguished which are partially derived from older Jewish Christian sources.[21]

These books contain elaborate reports of the preaching of Peter and a few of his companions. They begin by stating that Clement, prompted

19 An interesting Arabic text of 'Abd al-Jabbār, dating from the tenth century, is presented by Shlomo Pines (1966), *The Jewish Christians of the Early Centuries According to a New Source*. Jerusalem: The Israel Academy of Sciences and Humanities. It generally confirms the information of the church fathers about Jewish Christians. This manuscript may date back to ancient, independent sources.

20 Georg Strecker (1958), *Das Judenchristentum in den Pseudoklementinen*. Berlin: Akademie-Verlag, pp. 35–96; Liugi Cirillo and André Schneider (1999), *Les Reconnaissances du pseudo Clément: Roman chrétien des premiers siècles*. Turnhout: Brepols, pp. 13–23; Pierre Geoltrain (2005), 'Roman pseudo-clémentin: Introduction', in idem, Jean-Daniel Kaestli, ed., *Écrits apocryphes chrétiens* II, [Paris]: Gallimard, pp. 1175–1187 (1186).

21 See, e.g., Bernard Pouderon (2001), 'Aux origines du roman clémentin: Prototype païen, refonte judéo-hellénistique, remaniement chrétien', in Mimouni and Jones, eds, *Le judéo-christianisme dans tous ses états*, pp. 231–256; Bauckham, 'The Origin of the Ebionites', in Tomson and Lambers-Petry, eds, *The Image of Judaeo-Christians*, pp. 162–181. Especially important for our purposes is that *Recognitions* I, 27–71 stems from an old Jewish Christian, perhaps Ebionite source (so Bauckham).

by Barnabas' preaching in Rome, makes his way to Caesarea in Palestine, where he becomes a disciple of Peter.[22] Subsequently, Peter takes him along on his missionary journeys. Here he regularly comes up against Simon the Magician, as is also described in Acts 8:9–24. In these works, Simon propagates gnostic and Marcionite ideas, but sometimes he also turns out to be the personification of the apostle Paul.[23] Thus, in a concealed way, a stark contrast is assumed between Peter and Paul. In these books, Peter represents the true faith in Jesus, which is distorted by Simon.

Peter proclaims that there is one God, the Creator of the world whose will is made known by the true prophet.[24] Since the beginning of the world this true prophet has appeared as Adam, as Moses, and finally in the person of Jesus.[25] This proves that Jesus' pre-existence is acknowledged. Sometimes the true prophet is conceived as the pre-existent Christ, who appeared to Abraham and Moses.[26] Barnabas and Peter call him the Son of God, but Peter emphatically declares that Jesus never called himself God. As Son he is, after all, begotten, while only God the Father is unbegotten and therefore truly God. As far as one still wants to call Christ God, he does not differ from the immortal souls who, in a certain way, can also be called 'gods', because they originate from God.[27] Yet the Christ can also be called eternal and, being God's Son who became man, he is considered the beginning of all things.[28]

In his capacity of prophet, Jesus made known how to live according to God's will, by doing what is right; his teachings generally correspond with the Gospel of Matthew. For all who believe in him, his function is similar to the position Moses had among the Hebrews or Jews. Peter states that if the Hebrews observe the commandments of Moses, God will accept them even without believing in Jesus. Those who are not Jews, but do believe in Jesus, will be accepted by God if they keep to Jesus' commandments. Therefore, there are two paths to salvation.[29] In

---

22 *Homilies* I, 6–22 (GCS 42); *Recognitions* I, 6–26 (GCS 51).
23 Cirillo and Schneider, *Les Reconnaissances du pseudo Clément*, pp. 40–49. For Simon the Magician and for Marcion see, e.g., Roukema, *Gnosis and Faith in Early Christianity*, pp. 14–22; 136–137. That Simon represents Paul is apparent from, among others, *Homilies* XVII, 13–15, 19 and *Recognitions* III, 49, 5.
24 E.g., Homilies II, 12; III, 6, 1; XVI, 14, 3. See Strecker, *Das Judenchristentum in den Pseudoklementinen*, pp. 145–153.
25 *Homilies* I, 19; III, 11–13; III, 20–21; III, 53, 3 – 54, 1; VII, 8, 1; VIII, 10, 1–3; cf. *Recognitions* I, 45, 4; 52, 3; 63, 1.
26 *Recognitions* I, 33, 1; 34, 4; 37, 2; 45, 1–5; these texts stem from the Jewish Christian source mentioned in note 21.
27 *Homilies* I, 7–9; XVI, 15–16; cf. XVIII, 13, 1–5; *Recognitions* II, 41–42.
28 *Recognitions* I, 44, 2; 45, 2–5; 52, 3; 63, 1 (originating from the ancient Jewish Christian source, see note 21).
29 *Homilies* VIII, 5–7.

his preaching, Peter hardly mentions Jesus' death and he does not refer to his resurrection at all. He quotes Jesus' prayer for those who crucified him, 'Father, forgive them their sins, for they know not what they do.' Peter also says that the prophet is nailed to the cross by wrongdoers, but that this fact worked out for the best through his power.[30] Salvation is not based on Jesus' death (let alone his resurrection), but is the result of belief in him as the true prophet, of conversion and of the right *gnosis*.[31] It is not necessary for non-Jews to be circumcised, but they must be baptized in the name of the Father, the Son and the Holy Spirit.[32]

These novels – of which we have not discussed the plot – reflect the beliefs of factions in Syria who practised a Jewish form of Christianity. Apparently, their communities had members of Jewish as well as non-Jewish origin. We are not concerned, however, with the historical context of these novels in the second, third and fourth centuries, but with the view on Jesus expressed in them. Although Jesus is acknowledged as Christ and as God's Son, it is denied, or at least greatly relativized, that he himself is also God.[33] Jesus is particularly described as the true prophet who speaks in name of the only true God. Whoever believes in him, obeys his teachings, and is baptized in the name of the Father, the Son and the Holy Spirit, will be redeemed from his sins and from God's judgement. As Jesus Christ is the true prophet who appeared on earth since the beginning of the world, his pre-existence is acknowledged in these books.

6.3 *An ancient form of Christianity?*

We saw that the church fathers speak of Jewish Christians who maintained their positions especially in Syria without being a part of the catholic church. The Pseudo-Clementine writings indicate that there were also Christians of non-Jewish origin whose religious views were related to Jewish Christianity. They confessed Jesus as God's Son who at his baptism had received the Holy Spirit. In the Pseudo-Clementine writings, he is

---

30 *Homilies* XI, 20, 4 (cf. Luke 23:34); *Recognitions* I, 41, 2; VI, 5, 5; cf. I, 53, 2. *Homilies* III, 19, 1 reads that the prophet neglected his own blood; this has to refer to his kinsfolk (just prior to this is mentioned that he had mercy on the gentiles). *Recognitions* I, 43, 3 mentions the period of seven years after the Lord's passion, but this reference only serves as an indication of time.
31 *Homilies* III, 18, 2–3; VII, 8, 1–2; XI, 19, 2–3; *Recognitions* I, 14, 5; VI, 4, 1–6.
32 Recognitions V, 34, 2; *Homilies* XI, 26, 2.
33 Peterson, 'The Matrix of Judaic Christianity', pp. 140–143, points to a similar, yet slightly more orthodox argument of the Syrian-Persian church father Aphrahat, *Demonstrations* 17, 2–8 (from 344 CE; SC 359).

regarded as a manifestation of the pre-existent prophet, but it is denied that he was God next to God the Father. His death and resurrection generally had no redemptive value for the Jewish Christian groups, although this did seem to apply for the Nazoreans. Generally speaking, these Christians were all about converting to the lifestyle which Jesus preached. They appealed to the synoptic gospels, of which the Gospel of Matthew especially had authority, and to other herewith related gospels. The letters of Paul and the Gospel of John had no authority for these groups.

As already mentioned, our main interest is not in the various Jewish Christian communities in and around Syria in the second to the fourth centuries, but in the question of whether the faith that was confessed and practised there goes back to the first century. That is after all the time in which the New Testament books were written. If this branch of Christianity goes back to the first century, then, from a historical perspective, it could lay just as valid a claim to ancient traditions as the type of Christianity that does appeal to Paul and John.

There are good reasons to assume that Jewish Christianity, with its own view on Jesus as a prophet, does indeed goes back to the beginning of Christianity. This can be concluded from the oldest sources – which are the New Testament writings. Furthermore, the Gospel of Thomas also includes sayings originating from the oldest Jewish Christianity.[34] From the synoptic gospels it is apparent that Jesus' contemporaries had no idea that in him the LORD himself had come. It is mentioned more than once that they regarded him as a prophet sent by God.[35] This is confirmed by the Gospel of John.[36] It is evident that Jesus' demeanour gave cause for this designation. Jesus said about himself that a prophet is not acknowledged in his home town.[37] According to Luke 13:33, he said about his approaching death that it is impossible for a prophet to be killed outside Jerusalem. From this, it is apparent that in any case Jesus resembled Israel's prophets, as did John the Baptist.[38]

Many of Jesus' contemporaries who initially regarded him as a prophet, later apparently came to see him as the Son of God and the Messiah, i.e. the Christ. The idea also arose that he, as an exceptional human being, was proclaimed the Son of God at his baptism in the river Jordan, when

---

34 See, e.g., the conclusion of section 1.3 about Gospel of Thomas 12, which deals with the position of James as the leader of the Jewish Christian community in Jerusalem.

35 Matthew 16:14; 21:11; 21:46; Mark 6:15; 8:28; Luke 7:16; 7:39; 9:8; 9:19; 24:19; cf. Acts 3:22–23.

36 John 4:19; 6:14; 7:40; 7:52; 9:17.

37 Mark 6:4; also Matthew 13:57; Luke 4:24; John 4:44; Gospel of Thomas 31.

38 For John the Baptist as a prophet, see Matthew 14:5; 21:26; Mark 11:32; Luke 1:76; 20:6.

the Spirit descended upon him. But it seems that not everyone shared the view that in him the LORD himself had appeared, or that Jesus was the Word through which God had created the world. Nor did everyone agree with the thought expressed by Paul in 1 Corinthians 10:4 that Christ, in his pre-existence, travelled with the Israelites through the wilderness.

In section 2.1 we saw that after Paul had founded a few churches in Galatia, preachers arrived there who proclaimed a Jewish form of Christianity. Contrary to Paul, they believed that whoever wanted to be a real Christian – although this does not mean that they used this term[39] – had to abide by the Mosaic law. In their view this implied that Jews and non-Jews could not share a meal, not even in the Christian church. Men who became Christians had to be not only baptized, but also circumcised.[40] In other letters, Paul aims against opponents who in their preaching about Jesus emphatically appealed to their Jewish (actually 'Hebrew' is the term used) identity. According to Paul, they preached 'another Jesus' and 'another gospel'.[41] The book of Acts confirms that there were Jewish Christians who abided by the Mosaic law.[42] With his polemic terms 'another Jesus' and 'another gospel', Paul probably refers to a Jewish type of Christianity which on the one hand regarded Jesus Christ as God's prophet who was also God's Son. On the other hand, his opponents preached that Jesus had held on to the observance of Mosaic law and that he had not relativized its importance as Paul later did.

Our knowledge about the exact beliefs of Paul's opponents about Jesus is limited because none of their writings from the first decades have been handed down.[43] Although the New Testament letter of James is sometimes regarded as a polemic against Paul, it is not in the least certain whether this is correct.[44] However, it is likely that this letter comes from Jewish Christianity which, according to Paul, held on too tightly to the

39 According to Acts 11:26 this name was used for the first time in Antioch (perhaps about the year 40 CE), but this does not mean that this name was widely accepted at once.
40 Galatians 1:6–9; 2:11–14; 5:1–12; 6:12–16.
41 2 Corinthians 11:4–5; 11:13–15; 11:22–23; 12:11–12; Pilippians 3:2–11; cf. Galatians 1:6–9.
42 Acts 15:1; 15:5; 21:20–26.
43 A creative effort to give voice to Paul's opponents was made by J. S. Vos (2000), '"The Letter of Simon to Amion": A Hotly Debated Antipauline Document', *Gereformeerd Theologisch Tijdschrift*, 100, 184–189.
44 See Franz Mussner (1987), *Der Jakobusbrief* (5th edn). Freiburg: Herder, pp. 12–23; Klaus Berger (1995), *Theologiegeschichte des Urchristentums: Theologie des Neuen Testaments* (2nd edn), Tübingen, Basel: Franke Verlag, pp. 186–195; René Krüger (2003), *Arm und reich im Jakobusbrief von Lateinamerika aus gelesen: Die Herausforderung eines profetischen Christentums*. PhD thesis Free University Amsterdam, pp. 31–46; 199–212.

observance of the Mosaic law. Jesus Christ is designated here as 'our glorious Lord' (2:1). The author does not elaborate upon Jesus' death, resurrection and exaltation and therefore neither upon his heavenly position next to God. He does mention, though, 'the coming of the Lord' (5:7–8), meaning his second coming from heaven. We can conclude that the letter of James does not contain a polemic towards other ideas about Jesus.

The Gospel of Matthew can also be named as a possible witness of Christians who did not agree with Paul. After all, this gospel includes sayings of Jesus about the precise observance of Mosaic law.[45] We saw in section 3.2 that this observance was also relativized in this gospel. Yet it evaluates the law in a quite different way than Paul did, and therefore it is understandable that this gospel was cherished among Jewish Christians. In sections 2.3 and 4.3 it was made apparent, however, that in the Gospel of Matthew, Jesus is described in his high position as Son of God who acts with divine authority as the LORD himself. Therefore this gospel does not testify to a simple Jewish Christian view of Jesus as an exceptional prophet.

Another document with a strong Jewish Christian flavour is the *Didache*, dating from about 100 CE.[46] Jesus is simply called 'God's servant' there, but he is also designated as 'the Lord' and as 'the Son'.[47] At the congregational supper, thanks are given to God for the life and the knowledge which he made known through Jesus, his servant (9:3). That his death led to the forgiveness of sins is not mentioned explicitly. However, thanks are given for eternal life, which God granted through Jesus (10:3). No more than the letter of James and the Gospel of Matthew does the *Didache* contain any polemic against certain beliefs about Jesus.

6.4 *Conclusion*

The New Testament writings clearly indicate that there were Jewish Christians who did not go along with Paul's ideas that the observance of the Mosaic law is unnecessary and undesirable for non-Jewish Christians. The debate, however, seems not to be about the person of Jesus, but about

---

45 Especially Matthew 5:17–20; 23:3.
46 Van de Sandt and Flusser, *The Didache*, pp. 48–52.
47 'Servant' (or 'child'), Didache 9:2–3; 10:2–3; 'the Lord' (also used for God), e.g., in the heading; 4:1; 6:2; 8:2; 9:5; 11:2; 11:8; 12:1; 14:1; 15:4; 'the Son' (in the baptismal formula 'in the name of the Father and of the Son and of the Holy Spirit'), 7:1–3 (LCL 24). Van de Sandt and Flusser, *The Didache*, pp. 286–291, argue for the originality of the baptismal formula in this text, but their argument that this baptismal formula was later added to Matthew 28:19 is not convincing (see also section 4.3, note 25).

his teachings. There were Jewish followers of Jesus who believed in him as God's prophet and Messiah, who had taught how to abide by the Mosaic law. They did see Jesus as God's beloved Son, but it is uncertain that they agreed with the conviction that Jesus, as God's Son, was the Logos and the LORD himself. We saw in the preceding chapters that this conviction took hold early on. In chapter 8 we will discuss its Jewish background. Probably the factions which held on to the observance of Mosaic law limited themselves, with respect to Jesus, to the 'simpler' belief that, in his capacity of prophet, Messiah, and Son of God, he had proclaimed the coming of God's kingdom and his will. They saw Jesus, however, not as God next to God the Father. During the second and third centuries, they existed next to mainline 'catholic' Christianity. In this way these Jewish Christians and their descendents went their own way and preserved an ancient form of Christianity. A part of these Jewish Christian groups only wanted to include non-Jews if they were prepared to observe the Mosaic law, which also included circumcision. Another part, which comes to light in the Pseudo-Clementine writings, however, did recruit among non-Jews and did not require that gentile men be circumcised. In those circles it was believed that Jesus, as the true prophet, had a pre-existent life behind him, but they denied that he was God alongside God the Father.

So far we gave a concise historical survey of a few variants of Jewish Christianity. It is too early for a theological evaluation of their convictions; for that purpose we first want to discuss the Jewish background of the other views on Jesus. In any case, it is clear that these Jewish Christian views have not permanently left their mark on mainline Christianity, although we will see that again and again there have been Christians who were inspired by it.

CHAPTER 7

Did Jesus Have a Secret Teaching?

As stated earlier, the question whether Jesus, in addition to his public teaching, had a secret instruction not recorded in the New Testament gospels deserves separate discussion. We have seen that the Gospel of Thomas pretends to include, according to its heading, 'the secret words' of Jesus. In Gospel of Thomas 13 we read (in section 1.3) of the three words which Thomas heard and which Jesus' other disciples would not be able to comprehend. In saying 62 of this gospel Jesus says, 'I tell my mysteries to [those people who are worthy of my] mysteries'. The heading of the Gospel of Judas announces 'the secret doctrine' of Jesus, to which only Judas was initiated. In the Gospel of Mary (10, 8), Mary Magdalene tells Jesus' other disciples what was hidden from them; the Coptic word for 'hidden' is the same as that translated as 'secret' in the headings of the Gospels of Thomas and Judas. The *Secret Book of John* and the *Book of Thomas the Contender* lay claim to representing the secret teaching of the Saviour, namely the risen Christ, with the same term.[1] The church father Irenaeus regularly confirms that 'heretical' factions appealed to secret oral traditions and to books which were not included in the Scriptures.[2] It is apparent from these testimonies that the groups who handed down these traditions and books assumed that the included teachings of Jesus were unknown to the believers of 'catholic' Christianity. On the one hand, these traditions and books were therefore meant as supplements to the gospels that were read in the Christian communities. As is known, in the course of the second century, the gospels of Mark, Matthew, Luke and John

---

1   The *Secret Book of John*, Nag Hammadi Codex II, 1, 1, 1–4; Berlin Codex 75, 15–20; the *Book of Thomas the Contender*, Nag Hammadi Codex II, 7, 138, 1–2.
2   Irenaeus, *Against Heresies* I, 3, 1; 8, 1; 8, 5; 24, 6; 25, 5; 30, 14; III, 2, 1 (SC 264; 211).

were acknowledged as the most authoritative in 'catholic' Christianity.[3] On the other hand, the 'secret' books could also be intended to compete with these gospels and to correct the views on Jesus described in them.

7.1 *Jesus' unwritten teachings in the 'catholic' church*

It has always been acknowledged in early catholic Christianity that, in addition to the teachings of Jesus that were written down in the acknowledged gospels there were also oral traditions believed to date back to Jesus. Bishop Papias of Hierapolis (in the western part of modern Turkey) testified at the beginning of the second century that he preferred the oral traditions of Jesus' teachings, which dated back to eyewitnesses, over the written testimonies.[4] Irenaeus of Lyons approvingly cites a conversation between Jesus and Judas Iscariot about the fertility of the earth during the future millennium from Papias' written collection of words of Jesus.[5] Apart from the traditions collected by Papias, other sayings of Jesus which were not included in the four authoritative gospels, were also quoted in the early church. These sayings are called *agrapha*, which means 'unwritten'. With respect to their content, however, these words accredited to Jesus add hardly anything to that which is known from the New Testament gospels.[6]

At the end of the second century, Clement of Alexandria, who explicitly considered himself as belonging to the 'catholic church', testified that the teachings of and about Jesus exist in both unwritten and written form.[7] He writes that Christ left behind a 'gnostic tradition' to the apostles and that they passed on this gnosis in unwritten form to a small number of people.[8] Clement declares elsewhere that the Lord transmitted the gnosis after his resurrection to James the Righteous One, John and Peter, and that

---

3   As an authoritative collection they first appear about the year 180 CE in Irenaeus, *Against Heresies* III, 11, 7–8 (SC 211). Initially the churches did not read this collection of four, but merely one or a few of these gospels and sometimes other gospels also, e.g. the gospel attributed to Peter (see Eusebius, *Church History* VI, 12, 2–6; LCL 265). See also Roukema, 'La tradition apostolique et le canon du Nouveau Testament'.

4   See Eusebius, *Church History* III, 39, 1–17 (LCL 153); Bauckham, *Jesus and the Eyewitnesses*, pp. 12–38.

5   Irenaeus, *Against Heresies* V, 33, 3–4 (SC 153).

6   See Tom Riemer Roukema (forthcoming), 'Jesus Tradition in Early Patristic Writings', in Tom Holmén and Stanley E. Porter, eds, *Handbook for the Study of the Historical Jesus* 3. Leiden: Brill.

7   Clement of Alexandria, *Stromateis* I, 7, 1 (SC 30); for his references to the 'catholic church', see *Stromateis* VII, 106, 3 and 107, 5 (SC 428).

8   Clement of Alexandria, *Stromateis* VI, 61, 1–3 (SC 446).

they in turn passed it on to other apostles who subsequently passed it down to the seventy, to whom Barnabas belonged.[9] Clement is convinced that he himself also stands in this tradition. He states that what he has written in his books is derived from the trustworthy tradition which, through his own teachers, originates from the apostles Peter, James and John.[10] It follows that, according to Clement, the contents of this gnosis are to be found in his own books. It must be noted, however, that he uses the terms 'gnosis' and 'gnostic' to characterize the knowledge of advanced Christians of the 'catholic church', and that he repudiates the 'heretic'-gnostic factions.[11] These testimonies of Clement show that in catholic Christianity of the second century, one could also appeal to a secret oral tradition of Jesus' teachings that were intended for a limited group. On the grounds of various passages in Clement's works, Jean Daniélou demonstrated that he refers to traditions about the hierarchy of the angels, the heavenly dwelling places and the ascension of the souls to heaven, where they can behold God with the angels. Daniélou shows that Clement has for the greater part derived these traditions from Jewish and Christian apocryphal writings.[12] It is indeed plausible that Jesus also knew of such traditions. Therefore, it is also possible that he spoke about them in a small circle. In the synoptic gospels, after all, he is regularly related to heaven, angels and demons, and he speaks about these.[13] The Gospel of John confirms the image of Jesus as a visionary apocalyptic who speaks about heavenly matters.[14] However, this does not prove that everything which Clement writes about the angels and heaven in this form originates from Jesus' oral teachings.

The fact that catholic Christianity acknowledged not only written, but also unwritten traditions, is confirmed at the beginning of the third century by Tertullian of Carthage. He points to customs which are not written anywhere in Scripture, but have been passed on orally. Thus people who are to be baptized first renounce the devil and his angels, are then

---

9   Clement of Alexandria, *Hypotyposeis* VII, in Eusebius, *Church History* II, 1, 4 (LCL 153); Eusebius explains that James the Righteous One is Jesus' brother (cf. Mark 1:19; 3:17; 6:3; Galatians 1:19). For the seventy, see Luke 10:1.

10 Clement of Alexandria, *Stromateis* I, 11, 1–3 (SC 30). Given the previously mentioned text, Clement means James to be Jesus' brother and he considers him an 'apostle'; this corresponds to 1 Corinthians 15:7.

11 Clement of Alexandria, *Stromateis* VII, 106–110 (SC 428); cf. Riemer Roukema, *Gnosis and Faith in Early Christianity*, pp. 151–153.

12 Daniélou, *Théologie du judéo-christianisme*, pp. 59–64; Daniélou (1961), *Message évangélique et culture hellénistique aux IIᵉ et IIIᵉ siècles*. Paris: Desclée, pp. 409–425; see also Guy G. Stroumsa (1996), *Hidden Wisdom: Esoteric Traditions and the Roots of Christian Mysticism*. Leiden: Brill, pp. 27–45; 109–131.

13 E.g., Mark 1:10, 13, 24; 3:11, 23–27; 5:7; 8:38; 9:2–8; 12:25; 13:27, 32; Matthew 19:28; 26:53; Luke 10:18; 12:8–9.

14 E.g., John 1:5; 3:12–13, 31; 6:38, 51; 8:23. See also sections 7.3–4.

submerged three times, consume a mixture of milk and honey and do not bathe for an entire week. Furthermore, Tertullian mentions traditions about fasting, kneeling and making the sign of the cross. For the origin of these, he mentions the Holy Spirit, who guides into all the truth (John 16:13).[15] Because Jesus says in the Gospel of John that he would send this Spirit to his disciples (John 15:26; 16:7), Tertullian traces the unwritten traditions along this path indirectly to Jesus himself. At the end of the fourth century, the church father Basil of Caesarea explicitly appeals to Jesus' unwritten teachings which have been transmitted by the apostles. He then mentions, for example, the making of the sign of the cross, the direction of prayer facing east, the prayer said during the consecration of bread and wine, and the blessing of baptismal water, the chrism and the person to be baptized.[16] For the existence of the oral tradition, Basil appeals to texts of Paul that refer to his oral teachings.[17] Yet this does not in the least prove that the practices which Tertullian and Basil mention do indeed go back to Paul and other apostles, let alone to Jesus himself. Anyway, the traditions which Tertullian and Basil mention concern entirely different matters than are to be found in Clement or in the extracanonical gospels.

7.2 *Private teachings in the synoptic gospels*

We will now examine whether there are clues to be found in the New Testament gospels of teachings of Jesus for a secret, limited group, not put on paper, but passed down orally.

The synoptic gospels mention that Jesus, in his teachings, made a distinction between what he told the multitudes and what he passed on to a smaller circle of his disciples. Mark 4:10-11 reads,

> When he was alone, those who were around him along with the twelve asked him about the parables. And he said to them, 'To you

---

15 Tertullian, *The Chaplet* 3–4 (CCSL 2). When Tertullian wrote this book (*De Corona*), he had already been introduced to Montanism (*The Chaplet* 1, 4), where it was common to appeal to the inspiration of the Spirit. Still, he can be considered a representative of catholic Christianity with regard to these unwritten traditions; the aforenamed traditions originate from it and, furthermore, Tertullian never left the catholic church. See David I. Rankin (1995), *Tertullian and the Church*. Cambridge: Cambridge University Press; Eric Osborn (1997), *Tertullian: First Theologian of the West*. Cambridge: Cambridge University Press, pp. 176–177.

16 Basil of Caesarea, *The Holy Spirit* 27, 66 (SC 17bis).

17 Basil of Caesarea, *The Holy Spirit* 29, 71; he quotes 1 Corinthians 11:2 ('I commend you because you remember me in everything and maintain the traditions just as I handed them on to you') and 2 Thessalonians 2:15 ('Stand firm and hold fast to the traditions that you were taught by us, either by word of mouth or by our letter').

has been given the secret (*musterion*) of the kingdom of God, but for those outside, everything comes in parables.'

This means that Jesus' parables, for example the one of the sower (Mark 4:1–9), were not clear to all of his listeners. In the Gospel of Mark, we see that the group of Jesus' closest disciples, which asks about the reason for this, not only consists of the twelve men which he had especially chosen (Mark 3:13–19), but is wider. It is explicitly written, after all, 'Those who were around him along with the twelve'. Esther de Boer has pointed out that this distinction between the twelve and a larger group of disciples of Jesus, men and women, appears in more places in the Gospel of Mark.[18] From Mark 4:10–11 therefore can be deduced that in the description of this gospel, it made a difference to Jesus whether he addressed the circle of his disciples, which consisted of the twelve and a group around them, or others interested, who were designated as outsiders. As far as we can deduce from the Gospel of Mark that Jesus passed on a secret teaching, this was not intended for merely one of his disciples, neither only for the twelve, but for a larger group. In accordance with this, it is also stated in Mark 4:33–34 that Jesus spoke in parables as the people who listened to him were able to hear it, and that he explained everything in private to his own disciples.[19]

According to Mark it does happen, however, that on several occasions Jesus only takes three of the twelve male disciples with him. Only Simon Peter and the brothers James and John are mentioned in Mark's account of Jesus raising the daughter of Jairus from the dead (5:37–43), when he is transfigured on a mountain and meets Moses en Elijah (9:2–10) and when he goes to pray just before his arrest in Gethsemane (14:32–33). This threesome and Andrew, the brother of Simon Peter, were the first four disciples whom Jesus had called, according to Mark (1:16–20, cf. 1:29). Jesus addressed his sermon about the future of Jerusalem and the world to these four (13:3–37). The Gospel of Mark indicates therefore that Jesus gave teachings on various levels, for larger and smaller groups of his closest followers and for outsiders, and this perhaps gives the impression that he also had secret teachings in addition to what he said in public. Yet this does not in the least mean that the Gospel of Mark is

---

18 De Boer, *The Gospel of Mary*, pp. 103–109; see Mark 10:32 (those who followed Jesus and the twelve), 14:13 (two of his disciples) and 14:17 (the twelve); 15:40–41 (also women had come up with Jesus from Galilee to Jerusalem).

19 For Mark 4:33–34, see Gnilka, *Das Evangelium nach Markus (Mk 1–8,26)*, pp. 190–191.

therefore an esoteric document. The essence of Jesus' teachings to his closest disciples is after all included in this gospel.[20] These teachings, which Jesus stated in parables for the outsiders, concerned the coming of God's kingdom. His sermon, pronounced to four disciples, about the things that will precede the coming of that kingdom (13:3–37), is not kept secret, but is included in this gospel. That Jesus first had to suffer and die, and was to be lifted up as the Son of Man in the heavenly glory of his Father, he did not tell the outsiders, but only his disciples. As it is, this part of his teaching, however, can be read by everyone.[21] Characteristic for the Gospel of Mark is that it repeatedly mentions that Jesus did not want the demons he had exorcized, the people he had helped and his own disciples to make known who he really was.[22] Afterwards, however, this initial secret of Jesus' true identity is mentioned in this gospel without secrecy; he is then called 'the Holy One of God' (1:24–25), 'the Son of God' (3:11–12) and 'the Christ' (8:29–30). The Gospel of Mark therefore possibly gives the impression that it refers to a separate esoteric teaching of Jesus which is not included in this gospel, but these appearances are deceiving. It is not stated anywhere in this gospel that certain elements of Jesus' teachings to his closest followers had to be kept secret.[23]

The American scholar Morton Smith, who died in 1991, has given nurture to the supposition that alongside the Gospel of Mark which has been included in the New Testament there was also a 'Secret Gospel of Mark'. In 1973 he published a book in which he explained that in 1958 he had discovered two fragments of this secret Gospel of Mark in a monastery near Jerusalem. Smith declared that he came across these fragments in an unknown letter of Clement of Alexandria, which he had found in the library of the monastery.[24] He concluded that there had been a text of the Gospel of Mark which included a few secret passages intended for insiders only. Because no one besides Smith himself had seen the manuscript of the letter including these fragments, his discovery evoked scepticism from the beginning. In spite of this, various scholars gave credence to Smith's discovery and accepted the alleged fragments of this secret gospel as a serious or at least a possibly serious source

---

20 Cf. Hurtado, *Lord Jesus Christ*, p. 458.
21 Mark 8:31–38; 9:31; 10:33–34.
22 Mark 1:34; 3:12; 5:43; 7:36; 8:30.
23 It may seem obvious to point to Jesus' private explanation of the parable of the sower according to Mark 4:13–20. In any case this demonstrates that it was not Mark's intention to keep the explanation of this parable a secret. We cannot be sure, however, whether this explanation comes from Jesus himself or originates from the early church. See, e.g., Gnilka, *Das Evangelium nach Markus (Mk 1–8,26)*, pp. 173–174.
24 Morton Smith (1973), *Clement of Alexandria and a Secret Gospel of Mark*. Cambridge MA: Harvard University Press.

from early Christianity. Thus, they were included in several collections of early Christian apocryphal writings.[25] In 2005 the lawyer Stephen Carlson, however, irrefutably demonstrated that this letter of Clement of Alexandria and the fragments of the secret Gospel of Mark included in it are a falsification fabricated by Morton Smith himself.[26] One can therefore no longer point to these fragments as testimonies to secret teachings of Jesus.

We return to the references to Jesus' teachings to a limited group of his followers in the synoptic gospels. In the Gospel of Matthew, the relationship between the small circle of insiders and the others is presented differently than in Mark, but with regard to the secret teachings there is no essential difference between these two gospels. In Matthew 13:10 'the disciples' are the ones asking Jesus the question of why he speaks in parables, and Mark's distinction between the twelve and the other group around Jesus is lost. As opposed to the Gospel of Mark, the term 'the disciples' in the Gospel of Matthew often, although not always, means the twelve. Just before the passage about the parables, in Matthew 12:49–50, Jesus points to his disciples and says of them, 'Here are my mother and my brothers. For whoever does the will of my Father in heaven is my brother and sister and mother.' This saying proves that in the Gospel of Matthew too the circle of Jesus' disciples was larger than the twelve and included women as well.[27] According to Matthew, as far as Jesus had separate teachings about the mysteries of the kingdom of heaven for a smaller circle (Matthew 13:11), this was meant for these disciples; but it is true of this gospel too that the teachings for this group are included in the gospel itself. They can be found, for example, in Matthew 10:5–42, where Jesus instructs his twelve disciples before sending them out to proclaim the coming of God's kingdom. Jesus' sermons in Matthew 18 and 24–25 are, according to the evangelist, only directed toward his disciples and therefore not to a larger multitude. Yet these sermons of Jesus were not kept secret, but written down.[28]

25 Elliott, *The Apocryphal New Testament*, pp. 148–149, included the fragments, but he admitted that the antiquity and genuineness of this text are questioned by many scholars.

26 Stephen Carlson (2005), *The Gospel Hoax: Morton Smith's Invention of Secret Mark*. Waco TX: Baylor University Press. See also Peter Jeffery (2007), *The Secret Gospel of Mark Unveiled: Imagined Rituals of Sex, Death, and Madness in a Biblical Forgery*. New Haven CT: Yale University Press.

27 De Boer, *The Gospel of Mary*, p. 129.

28 Matthew 13:36–43 has an explanation of the parable of the tares (Matthew 13:24–30), which alludes to the fact that this explanation did not have to be kept a secret. We cannot be sure, however, whether this explanation comes from Jesus himself or goes back to a later tradition, as may also have been the case in the explanation of the parable of the sower (note 23). See, e.g., Joachim Gnilka (1986), *Das Matthäusevangelium* 1, Freiburg: Herder, pp. 499–500.

In the Gospel of Luke (8:9) 'his disciples' ask Jesus, in slightly different terms than in the Gospels of Mark and Matthew, about the meaning of the parable of the sower. In this gospel the term 'disciples' also refers to a larger group than the twelve.[29] For example, Luke 8:1–3 explicitly mentions that women travelled along with Jesus.[30] Jesus' answer to the question of his disciples in Luke 8:9 is that to them has been given to know the secrets of the kingdom and that these come to the others in parables (8:10). In other passages in this gospel, Jesus sometimes directs his teachings especially to these disciples, but in the text as we have it there is no allusion to any secrecy.[31] When in Luke 10:38–42 Mary, Martha's sister, listens to his words at Jesus' feet, the content of these words is indeed not mentioned, but this is not to keep these words secret – the reason being that Jesus' words to Martha that are included (Luke 10:41–42) form the essence of this story. These words are, 'Martha, Martha, you are worried and distracted by many things; there is need of only one thing. Mary has chosen the better part which will not be taken away from her.'

7.3 *Private teachings in the Gospel of John*

The Gospel of John refers in a different way than the synoptic gospels to Jesus' teachings to a restricted group. Initially, more than in the synoptic gospels, in the Gospel of John it is openly declared who Jesus is: the Lamb of God, the Son of God, the Saviour of the world, the light of the world, etc.[32] When bystanders do not understand Jesus' metaphors of the sheep and the sheepfold, he explains that he himself is the door for the sheep and the good shepherd (10:1–16). After his public appearance, however, in this gospel Jesus also gives instruction to a smaller circle of his disciples, during and after a meal (John 13–16).[33] Initially Judas Iscariot is present, but he soon leaves (13:26–30). In John 17, Jesus concludes these conversations with a meaningful prayer. Although the group of disciples present at these conversations and this prayer according to the

---

29 As appears from Luke 6:13; 6:17; 14:26–27.

30 See de Boer, *The Gospel of Mary*, pp. 139–149.

31 E.g., Luke 10:23–24; 11:1–13; 12:22–53; 16:1–13 (also heard by the Pharisees, 16:14); 17:1–10; 17:22–37; 22:14–38.

32 See, e.g., John 1:29; 1:34 (an important variant of 'the Son of God' that may be original, however, reads 'the Elect of God'); 4:42; 6:35; 8:12; 10:25–38; 12:44–50. Apart from these public characterizations of Jesus, he is called 'the Messiah' in a smaller circle from the beginning (John 1:41; also 4:25–26).

33 They are called 'disciples' in John 13:5; 13:22–23; 13:35; 15:8; 16:17; 16:29; 'his own' in 13:1.

traditional image consisted of the eleven – the twelve without Judas –
this is not explicitly mentioned. The expression 'the twelve' occurs only
a few times in this gospel, while the term 'disciple' also can be applied
to others than the twelve.[34] However this may be and whoever may have
been present at this last gathering, it is obvious that Jesus' last teachings
were intended for a restricted circle. To be sure, we can ask ourselves if
these conversations literally took place in this way, but what is important
here, is that they have been included in the gospel in this form and the
evangelist therefore had no reason to keep their contents a secret. That
the evangelist believed that in these teachings Jesus had not withheld
anything essential is evident from the saying of Jesus to his disciples thus
reported by him, 'I have called you friends, because I have made known
to you everything that I have heard from my Father' (15:15).

In spite of this, there is an indication that Jesus' teachings to his disciples
were not entirely clear and had to be explained later. It so happens, that
at the end of the conversations he says, 'I have said these things to you
in figures of speech. The hour is coming when I will no longer speak to
you in figures, but will tell you plainly (*parrhêsiai*) of the Father' (16:25).
When the disciples thereupon say (in 16:29), 'Yes, now you are speaking
plainly (*en parrhêsiai*), not in any figure of speech,' they seem to have
understood everything at that moment, but according to commentators
such as Barrett and Schnackenburg, this is an example of the irony of
this gospel; the disciples indeed thought at that moment that they had
understood everything, but they were mistaken.[35] This means that Jesus'
teachings in the Gospel of John were not completely comprehensible even
to his closest disciples. Exegetes correctly point out that Jesus' words
in John 16:25 must be understood in relationship to the period after
his resurrection, when he will again speak to them through the Spirit,
as he had announced according to this gospel. The Spirit, who is also
called 'the Advocate' (*paraklêtos*) will then speak on behalf of Jesus, will
remind his disciples of all that he had said to them and will guide them
into all the truth.[36] According to Schnackenburg this means that the Spirit

34 'The twelve' in John 6:67; 6:70; 20:24; other disciples in John 4:1; 6:60–61; 6:66; 8:31;
    19:38 (Joseph of Arimatea); 21:2 (Nathanael, cf. 1:45–49). Raymond Brown, *The
    Community of the Beloved Disciple*, pp. 31–34, supposes that the 'beloved disciple'
    who is thus called in this gospel (13:23; 19:26; 20:2 [?]; 21:7; 21:20) did not belong
    to 'the twelve'. Esther de Boer, *The Gospel of Mary*, pp. 157–163, argues that in this
    gospel Mary Magdalene belonged to Jesus' disciples.
35 Rudolf Schnackenburg (1975), *Das Johannesevangelium* 3. Freiburg etc.: Herder, p.
    185; C. K. Barrett (1978), *The Gospel According to St John: An Introduction with
    Commentary and Notes on the Greek Text* (2nd edn). London: SPCK, pp. 496–497.
36 John 14:16–17; 14:26; 15:26; 16:7–15; 20:22; see Schnackenburg, *Johannesevangelium*
    3, 182; Barrett, *St John*, p. 495; Herman Ridderbos (1992), *The Gospel According to
    John: A Theological Commentary*. Grand Rapids MI: Eerdmans, pp. 540–541.

will continue Jesus' revelation and will give a deeper insight into this, but with respect to content will not proclaim anything new compared to that which Jesus has already revealed in this gospel.[37] That the Gospel of John does not suggest that, besides what is written in it, there is also a secret, esoteric doctrine of Jesus, is finally confirmed by what he says when he is interrogated by the high priest Annas. Jesus then states,

> I have spoken openly (*parrhêsiai*) to the world; I have always taught in the synagogues and in the temple, where all the Jews come together. I have said nothing in secret. (18:20)

This seems to be contrary to the fact that, according to this gospel, Jesus engaged in lengthy, separate discussions with his closest disciples just prior to this. From this ambivalence, we can establish that it was not the intention of the evangelist that these concluding discussions would be regarded as an essentially different or deeper doctrine than that which Jesus had stated previously in public.[38] The dual conclusion of this gospel also contradicts that alongside this gospel there would be secret teachings of Jesus. Reference is indeed made to 'yet much more' that Jesus had done, but this has not been written down for the simple reason that the book would then become too voluminous (21:25). The writer states straight out what the purpose of that which has been included is: namely that the reader on its basis believes that Jesus is the Christ, the Son of God, and through believing may have life in his name (20:31).

7.4 *A secret teaching after all? Conclusion*

From the New Testament gospels it can therefore not be concluded that an essential part of Jesus' teachings, which was intended for a small group of insiders only, has deliberately been left out. Yet, we concluded with reference to Clement of Alexandria that by oral tradition some elements of Jesus' teachings could have been preserved that were later integrated in early Christian beliefs. It is not impossible that the New Testament gospels may unintentionally have preserved some of these elements. We can think of Jesus' experiences with angels, demons and visions, to which we have previously referred. Jesus says in Luke 10:18 that he has seen Satan fall from heaven like a flash of lightning. It is

---

37 Schnackenburg, *Johannesevangelium* 3, pp. 151–181.
38 Schnackenburg, *Johannesevangelium* 3, pp. 268–270.

conceivable that a vision underlies this statement about which he has
said more to his disciples than in this extremely short description.[39] That
Jesus had visionary experiences can be deduced from the descriptions
of his baptism, in which the heavens were opened to him, and of his
transfiguration on the mountain, when Moses and Elijah appeared to
him.[40] In the Gospel of John the following sayings of Jesus are recorded,
which we have linked up here as follows,

> Very truly, I tell you, you will see heaven opened and the angels of
> God ascending and descending upon the Son of Man (1:51). We speak
> of what we know and testify to what we have seen; yet you do not
> receive our testimony. If I have told you about earthly things and
> you do not believe, how can you believe if I tell you about heavenly
> things? (3:11–12). I have come down from heaven, not to do my own
> will, but the will of him who sent me (6:38). Then what if you were to
> see the Son of Man ascending to where he was before? (6:62). No one
> has ascended into heaven except the one who descended from heaven,
> the Son of Man (3:13).

That Jesus had descended from heaven is certainly the view of the
evangelist, who saw in him the divine and therefore heavenly Logos.
Yet these sayings can likewise go back to visions of Jesus in which he
experienced that he himself had been taken up into heaven. From this he
may have deduced that he had descended from heaven. Such visionary
experiences were after all known in those days. They are, for example,
elaborately described in the books attributed to Enoch. Paul also briefly
tells that he was taken up into the third heaven, and that there, in paradise,
he heard inexpressible words that he was not permitted to repeat (2
Corinthians 12:2–4). Applying the latter to Jesus, this may explain the
reticence of the gospel writers in reporting more fully on this. Remarkably
enough, Paul refers to traditions about the end of the world, which he
once calls a 'mystery' (*mustêrion*) and another time a 'word of the Lord'
(i.e. Jesus). He then speaks of an archangel who will raise his voice and
of God's trumpet which will sound.[41] Certainly, a similar announcement

39 Heinz Schürmann (1994), *Das Lukasevangelium* 2. Freiburg: Herder, p. 89; Bovon,
    Das Evangelium nach Lukas (9,51–14,35), p. 57; Ulrich B. Müller (1974), 'Vision und
    Botschaft: Erwägungen zur prophetischen Struktur der Verkündigung Jesu', *Zeitschrift
    für Theologie und Kirche*, 74, 416–448. The imperfect tense 'I watched' (*etheôroun*)
    points to the lengthy and impressive character of this vision.
40 Matthew 3:16; 17:1–5; Mark 1:10; 9:2–8; Luke 9:28–32.
41 1 Corinthians 15:51–57; 1 Thessalonians 4:13–17. Cf. *mustêrion* in Romans 11:25; 1
    Corinthians 2:7; 4:1; 13:2.

is to be found in the synoptic gospels.[42] Still, it is possible that in Paul we find a fragment of traditions going back to Jesus' teachings which in these terms are not included in the New Testament gospels.

Of a totally different order are the sayings of Jesus in the Gospel of Thomas that are not included in the New Testament gospels but could still go back to Jesus himself. As examples of these Gerard Luttikhuizen mentions the following two parables:[43]

Jesus said,
The Kingdom of the Father is like a woman carrying a [jar] filled with meal.
While she was walking [on the] road still a long way out,
the handle of the jar broke.
Behind her, the meal leaked out onto the road.
She did not realize it. She had not noticed a problem.
When she arrived at her house,
she put the jar down and found it empty. (97)

Jesus said,
The Kingdom of the Father is like someone who wished to kill a prominent man.
While at home, he drew out his knife.
'He stabbed it into the wall to test whether his hand would be strong (enough).
Then he murdered the prominent man. (98)

It is, however, clear that these parables, just as well as the previously mentioned *agrapha*, do not add anything essentially new to the teachings of Jesus that we know from the New Testament gospels. Their contents are totally different from the three secret words which, according to Gospel of Thomas 13, Jesus had intended for Thomas only and which would be unacceptable to his other disciples.[44]

We can therefore conclude that besides the teachings of Jesus that have been recorded in the New Testament gospels, more traditions circulated which could in part originate from him. It is plausible that in the intimate circle of his disciples Jesus has spoken about his mystical and visionary experiences. It is, however, completely unproved and, in

---

42 Mark 13:24–27; Matthew 24:29–31; cf. Luke 21:25–27.
43 G. P. Luttikhuizen (2002), *De veelvormigheid van het vroegste christendom*. Delft: Eburon, p. 56.
44 See sections 1.3 and 2.7.

fact, out of the question that Jesus, in addition to his public teachings, had a secret, esoteric doctrine that has now resurfaced in the gospels in the name of Thomas and Judas, for example. The popular belief that the church suppressed the true teachings of Jesus and that these were preserved by the 'heretics'[45] is fiction and has no historical foundation.

---

45 As propagated by, e.g., Dan Brown, *The Da Vinci Code*, pp. 312–317.

CHAPTER 8

Does Jesus as LORD *and Son of God Fit into Early Judaism?*

In early Christianity Jesus is regarded as the Son of God and as the LORD, and therefore as divine. It is often thought that this elevated idea cannot go back to Jesus himself, nor that it fits into the Judaism of his time. The Dutch systematic theologian H. M. Kuitert, for example, admits that we must not conceive of the Judaism of Jesus' time as being very uniform, but emphasizes that the diverse factions still had the monotheistic belief in one God in common.[1] Consequently, in his view Jesus could not have regarded himself as God, and the early Christian view about Jesus as God is too far removed from the historical Jesus and contemporaneous Judaism to be acceptable.

To be sure, we can no longer find out, strictly historically speaking, how Jesus thought about himself, because all the testimonies about him were written by his followers after his life on earth. From these testimonies we can establish that soon after Jesus' death at least an important part of his followers believed that he had occupied a high position alongside God and that in him God's Son, or God the LORD himself, had appeared on earth. Although we cannot establish with absolute certainty how Jesus viewed and presented himself to his followers, we can, however, examine if the Judaism of the time offered clues for the elevated conceptions associated with him.

---

1   H. M. Kuitert (1998), *Jezus, nalatenschap van het christendom: Schets voor een christologie.* Baarn: Ten Have, pp. 155–156.

8.1 *The Old Testament*

The Old Testament includes clear declarations of Israel's faith that its God is the only true God. Thus in Deuteronomy 4:35 is said to Israel 'that the Lord is God; there is no other besides him'. Shortly thereafter we read, 'Hear, O Israel: the Lord is our God, the Lord alone,'[2] and later, 'See now that I, even I, am he; there is no God besides me' (32:39). In the book of Isaiah, the prophet says in name of the Lord, 'I am the Lord, and there is no other, besides me there is no god' (45:5).[3] These sayings are directed against the worship of other gods, as practised by the gentiles.

These verses indeed give the impression of a monotheistic view of God, although it must be added that in other texts the existence of the gods of gentile peoples is not denied; they are, however, regarded as idols.[4] Concerning the worship of the Lord as Israel's God, however, it is apparent that, according to the Old Testament, he was surrounded by other heavenly figures. The book of Job tells that besides the Lord, there were also the 'sons of God', of whom Satan was one. From Job 1:6 and 2:1, it appears that these sons of God belong to the household of the Lord. In Job 38:7 is written that all the sons of God sang together when the Lord laid the foundation of the earth. In the Septuagint, 'sons of God' in these verses is translated as 'the angels of God' and 'my angels'.[5] In Genesis 6:2 and 4 it is told that the sons of God took wives for themselves on earth and that from these relationships heroes were born.[6] In 1 Enoch 6–10, this episode is told more elaborately as a story about the descent of angels to the earth. In Psalm 29:1 the 'sons of gods' are called upon to praise the Lord; Psalm 89:6 asks, 'who among the sons of gods is like the Lord?'[7] In both verses the Septuagint reads 'sons of God'. According to Psalm 82, God stands in the council of the gods,

---

2   Deuteronomy 6:4. Literally it reads, 'YHWH our God YHWH one'.

3   See also Isaiah 44:6–8.

4   See, e.g., Judges 2:13; 3:7; 8:33; 10:6; 11:24. In any case, ancient Israel did not know philosophical monotheism. See, e.g., K. van der Toorn (1999), 'God (I)', in Karel van der Toorn, Bob Becking and Pieter W. van der Horst, eds, *Dictionary of Deities and Demons in the Bible* (2nd edn). Leiden: Brill, pp. 352–365 (363).

5   Job 16:19–21 testifies to a completely different contrast in heaven; there the tormented Job appeals to God as his witness and advocate in heaven, in order that he – paradoxically – will do him justice against God. Thus one aspect of God is placed opposite another.

6   In Genesis 6:2, 4; Job 1:6; 2:1, the Hebrew expression is *bᵉnē haᵉlōhīm*. Job 38:7 reads *bᵉnē ᵉlōhīm*.

7   In Hebrew both texts read: *bᵉnē ēlīm*. (In the Hebrew Bible, the second text is numbered Psalm 89:7.)

who are called sons of the Most High, and who are nevertheless told that they will die as mortals.[8]

A very interesting text occurs in the book of Deuteronomy, from which we just quoted a few very monotheistic sounding statements. In the 'Song of Moses' is written, according to the common Hebrew Masoretic text:

> When the Most High divided to the nations their inheritance,
> when he separated the sons of Adam,
> he set the bounds of the people
> according to the number of the sons of Israel.
> For the LORD's portion *is* his people,
> Jacob *is* the lot of his inheritance. (Deuteronomy 32:8–9)[9]

The older Hebrew text of the Dead Sea scrolls, however, does not read, 'according to the number of the sons of Israel', but 'according to the number of God's sons'. In the Greek manuscripts of the Septuagint is written either 'according to the number of God's angels' or 'according to the number of God's sons'. Generally the conclusion is drawn that Deuteronomy 32:8 originally read that the Most High fixed the boundaries of the peoples according to the number of God's sons, i.e. his angels.[10] This means that to each nation an angel was assigned. This idea is confirmed by the book of Daniel, which mentions 'princes', i.e. angels, who are in charge of Persia and Greece, and Michael, the 'prince' of Israel.[11] Related to this is Joshua 5:13–15, which tells that near Jericho, Joshua met the commander of the army of the LORD and bowed down before him.[12]

---

8   The older explanation that the gods refer to judges or princes is outdated; see Hans-Joachim Kraus (1978), *Psalmen* 2 (5th edn). Neukirchen-Vluyn: Neukirchener Verlag, p. 736.
9   According to the King James Version, except for the phrase 'according to the number of the sons of Israel', where the KJV reads 'according to the number of the children of Israel'.
10 E.g., S. B. Parker (1999), 'Sons of (the) Gods', in Karel van der Toorn, Bob Becking and Pieter W. van der Horst, *Dictionary of Deities and Demons in the Bible* (2nd edn). Leiden: Brill, pp. 794–800 (796–797).
11 Daniel 10:13; 10:20–21; 12:1; also 8:11. In numerous other Jewish texts Michael appears as Israel's guardian angel and as the ruler of the angels; see M. Mach (1999), 'Michael', in Karel van der Toorn, Bob Becking, Pieter W. van der Horst, *Dictionary of Deities and Demons in the Bible* (2nd edn). Leiden: Brill, pp. 569–572.
12 J. H. Kroeze (1968), *Het boek Jozua verklaard*. Kampen, pp. 73–74, explains that the commander in Joshua 5:14 belongs to the company of princes, of whom Michael was also one and that he is a divine being. Kroeze therefore speaks of a theophany, which term is also used by John Gray (1967), *Joshua, Judges and Ruth*. London: Nelson, pp. 71–72. A later Jewish tradition (*Aggadat Bereshit* 32) reads that the prince

Subsequently, Deuteronomy 32:9 says that in this division Jacob – i.e., Israel – became the lot of the LORD's inheritance, or, according to the New Revised Standard Version, the allotted share of the LORD. It is obvious that, according to the author of the book of Deuteronomy as we now know it, the Most High and the LORD are the same God; this is apparent from the many 'monotheistic' verses elsewhere in the book.[13] In other Old Testament verses also, the LORD is considered the Most High.[14] In this case, according to Deuteronomy 32:8–9, the LORD as the Most High God has himself taken the people of Israel under his protection. But often this passage, with the reading 'according to the number of God's sons', is interpreted as a fragment of an older text. Then it is most natural to read here that the Most High divided the nations and that he apportioned to each of his sons – i.e., his angels – a nation, and that he assigned the people of Israel to Yahweh, the LORD. In that case, the LORD would initially be considered as one of the sons of the Most High God, who was in charge of the people of Israel.[15]

With regard to Israel's monotheism, the angel of the LORD is an interesting figure, since he is told to act on earth on behalf of the LORD. This angel encourages Hagar in the wilderness, after which she concludes that the LORD has spoken to her. Furthermore, this angel speaks on behalf of the LORD to Abraham when he wants to sacrifice his son Isaac, he appears to Moses in the burning bush and precedes the people of Israel to the promised land.[16]

who appeared to Joshua was Michael himself; see Lieve M. Teugels (2001), *Aggadat Bereshit*. Leiden: Brill, pp. 100–101. The Syrian-Persian Christian Aphrahat also gives this explanation in his *Demonstrations* III, 14 (of 337 CE; SC 349).

13 This text is also explained thus in Sirach 17:17 (this comes to light even more clearly in a few Greek manuscripts which have a longer text here), in Jubilees 15:30–32 (a free narration of Genesis from the second century BCE) and in Philo, *The Posterity and Exile of Cain* 89–92; *Noah's Work as a Planter* 59–60.

14 Thus in Psalm 47:3; 83:19; 97:9; see also the parallelism in Psalm 7:18; 9:3; 21:8; 46:5; 91:1–2. In Genesis 14:22 Abram swears to the LORD, the Most High God, but in the Genesis Apocryphon from Qumran (1QapGen 22, 16), in the Septuagint and in the Syrian translation the name of the LORD is absent; one can conclude that this name must have been added later to the Hebrew text.

15 See for this explanation, e.g., O. Eissfeldt (1956), 'El and Yahweh', *Journal of Semitic Studies*, 1, 25–37 (29); S. B. Parker, 'Sons of (the) Gods', p. 796; more literature in Riemer Roukema (2002), 'Le Fils du Très-Haut: Sur les anges et la christologie', *Études Théologiques et Religieuses*, 77, 343–357 (footnotes 7 and 10).

16 Genesis 16:7–13; 22:11, 15; Exodus 3:2; 23:20–23; 32:34; 33:2; Numbers 20:16. See also Numbers 22:22–35; Judges 2:1, 4; 6:11–12; 13:3, etc. See Aubrey R. Johnson (1961), *The One and the Many in the Israelite Conception of God* (2nd edn). Cardiff: University of Wales Press, pp. 28–33.

Another heavenly figure is Wisdom, who, according to Proverbs 8, was already with the LORD since the beginning of creation.[17] In this text she says:

> The LORD created me at the beginning of his work,
> the first of his acts of long ago.
> Ages ago I was set up,
> at the first, before the beginning of the earth. (...)
> When he established the heavens, I was there,
> when he drew a circle on the face of the deep,
> when he made firm the skies above,
> when he established the fountains of the deep,
> when he assigned to the sea its limit,
> so that the waters might not transgress his command,
> when he marked out the foundations of the earth,
> then I was beside him, like a master worker;
> and I was daily his delight,
> rejoicing before him always,
> rejoicing in his inhabited world
> and delighting in the human race. (Proverbs 8:22–23, 27–31)

Less conspicuous, but for our argument rather important, is that sometimes God is said to act and to speak through his word. He begins to create the heavens and the earth by saying, 'Let there be light.'[18] Therefore Psalm 33:6 says, 'By the word of the LORD the heavens were made.' Psalm 107:20 reads, 'He (the LORD) sent out his word and healed them,' and Psalm 147:15 declares, 'He (the LORD) sends out his command to the earth; his word runs swiftly.' In these verses, the Hebrew term *dabar* is used for 'word'; in the Greek translation of the Septuagint *logos* is used. In Isaiah 55:11 the prophet speaks in the name of the LORD about 'my word (*dabar*) that goes out from my mouth; it shall not return to me empty' (here in the Greek translation *rhêma* is used). In these texts, we see the beginning of the conception that the word of God is a separate, almost personified figure through whom the LORD acts and makes himself known.[19]

---

17 See furthermore, e.g., Job 28:12–28; Proverbs 9; also B. Lang (1999), 'Wisdom', in Karel van der Toorn, Bob Becking, Pieter W. van der Horst (eds), *Dictionary of Deities and Demons in the Bible* (2nd edn). Leiden: Brill, pp. 900–905.

18 Genesis 1:3; also 1:6, 9, 14, 20, 24, 26.

19 See Kraus, *Psalmen* 2, p. 1138; P.-E. Bonnard (1972), *Le Second Isaïe: Son disciple et leurs éditeurs: Isaïe 40–66*. Paris: Gabalda, pp. 309–310. J. L. Koole (1998), *Isaiah Part 3, Volume 2: Isaiah 49–55*. Leuven: Peeters, p. 438 remarks that the 'word' in Isaiah 55:11 has not yet become a hypostasis of God. Later, however, it was interpreted as such. Cf. Johnson, *The One and the Many in the Israelite Conception of God*, 17.

We just saw that the angels in the Old Testament are sometimes designated as the 'sons of God'. Often it is asserted that Israel's king is also called 'son of God', but this is not completely correct.[20] The king always counts as son of the LORD, even though he is never literally designated as such (as 'son of the LORD'). It is declared several times, however, that the LORD calls the king his son.[21] In Psalm 2:7 the LORD speaks to the king, 'You are my son; today I have begotten you.' This is usually said to refer to the adoption of the king by the LORD on the day of his enthronement.[22] It is even better to say that this adoption counts as a new birth.[23] In Psalm 89:27–28 the king addresses the LORD as 'my Father' and the LORD makes him his first-born. According to many Hebrew manuscripts, the LORD speaks to the king in Psalm 110:3, 'On the holy mountains from the womb of the morning, like dew, I have begotten you.' The Greek translation of this verse reads, 'From the womb, before Morning-star, I brought you forth.'[24] This tribute refers to a heavenly generation and pre-existence.[25] On grounds of the Father–son relationship of the LORD and the king, the king himself may also be called 'god'. In Psalm 45:6a, the king is thus addressed, 'Your throne, O god, endures forever and ever,' and Psalm 45:7b can be thus translated, 'Therefore, o god, your God has anointed you.'[26] In Isaiah 9:6 the new king is addressed as a newborn son who is named 'Wonderful Counselor, Mighty God, Everlasting Father'. For 'Wonderful Counselor', however, the Septuagint reads, 'angel of great

20 E.g., J. Fossum (1999), 'Son of God', in Karel van der Toorn, Bob Becking and Pieter W. van der Horst, *Dictionary of Deities and Demons in the Bible* (2nd edn). Leiden: Brill, pp. 788–794 (789). Margaret Barker (1992), *The Great Angel: A Study of Israel's Second God*. London: SPCK, pp. 4–10, correctly points to the distinction between 'sons of God' and 'son of the LORD'.

21 2 Samuel 7:14; 1 Chronicles 17:13; 22:10; 28:6.

22 E.g., Hans-Joachim Kraus (1978), *Psalmen* 1 (5th edn). Neukirchen-Vluyn: Neukirchener Verlag, pp. 151–153.

23 Peter C. Craigie and Marvin E. Tate (2004), *Psalms 1–50* (2nd edn). Waco TX: Word Books, p. 67.

24 Psalm 109:3 LXX (New English Translation of the Septuagint); in Hebrew, instead of the vocalization of the Masoretic text *jaldutêkā* (your youth) must then be read: *jᵉlīdᵉtīkā* (I have begotten you); for this the vowels only, and not the consonants have to be changed. See Kraus, *Psalmen* 2, pp. 926–927; 933.

25 See Joachim Schaper (1995), *Eschatology in the Greek Psalter*. Tübingen: J. C. B. Mohr, pp. 101–107; Eberhard Bons (2003), 'Die Septuaginta-Version von Psalm 110 (Ps 109 LXX): Textgestalt, Aussagen, Auswirkungen', in Dieter Sänger, ed., *Heiligkeit und Herrschaft: Intertextuelle Studien zu Heiligkeitsvorstellungen und zu Psalm 110*. Neukirchen-Vluyn: Neukirchener Verlag, pp. 122–145 (134–137).

26 Psalm 45:7b is thus understood by the Septuagint at least (Psalm 44:8 LXX). This may also be translated as, 'Therefore God, your God, has anointed you.' In Hebrews 1:8–9, Psalm 45:6–7 (44:7–8 LXX) is quoted in relation to Jesus as God's Son. See Kraus, *Psalmen* 1, pp. 490–491; Schaper, *Eschatology in the Greek Psalter*, pp. 80–83.

counsel' (Isaiah 9:5 LXX), which suggests that the king takes part in the heavenly council.[27] In other texts too the king is compared to an angel of God.[28] The close relationship of the king to the LORD is also apparent in 1 Chronicles 29:20, where, on the day of Solomon's enthronement, David summons the people to worship the LORD. It is written that the people 'bowed their heads before the LORD and the king'. Subsequently, 'Solomon sat on the throne of the LORD' (1 Chronicles 29:23). According to the writer of Chronicles, the LORD turns out, as a reflection of his throne in heaven, also to have a throne in Jerusalem upon which the king sits and where he accepts the honour on behalf of the LORD.[29]

Finally, the people of Israel as a whole also count as son of the LORD;[30] it ensues that the Israelites are called his sons and daughters.[31]

8.2 *Philo of Alexandria*

In the first half of the first century, the Jew Philo of Alexandria concludes that Moses' account of the creation of the world teaches, among other things, 'that God is one. This with a view to those who propound polytheism.'[32] He has, however, more to report about God than this fundamental creed.[33] He regularly distinguishes between God (*theos*) and the Lord (*kurios*). He considers God as the creative power and the Lord as the royal power. Both these powers (*dunameis*) are, according to Philo, manifestations of the one God whom he calls, on the basis of Exodus 3:14 in the Septuagint, 'The One Who Is' (*ho ôn*). He explains the appearance of the three men to Abraham (Genesis 18:2) with regard to the one God (the One Who Is), who manifested himself together with his powers Lord and God.[34]

27 Cf. Psalm 82:1; 89:8.
28 1 Samuel 14:17, 20; 19:27.
29 Cf. 1 Chronicles 17:14; 28:5; 2 Chronicles 9:8; Barker, *The Great Angel*, p. 36.
30 Exodus 4:22–23; Jeremiah 31:9, 20 (where the people are also called 'Ephraim'); Hosea 11:1.
31 E.g., Deuteronomy 14:1; 32:5–6; 32:18–19; Isaiah 30:1; 43:6; 45:11; 63:16; Jeremiah 3:4; 3:19; Ezekiel 16:20; Hosea 1:10.
32 Philo of Alexandria, *Creation* 171; see also *Allegorical Interpretation* III, 82; *Dreams* I, 229; *Virtues* 214.
33 For this section cf. Roukema, 'Le Fils du Très-Haut', pp. 346–348.
34 *Abraham* 121–124; *Life of Moses* II, 99–100; *Questions and Answers on Genesis* I, 57; II, 51; II, 53; IV, 2; IV, 8 (he uses the term *trias* there); furthermore *Who is the Heir* 166; *Allegorical Interpretation* III, 73; *Noah's Work as a Planter* 86; *The Change of Names* 11–14; 28–29. See Jean Daniélou (1958), *Philon d'Alexandrie*. Paris: Fayard, pp. 143–167; Mireille Hadas-Lebel (2003), *Philon d'Alexandrie: Un penseur en diaspora*. [Paris]: Fayard, pp. 289–300.

In addition to a threefold, Philo also relates a sevenfold appearance of the one God. In the description of the Ark of the Covenant, God speaks to Moses, 'I will speak to you from above the propitiatory in between the two cherubim' (Exodus 25:22).[35] In his interpretation, Philo distinguishes (1) the One Who Is, (2) his Logos (the 'Word') with which he speaks between the two cherubim, who stand for (3) God, the creative power and (4) the Lord, the royal power; from these two originate respectively (5) the beneficent power and (6) the legislative power, symbolized in the mercy seat (the propitiatory) and the 'testimonies' in the ark; the ark itself stands for (7) the noetic cosmos, i.e. the spiritual world of the Platonic ideas. A human being cannot directly know the One Who Is, but only through his powers.[36] Elsewhere, Philo makes a similar sevenfold distinction between the One Who Is, his Logos, his creative power God and his royal power the Lord, his grace, his commandments and his prohibitions.[37] In passing, he also distinguishes seven powers, of which the Logos, being the seventh, stands in the middle, while all seven came forth from the One.[38]

In other texts, Philo does not make a three- or sevenfold distinction in the one God and among his powers, but only mentions God and his Logos.[39] He calls the Logos God's first-born, the oldest and ruler of the angels, i.e. the archangel, and furthermore the Beginning, the Name of God, Man after God's image, and Israel; he explains this name as 'he who sees God'.[40] The term 'God's first-born' is derived from Exodus 4:22, where the LORD commands Moses to tell the Egyptian Pharaoh, 'Israel is my first-born.'[41] The 'Name of God' indicates the name Yahweh, i.e. the LORD. The title 'Man after God's image' refers to Genesis 1:26–27 which states that God created man after his image; it proves that the

---

35 According to the New English Translation of the Septuagint.

36 *Questions and Answers on Exodus* II, 67–68; cf. E. R. Goodenough (1935), *By Light, Light: The Mystic Gospel of Hellenistic Judaism*. New Haven CT, reprint (1969) Amsterdam: Philo Press, pp. 23–28.

37 *Flight and Finding* 100–101; cf. Goodenough, *By Light, Light*, pp. 28–30.

38 *Who is the Heir* 215–216.

39 Thomas H. Tobin (1992), 'Logos', in David N. Freedman, ed., *The Anchor Bible Dictionary* 4. New York: Doubleday, pp. 348–356, concludes that for Philo the creative power God and the royal power Lord are two aspects of the Logos (350).

40 *Confusion of Tongues* 146–147; cf. *Allegorical Interpretation* III, 96; 175; 186; 212; *On Dreams* I, 215.

41 The Greek term for 'first-born' is not directly derived from the Septuagint version of Exodus 4:22, because this reads *prôtotokos* (which also means 'first-born'), while Philo, *Confusion of Tongues* 146, reads *prôtogonos*. In his work *Posterity of Cain* 63 Philo alludes to Exodus 4:22 using the term *prôtogonos*; here he does not follow the Septuagint either. Philo does not use *prôtotokos* anywhere in his works as a designation of the Logos.

Logos, according to Philo, is the archetype of mankind created by God. The designation 'he who sees God' is derived from Genesis 32:30, where Jacob after his wrestling with the unknown man was given the name Israel and says, 'I have seen God.'[42]

Philo identifies this Logos and first-born son with the angel from Exodus 23:20, who will go in front of Israel and upon whom the Name of the Lord rests. This angel too is called Lord and is the ruler over all powers.[43] Elsewhere, he identifies the Logos with God's Wisdom.[44] For Philo the Logos is a 'second god', whom he designates without the definite article 'the' (*ho*), the ruler of everything, through whom everything exists.[45] He is God for the people who are not perfect yet.[46] As ruler over the angels, he is neither uncreated like the Creator, nor created like human beings, and therefore he is midway between God and human beings.[47] He regularly appeared on earth to help people in need, like Hagar and Jacob.[48]

Without mentioning the title 'Logos', Philo refers to this figure in a passage about a man whose name is *Anatolê* in Zechariah 6:12, which can be translated as 'dawn'.[49] Philo sees in this the incorporeal figure who differs in nothing from the 'divine image' (Genesis 1:26–27). He calls him the eldest son whom God the Father has generated, and his first-born.[50]

We just mentioned that Philo also identifies the Logos with God's Wisdom. This identification is also apparent when he calls Wisdom the highest and first of God's powers, with which he quenches the thirst of the souls who love him.[51] The passage about Wisdom in Proverbs 8:22 he explains in the sense that God had intercourse with his knowledge (*epistêmê*), who subsequently brought forth the world. Thus, he calls Wisdom the mother of the entire creation.[52] Elsewhere, however, he calls her God's daughter.[53]

---

42 Genesis 32:24–30. The interpretation of Israel as 'he who sees God' is based upon the Hebrew *îš rō'ēh 'ēl*, 'man seeing God'.
43 *Husbandry* 51; *Migration of Abraham* 174; *Dreams* I, 157; 239–240.
44 *Allegorical Interpretation* I, 65; cf. *Who is the Heir* 191; *Dreams* II, 242–245.
45 *Questions and Answers on Genesis* II, 62; *Dreams* I, 227–230; *Cherubim* 36; *Allegorical Interpretation* II, 86.
46 *Allegorical Interpretation* III, 207; cf. *Confusion of Tongues* 146–147.
47 *Who is the Heir* 205–206.
48 *Dreams* I, 238–241; *Questions and Answers on Genesis* III, 34–35; *Allegorical Interpretation* III, 177; *Flight and Finding* 5; *The Unchangeableness of God* 182.
49 Cf. Luke 1:78, discussed in section 2.4.
50 *Confusion of Tongues* 62–63.
51 *Allegorical Interpretation* II, 86; also I, 65; *Who is the Heir* 91; *Dreams* II, 242.
52 *Drunkenness* 30–31.
53 *Flight and Finding* 50–52.

People who know the one God can, according to Philo, be called 'sons of God'; he then refers to Deuteronomy 14:1: 'you are sons (or children) of the LORD, your God'.[54] He who, like Abraham, is God's friend, has become God's adopted and only son.[55] Thus, Isaac is also called a son of God.[56]

Because Philo mainly comments on the books of Moses in his works, he does not consider those Old Testament texts which mention the king as a son of the LORD. Still, he does quote Exodus 7:1 several times, where the LORD says to Moses, 'I have made you like a god for Pharaoh' (NEB). From this, Philo infers that through this task Moses became a god to a certain degree, and that this goes for every wise man. Yet he adds that Moses and other wise men are not really gods except in comparison with fools.[57]

8.3 *Other early Jewish writings*

As in the book of Proverbs, in early Jewish texts Wisdom is described almost as a separate figure who can act on behalf of the LORD.[58] She is even called 'the fashioner of all things', which suggests that God has created the world through his Wisdom.[59] We have already seen that the idea that God acts by means of his word, i.e. Logos, appears in the Old Testament. This idea can also be found in early Jewish writings. Sirach (42:15) and Wisdom of Solomon (9:1) declare that God has created the world by his word.[60] One Ezekiel (not the biblical prophet) has written a Greek theatre adaption of the book of Exodus in the second century BCE. When he describes that Moses sees the burning bush (Exodus 3:2), a voice says that the divine Logos shines from the bush; Moses can after all not see God's face, but he can listen to his words (*logoi*). God then makes himself known as the God of Abraham, Isaac and Jacob.[61] According to

---

54 *Confusion of Tongues* 145; *Special Laws* I, 318.
55 *Sobriety* 56; Philo reads Genesis 18:17 thus, 'Shall I (the Lord) hide anything from Abraham my friend?'
56 *Change of Names* 131.
57 *The Worse Attacks the Better* 161–162; *Sacrifices of Abel and Cain* 9; *Migration of Abraham* 84; *Change of Names* 128; *Dreams* II, 189; *Every Good Man is Free* 43.
58 Sirach 24:1–22; Baruch 3:15; 3:29–38; Wisdom of Solomon 1:4–6; 6:12–10:21; 1 Enoch 42; 2 Enoch 30:8; 33:4 (OTP 1); see Georg Sauer (2000), *Jesus Sirach/Ben Sira.* Göttingen: Vandenhoeck & Ruprecht, pp. 180–181.
59 Wisdom of Solomon 7:22.
60 Thus also 4 Ezra 6:36 (from about 100 CE; OTP 1).
61 In Eusebius of Caesarea, *Preparation for the Gospel* IX, 29, 8 (SC 369; also in OTP 2, p. 813).

this Ezekiel, God therefore revealed himself by his Logos. In a similar way, Wisdom of Solomon 18:14–16 reads that in the night in which the people of Israel were to be delivered from Egypt, God's all-powerful Logos leapt from his royal throne in heaven and with his sword spread death everywhere in Egypt. According to Exodus 12:12–13 and 12:29, it was the LORD himself who would go round Egypt to kill all the first-born, except those of the Israelites, but the author of the book of Wisdom declares that this action is carried out by God's Logos.

To be sure, Ezekiel the dramatist and author of the book of Wisdom in all probability originated from Alexandria, just as did Philo whom we have discussed. One could therefore ask oneself if the Jewish traditions that appear in their works are relevant to the person of Jesus and his first disciples, who lived in Palestine or originated from there. With regard to the Logos, however, the same traditions appear in some of the Aramaic translations of the books of Moses, called the targums. In these books, which originate among others from Palestine, the LORD speaks, acts, and appears continually by his *Mēmra*, which is Aramaic for Word, i.e. Logos.[62] According to a few targums, the Mēmra of the LORD brings about the creation.[63] In conclusion of the story of the angel of the LORD who appears to Hagar at a well in the wilderness, a few targums read that the Mēmra of the LORD appeared to her, or had spoken to her.[64] In the story of the burning bush, according to the Targum Neofiti, it is the Mēmra of the LORD who appears to Moses.[65] This Mēmra goes through Egypt to kill the first-born.[66] The angel who precedes the people of Israel is identified with this Mēmra.[67] Also, the LORD says that he will meet Moses at the Ark of the Covenant through mediation of his Mēmra.[68]

---

62 George F. Moore (1927), *Judaism in the First Centuries of the Christian Era: The Age of the Tannaim* I (reprint 1971). Cambridge, New York: Schocken Books, pp. 417–418 denies that *Mēmra* in the targums corresponds to *dābār* in the above-mentioned Old Testament texts and to Philo's Logos. His argument is that *dābār* is not translated with *mēmra* but with *pitgama* or *milla* in such Old Testament texts. In view of the following similarities between the early Jewish writings written in Greek in which God acts through his Logos and the later targums, in which in the same texts his *Mēmra* is mentioned, Moore's denial is not tenable. Cf. Daniel Boyarin (2004), *Border Lines: The Partition of Judaeo-Christianity*. Philadelphia: University of Pennsylvania Press, pp. 112–135; 300.
63 Genesis 1:3–2:2 Targum Neofiti 1; Genesis 1:3–2:3 Fragmentary Targum.
64 Genesis 16:13 Targum Neofiti 1; Targum Pseudo-Jonathan; Fragmentary Targum.
65 Exodus 3:4–12 Targum Neofiti 1.
66 Exodus 12:12–13, 23, 29 Targum Neofiti 1; Exodus 12:12, 29 Targum Pseudo-Jonathan.
67 Exodus 23:22 Targum Neofiti 1; Exodus 23:21–22 Targum Pseudo-Jonathan.
68 Exodus 25:22 Targum Neofiti 1; Targum Pseudo-Jonathan.

To be sure, these targums are difficult to date; most targums are supposed to have been written, in the form in which they are now known, well after the first century CE. The Targum Neofiti is, however, dated to the first or second century CE.[69] Comparison with the Alexandrian writings just mentioned reveals in any case that, with regard to the Mēmra, the targums contain old traditions. In theory, it is possible that the authors who translated the Scriptures from Hebrew to Aramaic borrowed this element from Alexandrian Greek-speaking authors.[70] It is more likely, however, that the representation of God who reveals himself and acts through his Word (Logos, Mēmra), does not originate from Alexandria, but – also considering the Old Testament roots – goes back to the land of Israel, later called Palestine.

An interesting Greek text in which we do not find the term Logos, but other terms which also appear in Philo, is the *Prayer of Joseph*. This text is only known thanks to two quotations of Origen and is dated to the first century CE.[71] In his commentary on the Gospel of John, Origen poses the question of whether John the Baptist might be a incarnated angel. He thinks that this is indeed the case and quotes as an argument for this a fragment of the 'apocryphal' *Prayer of Joseph*.[72] Jacob says there that he is an angel of God, and that Abraham and Isaac were created before everything else; this refers to their pre-existence in heaven. Jacob continues that God called him 'Israel', 'the man who sees God', and that he is the first-born of all living beings. He tells that he descended to earth and came to live among men. There he met the angel Uriel, who was jealous of him and began to fight with him. Jacob then said to him,

> Are you not Uriel, the eighth after me? and I, Israel, the archangel of the power of the Lord and the chief captain among the sons of God? Am I not Israel, the first minister before the face of God?[73]

This passage offers an exceptional view on Jacob's wrestling with the unknown man, which is described in Genesis 32:24–30. According to Genesis 32:28, Jacob was given the name Israel after this wrestling. Hosea

69 Alejandro Díez Macho (1968), *Neophyti 1: Targum Palestinense: Ms de la Biblioteca Vaticana I*. Madrid, Barcelona: Consejo Superior de Investigaciones Científicas, pp. 57*–96*.

70 Cf. Boyarin, *Border Lines*, p. 128, who does not share this view.

71 J. Z. Smith (1985), 'Prayer of Joseph', in James H. Charlesworth, ed., *The Old Testament Pseudepigrapha* 2. London: Darton, Longman & Todd, pp. 699–723.

72 Origen, *Commentary on the Gospel of John* II, 186–191 (from about 231 CE; SC 120).

73 Origen, *Commentary on the Gospel of John* II, 189–190 (translation Smith, OTP 2, p. 713).

12:5 says that Jacob wrestled with an angel. In the *Prayer of Joseph* not only the unknown man but also Jacob himself is considered an angel in human form. Just as in Philo, Jacob (i.e. Israel) is called the one 'who sees God', 'the first-born'[74] and the 'archangel'. This means that Israel was considered God's pre-existent first-born son, who subsequently became incarnate in Jacob, to whom also was given the name Israel. Yet, the view of the *Prayer of Joseph* does not completely correspond to Philo, because he remarks that it was the Logos who gave Jacob his new name,[75] while in the *Prayer of Joseph* this angel is called Uriel. In a Greek version of the book of Enoch, Uriel is one of the seven archangels, among whom he is mentioned first.[76] The idea behind the *Prayer of Joseph* appears to be that Israel as the highest angel stands above these seven archangels and all other 'sons of God'.

One of the *Songs of the Sabbath Sacrifice* from Qumran also affirms that there are seven archangels.[77] It is striking that the number of seven archangels corresponds with the number of seven powers (*dunameis*) who, according to Philo, come forth from the one God.

In early Jewish writings the title 'son of God' is used not only for angels, but also for men. The Wisdom of Solomon describes how wrongdoers oppress a righteous poor man. They say about him:

He professes to have knowledge of God,
and calls himself a servant of the Lord (...)
He calls the last end of the righteous happy,
and boasts that God is his father.
Let us see if his words are true,
and let us test what will happen at the end of his life;
for if the righteous man is God's son, he will help him,
and will deliver him from the hand of his adversaries. (2:13, 16b–18)[78]

Here 'son of God' is synonymous with 'servant of the Lord' and 'the righteous man'. Similarly, the Hebrew text of Sirach 4:10 says that if someone acts mercifully and justly, God will call him 'son'; the Greek

---

74 Just as in Philo, *Confusion of Tongues* 146, the *Prayer of Joseph* reads *prôtogonos* and not *prôtotokos* (Exodus 4:22 LXX).
75 Philo, *Change of Names* 87.
76 Enoch 20 (ed. Black): Uriel, Raphael, Raguel, Michael, Sariel, Remiel, Gabriel.
77 4Q403 fragment 1, I, ('seven wonderful powers', seven 'chief princes'). Cf. also the seven spirits before God's throne in Revelation 1:4.
78 New Revised Standard Version, with minor changes.

version reads that he will then be 'like a son of the Most High'. In the Talmud it also occurs that God calls certain rabbis 'my son'.[79]

The Dead Sea Scrolls contain a lacunous text which announces an exceptional son of God. Someone – perhaps Daniel – explains a dream to a king and then speaks of a king who will conquer the enemies of God's people:

> He will be called son of God, and they will call him son of the Most High. (…) His kingdom will be an eternal kingdom, and all his paths in truth. He will judge the earth in truth and all will make peace. The sword will cease from the earth, and all the provinces will pay him homage. The great God is his strength, he will wage war for him; he will place the peoples in his hand and cast them all away before him. His rule will be an eternal rule, and all the abysses …[80]

From this fragment it is not clear who is meant by this son of God. The Messiah or a messiah could be meant, or another heavenly saviour, but the text could also speak of a future Jewish king.[81] It is not necessary to make a choice in this now; it is sufficient to remark that in Qumran a saviour could be considered son of God and son of the Most High.

Terms such as 'son of God' and 'sons of God' also occur in *Joseph and Aseneth*, which is a Greek document written in Egypt around the first century CE.[82] It narrates how Aseneth, the daughter of an Egyptian priest, becomes the wife of Joseph, the viceroy of Egypt (cf. Genesis 41:45). It tells that the 'commander of the whole host of the Most High' appears from heaven to Aseneth and informs her that she will be Joseph's bride. He calls 'Repentance' a daughter of the Most High and his own sister, who prays in heaven for Aseneth to the Most High God.[83] Afterwards, Aseneth converts to the Most High God and Joseph marries her. Joseph

---

79 Babylonian Talmud Berakoth 7a (rabbi Ishmael ben Elisa); Berakoth 17b and Taanith 24b–25a (rabbi Hanina ben Dosa); Taanith 25a (rabbi Eleazar ben Pedat).

80 4Q246 II, in Florentino García Martínez and Eibert J. C. Tigchelaar (1997), *The Dead Sea Scrolls Study Edition* I. Leiden: Brill, pp. 494–495. In Luke 1:32 and 35, the combination 'son of God' and 'son of the Most High' appears with regard to Jesus; see section 2.4.

81 Florentino García Martínez and Adam van der Woude (2007), *De rollen van de Dode Zee* (2nd edn). Kampen: Ten Have, p. 611, believe that this heavenly figure must be considered as messiah; Joseph A. Fitzmyer (1993), '4Q246: The "Son of God" Document from Qumran', *Biblica* 74, 153–174, prefers 'a coming Jewish ruler, perhaps a member of the Hasmonean dynasty' (173–174).

82 See C. Burchard (1985), 'Joseph and Aseneth: A New Translation and Introduction', in Charlesworth, ed., *The Old Testament Pseudepigrapha* 2, pp. 177–247 (187–188).

83 *Joseph and Aseneth* 14:1–15:12x.

is called 'son of God' and 'the first-born son of God' by Aseneth and other Egyptians.[84] Aseneth is also called 'daughter of the Most High' by Pharaoh.[85] The angelic prince who appears to Aseneth sums up all 'God's angels, God's chosen ones and all sons of the Most High', and Joseph refers to the Israelites as 'the sons of the living God'.[86] From this document it appears that human beings can be called sons and daughters of God or of the Most High and that the angel named Repentance counts as God's daughter. Since the angelic prince speaks about her as his sister, the conclusion may be drawn that he himself is also a heavenly son of God. He appears to be a similar figure as the Logos, i.e. the Mēmra whom we encountered in other texts, who appears to human beings and acts on behalf of God. In heaven he has a position which is comparable to that of Joseph in Egypt. He stands above all the angels, but under the Most High God, just as Joseph was put in charge of all of Egypt, but stood under Pharaoh.

To conclude, a few other texts about heavenly figures deserve our attention. In Ezekiel's theatre adaption of the book of Exodus, Moses tells about a dream to his father-in-law. On top of Mount Sinai stood a large throne upon which a noble man sat. This man invited Moses to mount the throne; he withdrew from it himself. Moses saw the whole earth, what is beneath the earth and what is above the heavens, and the stars served him. His father-in-law explained that Moses would establish a great throne, would be a leader of mortals and would see what is, what was and what will be.[87] So, according to this rendering of Exodus, Moses would be exalted up to heaven.

A similar motive seems to occur in a lacunous text from Qumran in which someone from the community is speaking. Some lines read:

> besides me no-one is exalted, nor comes to me, for I reside in [...], in the heavens ... I am counted among the gods (*ēlīm*) ... Who bea[rs all] sorrows like me? And who [suffe]rs evil like me? ... [f]or among the gods is [my] posi[tion, and] my glory is with the sons of the king.[88]

84 'Son of God': *Joseph and Aseneth* 6:3; 6:5; cf. 'your son' in 13:13; 'the first-born (*prôtotokos*) son of God': 21:4 (cf. 18:11); 'like the first-born son of God': 23:10.
85 *Joseph and Aseneth* 21:4.
86 *Joseph and Aseneth* 16:14; 19:8.
87 Eusebius, *Preparation for the Gospel* IX, 29, 6–7 (SC 369); see R. G. Robertson (1985), 'Ezekiel the Tragedian', in Charlesworth, ed., *The Old Testament Pseudepigrapha* 2, pp. 803–819 (811–812).
88 4Q491c fragment 1; García Martínez and Tigchelaar, *The Dead Sea Scrolls Study Edition* II, pp. 980–981.

It seems that here a man is speaking who declares that he has been exalted up to heaven and has become equal to the angels.[89]

Another fragmentary text from Qumran deals with the day of reconciliation in the jubilee at the end of time, when debts will be acquitted and prisoners will be released. There, Psalm 82:1 is quoted, 'God has taken his place in the divine council; in the midst of the gods he holds judgement' and applied to Melchizedek. This being, known from Genesis 14:18–20 and Psalm 110:4, acts in this text as a heavenly figure who is himself called 'God' (*elōhīm*). He will execute judgement over God's enemies and have leadership over the meeting of the heavenly powers (also called *elōhīm*).[90] He has the same function here as attributed to the Prince of light, meaning Michael, in other texts from Qumran.[91]

8.4 *Conclusion*

With regard to the question to what degree the high position which was attributed to Jesus Christ fits into early Judaism, many more early Jewish texts could be discussed. For our purpose the evidence treated thus far is, however, sufficient to give an impression of Jewish beliefs from the context in which Christianity originated. The texts discussed prove that so far as the early Jewish religion can be regarded as monotheistic this term needs to be qualified. Old Testament and early Jewish writings show, after all, that God the LORD in heaven has other figures next to him, who come forth from him or in whom an aspect of his being is personified, as it were. These figures can appear, speak and act on behalf of God. It was also considered possible that human beings could be exalted up to God.

Furthermore, around the beginning of our era there were even Jews who regarded the worship of other 'pagan' gods by other nations legitimate. These Jews regarded the 'pagan' gods as subordinate to their own God, whom they believed to be the Most High. In the light of the many figures next to God in early Judaism on the one hand, and this recognition of other gods (here discussed no further) on the other hand, William Horbury speaks of 'inclusive monotheism'.[92] This means

---

89 See e.g., Étienne Nodet (2002), *Le Fils de Dieu: Procès de Jésus et Évangiles*. Paris: Cerf, pp. 152–157; 184.

90 11Q13 = 11QMelch, in García Martínez and Tigchelaar, *The Dead Sea Scrolls Study Edition* II, pp. 1206–1207.

91 1QS III, 20; CD V, 18; 1QM XIII, 10; XVII, 6–7.

92 William Horbury (2004), 'Jewish and Christian Monotheism in the Herodian Age', in Loren T. Stuckenbruck, Wendy E. S. North, eds, *Early Jewish and Christian Monotheism*. London: T&T Clark, pp. 16–44.

that the worship of the one God of the Jews could co-exist with the recognition of other heavenly and divine figures. 'Inclusive' is opposed to 'exclusive'; exclusive monotheism means that there is only one God and that other gods and powers either do not exist, or are not worthy of any kind of worship. The Jewish religion is often thought to be exclusively monotheistic. For early Judaism, however, this was not true.

The question now is what this examination of early Jewish beliefs in the heavenly, divine figures next to God the LORD provides for our view of Jesus. In chapter 4 we discussed the fact that after his death, Jesus' earliest disciples worshipped him as the risen and exalted Lord. They regarded him as the Son of God, as the Logos and as the LORD who had appeared on earth. This is why the first Christians included him in their worship and adoration of God the Father. Inevitably, the early Jewish representations of God, who by his Wisdom or Word created the world and through his Word appeared to people and delivered Israel from Egypt, make one think of what Christians believed with regard to Jesus. In the Gospel of John he is, after all, called 'the Word' which was in the beginning with God and through which all things came into being (1:1–3). Abraham and Isaiah already knew him (8:56; 12:41). Paul also says that everything came into being through the one Lord, Jesus Christ, and that Christ accompanied the Israelites through the wilderness (1 Corinthians 8:6; 10:4). It is fascinating that Philo calls the Logos the ruler of the angels and God's oldest and first-born son. In a similar way, Jesus Christ counts as God's only Son (*monogenês*) in the Gospel of John (1:14, 18), and in numerous other New Testament verses he is called the Son of God. It is evident that this title is not only used in the meaning of a 'righteous man', but indicates a much higher position with God. Considering that in the Old Testament the angels are sometimes called the 'sons of God', it is possible to interpret Jesus' title of 'Son of God' with regard to this designation. Then he would be the angel or messenger (*aggelos*), i.e. the Son of God par excellence. According to Philo, the Logos is, among other things, called 'the Name of God' of which we said that this points to the name Yahweh, the LORD. In the New Testament it is regularly suggested that Jesus also carries the name of the LORD. Philo sometimes calls the Logos 'a second god', or a god for the people who are not yet perfect. Similarly, in the New Testament Jesus is also believed to be divine, as God next to or on behalf of God.

These similarities are, however, judged in various ways. Some scholars think that early Judaism already knew a pattern of the plurality in God, and that the first Christians applied this pattern to Jesus Christ. In this vein, the Jewish scholar Daniel Boyarin thinks that in early Judaism a 'logos theology' existed, which was used by the first Jewish Christians to make clear who Jesus Christ was for them. In defence against this, other

Jews would have removed this logos theology from their beliefs, which resulted in exclusive monotheism.[93] Loren Stuckenbruck also believes that the early Jewish belief in angelic powers next to God was of essential importance to the earliest expressions of faith in the exalted Lord Jesus. He tries to demonstrate that early Judaism not only believed in high angels, but that they were also invoked and worshipped. He points to *Joseph and Aseneth*, for example, where Aseneth honours and worships the angel who appears to her, to a few texts from Qumran and to the deuterocanonical book of Tobit.[94] He argues that some polemical texts from the first and second centuries CE demonstrate that there were Jews who worshipped angels at that time.[95] According to Stuckenbruck, the early Christian worship of Jesus could have originated analogously to this.

These data, however, are judged differently by Larry Hurtado. He emphasizes that the earliest worship of Jesus Christ goes much further than the Jewish belief in angels and other mediator figures, even though occasionally it is testified that they were also invoked and worshipped.[96] Hurtado thinks that the worship which fell to Jesus soon after his death was something new which fundamentally deviated from the Judaism of that time. This novelty, according to him, was instigated by religious experiences which Jesus' first – and therefore Jewish – followers had after his death and resurrection.[97]

Considering the formal similarities, a relationship unmistakably exists between the early Jewish conception of the Logos or Mēmra and other

93 Boyarin, *Border Lines*, pp. 89–147.
94 Loren T. Stuckenbruck (2004), '"Angels" and "God": Exploring the Limits of Early Jewish Monotheism', in Loren T. Stuckenbruck and Wendy E. S. North, eds, *Early Jewish and Christian Monotheism*. London: T&T Clark, pp. 45–70; more elaborate in Stuckenbruck (1995), *Angel Veneration and Christology: A Study in Early Judaism and in the Christology of the Apocalypse of John*. Tübingen: J. C. B. Mohr, pp. 45–204.
95 E.g. Colossians 2:18; The *Preaching of Peter* in Clement of Alexandria, *Stromateis* VI, 41, 1 (SC 446), 'Neither worship as the Jews; for they, thinking that they only know God, do not know Him, adoring as they do angels and archangels, the month and the moon' (translation ANF 2, p. 489); also Celsus in Origen, *Against Celsus* I, 26; V, 6 (SC 132; 147); The *Tripartite Tractate* (Nag Hammadi Codex I, 5) 112, 'Some (of the Jews) say that the god who made a proclamation in the ancient scriptures is one; others say that they are many' (translation Einar Thomassen, in Marvin Meyer, ed. (2007), *The Nag Hammadi Scriptures: The International Edition*. New York: HarperCollins, p. 90). See Stuckenbruck, *Angel Veneration*, pp. 111–119; 140–146; Horbury, 'Jewish and Christian Monotheism', p. 25.
96 Larry W. Hurtado (1998), *One Lord, One God: Early Christian Devotion and Ancient Jewish Monotheism* (2nd edn). Philadelphia: Fortress Press, pp. 17–92.
97 Hurtado, *One Lord, One God*, pp. 93–128; idem, *Lord Jesus Christ*, pp. 70–74; 134–153; 194–206.

figures who manifest themselves next to, or on behalf of God, on the one hand, and the early Christian views of Jesus as the LORD and God's Logos and Son, on the other. In this Boyarin, Horbury and Struckenbruck are right. Hurtado correctly remarks, however, that the worship of Jesus, which originated shortly after his death, is something new after all. The novelty is that this worship is not directed at a high angel who, according to certain stories and interpretations, appears to people, but at a concrete human being who had recently lived and died on a cross.

We can now answer the question of whether early Judaism offers clues for the exalted conceptions of Jesus. It turns out that these clues do indeed exist. That Jesus was considered the Son of God and the Logos and the LORD has ample analogies in contemporaneous Palestinian and Alexandrian Judaism.[98] So far it can be *historically* determined that the early Christian conviction that Jesus represented God and that he himself was divine and God himself was not completely unfamiliar to early Judaism. This does not mean that we can determine historically that God in his Logos did indeed take on a human form in Jesus Christ. One can only believe or reject this. For whoever wants to believe it, this conviction can be the starting point of theological consideration. However, this would lead us into a different language field.

98 Cf. Joseph A. Fitzmyer (1995), 'The Palestinian Background of "Son of God" as a Title for Jesus', in T. Fornberg and D. Hellholm, eds, *Texts and Contexts in their Textual and Situational Contexts.* Oslo: Scandinavian University Press, pp. 567–577; Boyarin, *Border Lines*, pp. 89–147; also Johnson, *The One and the Many in the Israelite Conception of God*, p. 37.

CHAPTER 9

Jesus and the Dogma of God's Trinity

We have established that early Judaism knew a plurality in the one God and left room to other heavenly figures besides God, so that the exalted conceptions which were made of Jesus were not completely unfamiliar to contemporaneous Judaism. Now we will continue with the question of how this fact relates to the view that Jesus Christ is the eternal Son of God and that he forms a *trias*, i.e. threesome, with the Father and the Holy Spirit. The catholic church declared this idea to be orthodox in the council of Nicaea of 325 CE and rejected other views. This arouses the question why this was so decided and which other views existed at that time. This chapter discusses the most important opinions and people who led to this decision.[1] Because the council of Nicaea was concerned with the relationship of God the Father and Jesus Christ, and the position of the Holy Spirit was not under debate at that time, this chapter will mainly deal with the relationship between the Father and the Son. In the second half of the fourth century an intense debate was held about the position of the Holy Spirit in God's trinity, but that is not the theme of this book.

9.1 *God the Father, the Son and the Holy Spirit in the New Testament*

First, we will deal with some New Testament texts in which God the Father, Jesus the Son and the Holy Spirit are named in the same breath. Subsequently, we will point to a few passages which demonstrate in which

---

1 Apart from some Dutch books, I used J. N. D. Kelly (1977), *Early Christian Doctrines* (5th edn). London: Adam & Charles Black.

way Jesus was seen as the Son of God the Father and to a few verses in which he himself is called 'God'.

In section 4.3 we saw that, according to the Gospel of Matthew, the risen Jesus commands his disciples to baptize the nations 'in the name of the Father and of the Son and of the Holy Spirit' (28:19). We remarked there that no theology of the trinity is formulated here, but that this verse does point into that direction. In the synoptic gospels, at the beginning of his public appearance, at his baptism, Jesus is named in the same breath with God's voice from heaven and the Spirit descending upon him; he is then called 'my beloved Son' by the voice from heaven.[2] Thus the Father, the Son and the Spirit appear in one short story.

The letters of Paul also contain a few texts in which he mentions the Father, the Son and the Spirit parallel to one another. He concludes the second letter to the Corinthians with the following blessing, 'The grace of the Lord Jesus Christ, the love of God, and the communion of the Holy Spirit be with all of you' (13:13). In 1 Corinthians 12:4–6, Paul mentions parallel to one another one Spirit, one Lord (i.e. Jesus) and one God in connection with the gifts of the Spirit. In Romans 8:9–10, Paul speaks first about the Spirit of God, subsequently about the Spirit of Christ and then again about Christ in the believers. He continually refers to the same spiritual reality and makes no distinction between the Spirit of God, the Spirit of Christ and the risen Christ. The letter to the Ephesians 1:3–14 contains a thanksgiving which is first addressed to 'the God and Father of our Lord Jesus Christ', subsequently deals with the redemption which is given through Jesus Christ, and finally mentions the Holy Spirit as a pledge of the promised inheritance.

The Gospel of John also contains a few statements in which the Father, the Son and the Spirit are named in the same breath. John the Baptist sees the Spirit descend upon Jesus and then calls him the Son of God (1:32–34).[3] About himself Jesus says, 'He whom God has sent speaks the words of God, for he gives the Spirit without measure' (3:34). In John 14:26, Jesus speaks about the Holy Spirit whom the Father will send on his behalf.[4] According to this gospel, Jesus also said, 'The Father and I are one' (10:30)[5] and, 'God is spirit' (4:24).

In 1 John 5:7 according to the King James Version, the Father, the Word (the Logos) and the Holy Ghost are presented as 'three that bear

---

2   Matthew 3:16–17; Mark 1:9–11; Luke 3:21–22 (see section 2.4 for the alternative reading in Luke 3:22).
3   See p. 40, n.88 about the alternative reading 'elect'.
4   See also John 14:17; 15:26.
5   For 'one' it reads the neuter *hen*, not the masculine *heis*; this implies that Jesus and the Father are not perceived as one person, but that they are of one will and intention. See also John 5:17, 19, 30; 8:16, 18.

record in heaven', about whom is said, 'and these three agree in one' (literally: 'and these three are one'). However, this verse is only found in later Latin and Greek manuscripts and is therefore to be considered an insertion in the original text.[6]

With the exception of the baptismal command in Matthew 28:19, the quoted verses speak as it were in passing of the threesome Father, Son and Spirit, in various terms and in various sequences. This implies that these three figures are indeed closely related to each other, but also that a doctrinal statement about their mutual relationship is made nowhere in the New Testament.

In chapter 2, which treated Jesus' origin and identity, numerous texts in which Jesus was represented as the Son of God were mentioned. Here, we will call to mind only a few of these texts. Paul confesses in 1 Corinthians 8:6 'one God, the Father, from whom are all things and for whom we exist, and one Lord, Jesus Christ, through whom are all things and through whom we exist'. In Matthew 11:27 and Luke 10:22, Jesus calls himself the Son who knows the Father in an intimate way and to whom the Father has handed over all things. The Gospel of John begins with a hymn about God and his Logos, who was with God from the beginning, through whom everything came into being and who is God's only Son, Jesus Christ (1:1–18).[7] Two New Testament passages were not mentioned in the previous chapters. Colossians 1:15–17 contains a hymnic passage about Christ that reads,

> He is the image of the invisible God,
> the first-born of all creation;
> for in him all things in heaven and on earth were created,
> things visible and invisible,
> whether thrones or dominions or rulers or powers –

6 See, e.g., Georg Strecker (1989), *Die Johannesbriefe*. Göttingen: Vandenhoeck & Ruprecht, pp. 279–282.

7 John 1:14 reads *monogenês* (the term which has often been translated as 'only begotten', but may rather mean 'only'); in John 3:16, 18 and in 1 John 4:9 *monogenês* is connected with *huios*, 'the only Son'. Perhaps *monogenês huios* is also the original reading in John 1:18; see section 2.5, p. 40. For the translation of *monogenês* as 'only begotten' or as 'only', see, respectively, Friedrich Büchsel (1969), '*monogenês*', in Gerhard Kittel and Geoffrey W. Bromiley, eds, *Theological Dictionary of the New Testament* 4. Grand Rapids MI: Eerdmans, pp. 737–741, and Dale Moody (1953), 'God's Only Son: The Translation of John 3:16 in the Revised Standard Version', *Journal of Biblical Literature*, 72, 213–219; furthermore Peter L. Hofrichter (1987), 'Das Verständnis des christologischen Titels 'Eingeborener' bei Origenes', in Lothar Lies, ed., *Origeniana Quarta*. Innsbruck: Tyrolia-Verlag, pp. 186–193; also in Hofrichter (2003), *Logoslied, Gnosis und Neues Testament*. Hildesheim: Olms, pp. 99–106.

all things have been created through him and for him.
He himself is before all things,
and in him all things hold together.

The letter to the Hebrews 1:2–3 also says that God created the worlds through the Son. There he is called 'the reflection of God's glory and the exact imprint of God's very being'. Psalm 45:6–7 (44:7–8 LXX) is quoted with reference to the Son, 'Your throne, o God, is forever and ever (...); therefore, God, your God, has anointed you with the oil of gladness beyond your companions' (Hebrews 1:8–9).

In the last quotation the Son himself is also addressed as 'God'. This corresponds to the prologue of the Gospel of John (1:1, possibly 1:18)[8] and to Thomas' confession 'my Lord and my God' (John 20:28). The use of the term 'God' for Jesus Christ occurs yet a few other times in the New Testament. Titus 2:13 speaks about 'the manifestation of the glory of our great God and Saviour, Jesus Christ'. 2 Peter 1:1 speaks with a similar formulation of 'the righteousness of our God and Saviour Jesus Christ'. In 1 John 5:20 it is said of Jesus Christ that 'he is the true God and eternal life'. Romans 9:5 reads, 'from them (the Israelites) according to the flesh, comes the Messiah, who is over all, God blessed forever'. Some exegetes presume, however, that in this text Paul expresses himself awkwardly and refers to God the Father.

These New Testament texts, which were for the most part written in the second half of the first century CE, demonstrate which high position was attributed, at that time, to Christ as the Son, who from the beginning had been with God the Father, through whom God created the world, and who could also be called God himself.

9.2 *The Father, the Son and the Holy Spirit in gnostic writings*

Before we continue with early Christian writings from the catholic tradition, it is useful to point out that the juxtaposition of the Father, the Son and the Spirit also occurs in gnostic texts. In Gospel of Thomas 44, the Father, the Son and the Holy Spirit are mentioned parallel to one another.[9] The Valentinian Gospel of Philip once speaks of 'the Father,

---

8   See p. 40, n.87.
9   See section 2.7. The lacunous Greek text of Gospel of Thomas 30 is often reconstructed in such a way that the translation reads, 'Wherever there are [three], they are without God and where there is one alone I say I am with him.' The Coptic text reads, 'Where there are three gods, they are gods; where there are two or one, I am with him' (Elliott, *The Apocryphal New Testament*, p. 139). However, April D. DeConick (2006),

the Son and the Holy Spirit' (11) and once of receiving the name of the Father, the Son and the Holy Spirit (67). To be sure, the author is very critical about the way in which catholic Christians interpret these names, but he does indicate that one still has to receive these names, at least in the gnostic sense. Since the Gospel of Philip probably consists of notes for baptismal instruction,[10] this entails that the Valentinian faction to which the author belonged most probably administered baptism in the name of the Father, the Son and the Holy Spirit. This is confirmed by Clement's *Excerpts* from the work of the Valentinian Theodotus, in which he quotes the baptismal commandment from Matthew 28:19, and refers to the sealing by the Father, the Son and the Holy Spirit.[11] Furthermore, in section 3.9 reference was made to a passage in the *Tripartite Tractate*, which spoke about baptism in the name of the Father, the Son and the Holy Spirit (127–128). To be sure, these texts do not presuppose a doctrine of God's trinity. In chapter 2 we saw that in the various gnostic works the relationship between God the Father and Jesus Christ is much more complex than in the New Testament writings. In spite of this, we can establish that not only 'catholic' Christianity spoke about the Father, the Son and the Holy Spirit.

9.3 *Some church fathers from the second century*

Subsequently, we will listen to some authors from 'catholic' Christianity.[12] At the beginning of the second century Ignatius, the bishop of Antioch, regularly calls Jesus Christ 'God'. Nowhere does he give the impression that he thus introduces something new.[13] He also emphasizes that Jesus was a real human being.[14] That Christ, at that time, was considered God, is confirmed by a letter of the Roman governor Pliny the Younger to the

---

'Corrections to the Critical Reading of the *Gospel of Thomas*'. *Vigiliae Christianae*, 60, 201–208 (201–204), argues that the Greek text must be read as follows, 'Where there are three, they are gods,' and that in the Semitic original this must have meant, 'Where there are three people, Elohim [God] is there.' Neither the Greek, nor the Coptic text therefore reacts to a developing or existing doctrine of God's trinity.

10 See Lubbertus K. van Os (forthcoming), *Baptism in the Bridal Chamber: The Gospel of Philip as a Valentinian Baptismal Instruction* (PhD thesis University of Groningen 2007). Leiden: Brill.

11 Clement of Alexandria, *Excerpts of Theodotus*, 76, 3; 80, 3 (SC 23).

12 For more authors and a more elaborate discussion of the second century, see, e.g., Kelly, *Early Christian Doctrines*, pp. 83–108.

13 Ignatius of Antioch, *Ephesians* heading; 1:1; 7:2; 15:3; 18:2; 19:3; *Trallians* 7:1; *Romans* heading; 3:3; 6:3; *Smyrnaeans* 1:1; *Polycarp* 8:3 (LCL 24).

14 Ignatius, *Ephesians* 7:2; 18:2; 19:3; 20:2; *Trallians* 9:1; *Smyrnaeans* 1:1-2 (LCL 24).

emperor Trajan. Former Christians in Bithynia (in the north-western part of Asia Minor) had told him that they sang 'a hymn to Christ as God' in their gatherings.[15]

From other 'catholic' authors of the second century, it is apparent that they were familiar with the view that Jesus is the LORD or the angel of the LORD, who was regularly mentioned in the Old Testament.[16] According to Justin Martyr (about 150 CE), the God who revealed himself to the patriarchs, Moses and the prophets is not the invisible God, the Father in heaven, but another God and Lord, who is also called Son, Wisdom, Angel, Logos and Christ.[17] According to Justin this Son has been begotten by the Father before all other creatures; he was with the Father when he said, 'Let us make humankind,' he was the Wisdom of whom Solomon spoke, he was the commander of the army of the LORD who appeared to Joshua,[18] he was the angel who led the people of Israel out of Egypt, etc.[19] Justin testifies of him that he became man in Jesus Christ.[20] Justin mentions God the Father, Jesus Christ and the Holy Spirit together with regard to baptism and the celebration of the Eucharist.[21]

Like Justin, Melito of Sardes also testifies in his *Homily on the Passion* (from 160–170 CE) that Jesus Christ is God's first-born who was generated before the morning star (Psalm 109:3 LXX). He brought about the creation of the world, he guided humanity from Adam to Abraham, and it was he who guided the patriarchs and delivered Israel from Egypt.[22] Melito also says that in the beginning God by his Logos created heaven

---

15 Pliny the Younger, *Letters* X, 96, 7 (LCL 59).

16 See for this Joseph Barbel (1941), *Christos Angelos: Die Anschauung von Christus als Bote und Engel in der gelehrten und volkstümlichen Literatur des christlichen Altertums: Zugleich ein Beitrag zur Geschichte des Ursprungs und der Fortdauer des Arianismus*. Bonn: F. J. Dölger-Institut, pp. 47–70.

17 Justin, *Dialogue with Trypho* 55–63, especially 56, 4 (*theos kai kurios heteros*); 58, 3; 60, 2; 61, 1; 63, 5; 126–128; *1 Apology* 62, 3–63, 17; *2 Apology* 13, 4 (ed. Goodspeed).

18 Justin, *Dialogue with Trypho* 62, 4; 63, 3; see Genesis 1:26; Proverbs 8:22-31; Joshua 5:13-15; Psalm 109:3 (LXX). Also *1 Apology* 23, 2; *2 Apology* 6, 3.

19 Justin, *Dialogue with Trypho* 75, 1–2, where the angel is even named Jesus (*Iêsous*) after Joshua (also *Iêsous*); 126–129.

20 Justin, *1 Apology* 5, 4; 23, 2; 32, 10; 66, 2; *2 Apology* 6, 5; 10, 1; *Dialogue with Trypho* 105, 1. See Christian Uhrig (2004), *'Und das Wort ist Fleisch geworden': Zur Rezeption von Joh 1,14a und zur Theologie der Fleischwerdung in der griechischen vornizänischen Patristik*. Münster: Aschendorff, pp. 72–100.

21 Justin, *1 Apology* 61, 3; 61, 10–13; 65, 3; also 13, 3. See Gerrit C. van de Kamp (1983), *Pneuma-christologie: een oud antwoord op een actuele vraag?* Amsterdam: Rodopi, pp. 71–73 for Justin's incidental identification of the Spirit and the Logos in *1 Apology* 33, 6.

22 Melito of Sardes, *Passion* 81–86; 104; also *Fragments* 15 (SC 123).

and earth, subsequently moulded man and placed him in paradise (47; cf. 104). Christ came from heaven to earth, suffered physically and killed death through his Spirit (66). He is buried as a human being, has risen from the dead as God; by nature he is God and man (8–9). Melito goes a long way in attributing qualities to the Son which usually belong to the Father: Christ encompasses everything (5), he is not only Son insofar as he has been begotten, but also Father insofar as he himself begets (9). The latter has been explained in the sense that Christ generates the believers unto new life in their baptism and regeneration, but this interpretation is not certain; Melito does not explain what he means by this.[23] He also says that Christ is sitting at the right hand of the Father, that he bears the Father and that he is borne by the Father (105). Melito makes a clear distinction between the Father and the Son when he says that it was the Father's will for the Son to suffer on the cross (76; cf. 103).

Theophilus of Antioch says in his work *To Autolycus* (dating from about 180 CE) that God had the Logos in himself and generated him together with his own Wisdom before the universe came into being. This Logos was therefore God's Son, the first-born of the entire creation. Through him and through his Wisdom God created the world, and it was his Logos who appeared to Adam in paradise.[24] Theophilus is the first Christian author who is known to write about God's trinity (*trias*); this he understood to be God, his Logos and his Wisdom (II, 15). In passing, he turns out to identify God's Wisdom with God's Spirit (I, 7). From his quotations, for example of John 1:1 and 3, and from his references to the gospels (III, 12) it becomes clear that with the Logos he means Jesus Christ, but in the one work that we have of him, he does not call him by name.

Irenaeus of Lyons (also from around 180 CE) belongs to the tradition which came to light with Justin, Melito and Theophilus. He confesses one God who is unknowable for men, but who has a Logos within himself through which he created the world; because God is Spirit, he arranged everything through his Spirit. The Logos is God's Son, Jesus Christ, who already appeared to the patriarchs and the prophets, and the Spirit is his Wisdom, through which the prophets have spoken.[25] Because Christ as the Logos is Creator, he can also be called Father. Thus Irenaeus quotes Deuteronomy 32:6 (LXX), which speaks about the LORD, with an eye to Christ, 'Did not he himself, your Father, acquire you and make you and

---

23 See Othmar Perler (1966), *Méliton de Sardes: Sur la Pâque et fragments* (SC 123). Paris: Cerf, p. 34, and van de Kamp, *Pneuma-christologie*, pp. 75–76.
24 Theophilus of Antioch, *To Autolycus* I,7; II,10; II,18; II,22 (ed. Grant).
25 Irenaeus, *Demonstration of the Apostolic Preaching* 5–6, with reference to Psalm 33:6 (32:6 LXX); 43–46; *Against Heresies* II, 30, 9; IV, 20, 1–12 (SC 406; 294; 100).

create you?'[26] It is therefore not surprising that according to Irenaeus, the Son is God as well because he is born of God.[27] He also calls the Son and the Spirit God's hands.[28] For the fact that God reveals himself in history as Father, Son and Spirit, Irenaeus uses the term *oikonomia*, which among other things can be translated as the 'plan of salvation' that God had in store for humanity.[29]

So we see that these witnesses from the second century believed in God the Father, who through his Logos, or his Logos and Wisdom, created and arranged the world. We can conclude that where these church fathers read about the LORD in the Old Testament, they as a rule interpreted this name as the pre-existent Logos who appeared to the patriarchs and the people of Israel and became a human being in Jesus Christ. They therefore made a distinction between God the heavenly Father and the LORD, through whom God had created the world and in whom he appeared to people and became a human being. The implication of this view is that the gnostic traditions of a high God, a lower, inferior Creator, and a Saviour who had elements of both gods within himself were rejected. Still, although these 'catholic' authors assumed God's unity, they distinguished in their own way between God the Father and the LORD as God's Logos who became a human being in Jesus Christ.

This conviction was concisely put in words in the 'rule of faith' which was essentially handed down orally, but which was sometimes also put in writing. At the beginning of the third century, Tertullian of Carthage formulates this rule of faith in these words:

that there is one only God, and that he is none other than the Creator of the world, who produced all things out of nothing through his own Word, first of all sent forth;
that this Word is called his Son, and, under the name of God, was seen in diverse manners by the patriarchs, heard at all times in the prophets, at last brought down by the Spirit and Power of the Father into the Virgin Mary, was made flesh in her womb, and, being born of her, went forth as Jesus Christ; thenceforth he preached the new law and the new promise of the kingdom of heaven, worked miracles; having

26 Irenaeus, *Against Heresies* IV, 10, 2; 31, 2 (SC 100).
27 Irenaeus, *Demonstration of the Apostolic Preaching* 47 (SC 406).
28 Irenaeus, *Against Heresies* IV praefatio 4; IV, 20, 1 (SC 100). See for God's hands Job 10:8 and Psalm 119:73.
29 For example Irenaeus, *Against Heresies* III, 1, 1 (SC 211); see for the many meanings of this term Jacques Fantino (1994), *La théologie d'Irénée: Lecture des Écritures et réponse à l'exégèse gnostique: Une approche trinitaire.* Paris: Cerf, pp. 79–126. The term appears in the sense of 'fulfilment' also in Ephesians 1:10; 3:9; as 'divine training (or plan)' in 1 Timothy 1:4. The word 'economy' is derived from it.

been crucified, he rose again the third day; then having ascended into the heavens, he sat at the right hand of the Father;
sent instead of himself the Power of the Holy Ghost to lead such as believe; will come with glory to take the saints to the enjoyment of everlasting life and of the heavenly promises, and to condemn the wicked to everlasting fire, after the resurrection of both these classes will have happened, together with the restoration of their flesh.[30]

Although there might be much to say about the strong lines at the end of this creed, we will now only examine the relationship between God the Father, the Son and the Holy Spirit. With the formulation, 'that there is only one God and that he is none other than the Creator of the world' and the mentioning of the activity of God's Word (the Logos) in Old Testament times, this rule of faith dissociates itself from other ideas of that time. Apart from numerous gnostics, the followers of Marcion also had little appreciation for God the Creator, the creation of the world and the Old Testament. That is why they distinguished between the unknowable high God from whom Jesus originated, and the lower, unreliable Creator. This distinction is implicitly rejected by this rule of faith.

We see that this creed is built up according to the threefold division of God the Father, the Son and the Holy Spirit, and that most words deal with the Son, Jesus Christ. On the one hand, the plurality in the one God goes back, as we have seen, to traditions which we encountered in the Old Testament, in Philo, in other early Jewish authors and in the New Testament. On the other hand, philosophers from the second century CE, who stood in the tradition of Plato and were not Christians, had ideas which resembled this to a certain degree. Alcinous and Numenius wrote about a first God and a deity subordinate to him who, instigated by the ideas of the first God, formed the world.[31] Numenius called the Creator (*dêmiourgos*) the second God. For him the world was the third God.[32] Moreover, Stoic philosophy of that time knew the Logos as a divine authority who guaranteed the order in the world.[33] A Christian, therefore, who in the second century professed to believe in one God, who

30 Tertullian of Carthage, *Prescription against Heretics* 13 (CCSL 1; translation ANF 3). See also Irenaeus, *Demonstration of the Apostolic Preaching* 6 (SC 406); *Against Heresies* I, 10, 1 (SC 264).
31 Alcinous, *Didaskalikos* 9–10; 27 (ed. Whittaker and Louis). See Roukema, *Gnosis and Faith in Early Christianity*, pp. 88–91.
32 Numenius of Apameia, *Fragments* 11–22 (ed. des Places).
33 See, e.g., Hermann Kleinknecht (1969), 'The Logos in the Greek and Hellenistic World', in Gerhard Kittel and Geoffrey W. Bromiley, eds, *Theological Dictionary of the New Testament* 4. Grand Rapids MI: Eerdmans, pp. 77–91; Tobin, 'Logos', pp. 348–349 .

through the Logos who came forth from God and was subordinate to God had created the world seemed to concur with respectable philosophical schools of that time. Thus this part of the Christian faith, being based on older Jewish and Christian traditions could at the same time be presented as philosophically justifiable.[34]

This second-century theology, however, contained some ambiguities. If Christians confessed that there was one God, but in fact distinguished between God the Father and the LORD, who was called his Logos and Son and God as well, did they not then actually believe in two gods? Did not this distinction remind one of the gnostic and Marcionite distinction between a high and a lower god? And how did this Logos or Son come forth from the Father? Could not the relationship between God the Father and the LORD as his Logos and Son also be seen in another way? These seem to be speculative questions, far removed from Jesus of Nazareth. In catholic Christianity of the time, however, one did not believe so much in Jesus as the inspiring rabbi of Nazareth but rather that in him God himself had visited mankind. Catholic Christians wanted to account for this conviction in terms that were current at the time. Whoever finds this second-century theology unnecessarily speculative must realize that it is a wonder of simplicity in comparison with the complex and very divergent gnostic systems of the same time. We will see, however, that in the Christianity of the time some attempts were made to express more simply belief in Jesus Christ as God's manifestation on earth.

9.4 *Adoptianism*

The first attempt to be mentioned here was put forward around 190 CE by Theodotus, a leather merchant from Byzantium. In fact, none of his writings nor those of his pupils have been preserved. For our knowledge of his ideas we must rely on the critical reproduction given by Hippolytus of Rome (early third century) and Eusebius of Caesarea (early fourth century). In Rome, Theodotus declared that he considered Jesus a mere man and not God. He believed that Jesus was born of the Virgin Mary by

---

34 Another question is whether the ideas of early Jewish authors like Philo and the author of the Gospel of John, with regard to the Logos, were also influenced by Platonic and Stoic philosophy. In Philo, this influence is very clear, although he draws from Jewish traditions in the first place. For the Gospel of John, this connection is found by George H. van Kooten (2005), 'The "True Light which Enlightens Everyone" (*John* 1:9): John, *Genesis*, the Platonic Notion of the "True, Noetic Light," and the Allegory of the Cave in Plato's *Republic*', in George H. van Kooten, ed., *The Creation of Heaven and Earth: Re-interpretations of Genesis 1 in the Context of Judaism, Ancient Philosophy, Christianity, and Modern Physics*. Leiden: Brill, pp. 149–194.

God's will, that he lived as a very devout man, and that the Spirit who at
his baptism in the river Jordan had descended upon him was the Christ.
Thanks to the Spirit, i.e. Christ, Jesus received powers that he did not
have before his baptism. Victor, bishop in Rome, thought that this view
did not do justice to Christ as God and therefore he expelled Theodotus
from the church. It goes without saying that the faction gathered around
Theodotus by then did not, because of this, simply disappear. His pupils
thought that their view of Jesus had good credentials since it went back
to an old tradition. According to Eusebius they said, however, that with
that purpose they 'had corrected' the Scriptures. A part of this faction,
for that matter, acknowledged that Jesus Christ became God after his
resurrection.[35]

Because Theodotus and his disciples believed that the man Jesus
became Christ at his baptism and that God the Father then adopted him
as his Son, this faction is called 'adoptianism'. According to Novatian of
Rome (around 240 CE), its adherents turned against the impression given
by the catholic church that there were two gods, the Father and the Son,
and wanted to do justice to God's unity.[36] Because at the time the term
monarchia was used for God's 'unity', and adoptianists assumed that
thanks to the Spirit God's power (*dunamis*) worked in Jesus, their faction
is also called 'dynamic monarchianism'.

The assertion of Theodotus' pupils that their view went back to an old
tradition is correct. In chapter 6 we saw that there were Jewish Christians
who believed that Jesus owed his special gift to the Spirit who had
descended upon him at his baptism. Moreover, there are some texts in the
New Testament which could be explained in an adoptianistic sense.[37] For
lack of written sources, however, it is difficult to assess how widespread
these ideas were in the Christianity of the second century.[38] That they
continued to exist is apparent from Paul of Samosata. He originated
from northern Syria and became bishop of the church in Antioch in 261

---

35 Thus Hippolytus of Rome, *Refutation of all Heresies* VII, 35 (PTS 25); Eusebius,
    Church History V, 28 (LCL 153); cf. also Epiphanius of Salamis, *Panarion* 54 (NHMS
    36). About Jesus' baptism in the river Jordan, see sections 2.2, 2.3 and 2.4, in particular
    pp. 37–38 about Luke 3:22.

36 Novatian of Rome, *Trinity* 30, 175 (ed. Weyer).

37 Apart from Luke 3:22, also Acts 2:36; 13:33; Romans 1:3-4. From this one might
    conclude that Jesus was Lord, Christ and Son of God only after his resurrection, See
    section 2.1 (pp. 21–22) for Romans 1:3-4. In Acts 2:36 and 13:33 is not written,
    however, that Jesus was not Lord, Christ and Son of God before his death and
    resurrection; that he was so indeed is confirmed in his resurrection. See Rowe, *Early
    Narrative Christology*, pp. 193–196.

38 Kelly, *Early Christian Doctrines*, p. 117, believes that the adoptianists were an isolated
    and unrepresentative movement in gentile Christianity.

CE. He turned out, however, to have adoptianistic ideas. According to him, Jesus Christ was a mere man who came 'from below' and not from heaven.[39] Although it was exceptional that the Logos came to live in him, Paul did not want to call the Logos, i.e. God's Son, a separate figure or manifestation of God; that would, after all, be in conflict with God's unity. He considered the Spirit as the Spirit in the Logos, and not as a separate figure either. Considering the later developments, it is remarkable that Paul of Samosata said that the Logos was 'of the same substance' as God; the Greek term for this was *homo-ousios*. Thus Paul thought that the man Jesus was full of God in a special way. Because of his local popularity and his good contacts with the authorities, it was quite difficult for the church to remove him from his episcopal see. After a long struggle, a local synod definitely dismissed him as bishop in 272 CE.[40]

The adoptianistic or dynamic-monarchianistic view on Jesus most probably continued to have adherents in those centuries. In catholic Christianity, however, it presumably remained marginal. In general, Christians believed in Jesus Christ as God without any difficulty. The philosopher Celsus confirms this (about 170 CE). He remarks that it did not occur to the Christians that their extravagant devotion to Jesus was inconsistent with monotheism.[41] For philosophically educated Christians and for those who kept in touch with Jews or Jewish Christians, belief in 'two gods' could, however, become a problem. For this, the adoptianists wanted to offer a solution.

9.5 Modalism

Another attempt from that time to present the relationship between God the Father and Jesus Christ more simply than was customary in the church, stems from Noetus of Smyrna. Hippolytus reports that, according to Noetus, the Father and the Son are one and the same God. In this way Noetus strictly held on to God's unity, i.e. *monarchia*. His emphasis on God's unity entailed that in his view God the Father was born of the Virgin Mary and had lived as a human being. He made himself known as God's Son, but to those who could grasp it, he had revealed that he actually was the Father. Thus, the Father died on the cross and had raised himself on the third day.[42]

---

39 Eusebius, *Church History* VII, 27, 2; 30, 11 (LCL 265).
40 Thus Epiphanius, *Panarion* 65, 1, 5–8 (NHMS 36). Also Kelly, *Early Christian Doctrines*, pp. 117–119; 140.
41 In Origen, *Against Celsus* VIII, 12 (SC 150).
42 Hippolytus of Rome, *Refutation of all Heresies* IX, 7, 1; 10, 9–12; X, 27, 1–2 (PTS 25). Also Pseudo-Hippolytus, *Against Noetus* 1–2 (ed. Schwartz); Epiphanius, *Panarion* 57

We see that Noetus, like the adoptianists, offered an alternative for the idea that the Father and the Son both are God, and therefore are two gods. He also dissociated himself from the Valentinian gnostics who assumed even more divine powers. Noetus acknowledged that Jesus had made himself known as the LORD. However, he did not distinguish between the LORD as God's Logos and God the Father, but he identified the LORD with God the Father. Noetus was expelled from the church of Smyrna because of his views,[43] but they were spread in Rome by one of his pupils, when Zephyrinus was bishop there (199–217 CE). Influenced by his deacon Callistus – an intriguer, according to Hippolytus – Zephyrinus was not opposed to these views. After Zephyrinus died, he was succeeded by Callistus. In his capacity of bishop of Rome, he initially turned against the idea that there were 'two gods'. In his time a certain Sabellius appeared in Rome. He harboured the same ideas as Noetus, but seems to have formulated them more subtly. He assumed one God, the Father, who could also manifest himself as Son and as Spirit. Callistus initially went along with Sabellius, but later judged that his ideas were not acceptable. He then expelled him from the church.[44]

Around 213 CE, Tertullian of Carthage wrote a book in Latin against the ideas of a certain Praxeas. Most likely this is a nickname which means something like 'busybody'. He probably referred to Noetus, or to one of his pupils, or perhaps even to Callistus. The ideas which Tertullian disputes correspond with the views that we just described: that there is one God, the Creator of the world, who was born of the Virgin Mary and suffered on the cross. This means that the Father and the Son would be one and the same figure.[45] It is difficult to imagine, however, that a father is his own son. In a discussion Praxeas therefore admitted that the Son was the man Jesus, and that the Father was identical with Christ and the

---

(NHMS 36). Although the document *Against Noetus* has been attributed to Hippolytus, it in fact dates from the fourth century, according to Josef Frickel (1993), 'Hippolyts Schrift Contra Noetum: ein Pseudo-Hippolyt', in Hanns Christoph Brennecke, Ernst Ludwig Grasmück and Christoph Markschies, eds, *Logos: Festschrift für Luise Abramowski zum 8. Juli 1993*. Berlin, New York: De Gruyter, pp. 87–123. For Noetus see Reinhard M. Hübner (1993), 'Der antivalentinianische Charakter der Theologie des Noët von Smyrna', in *Logos*, pp. 57–86; also in Hübner (1999), *Der Paradox Eine: Antignostischer Monarchianismus im zweiten Jahrhundert*. Leiden: Brill, pp. 95–129.

43 Pseudo-Hippolytus, *Against Noetus* 1 (ed. Schwartz).
44 Hippolytus, *Refutation of all Heresies* IX, 11; IX, 12, 14–19 (PTS 25); cf. Epiphanius of Salamis, *Pararion* 62 (NHMS 36). See for Sabellius: Wolfgang A. Bienert (1993), 'Sabellius und Sabellianismus als historisches Problem', in Brennecke, Grasmück and Markschies, eds, *Logos*, pp. 124–139.
45 Tertullian, *Against Praxeas* 1, 1; 5, 1; cf. 10, 1; 10, 7 (CCSL 2).

Spirit joining itself to Jesus. The Father would then have suffered with the Son on the cross.[46] If Praxeas indeed meant it this way, then his view would appear to be closely related to adoptianism.

Because it is said that in the view of Noetus and Sabellius the one God has revealed himself in two or three *modi* (modes of existence), this movement is called 'modalism'. Because the modalists strongly held on to God's unity, i.e. *monarchia*, one also speaks of 'modalistic monarchianism'.[47] The adherents of this view wanted to do justice to God's unity which is proclaimed in the Old Testament. It proves difficult, however, to imagine that God the Father is born of a woman as his own Son and dies on a cross. With a term deriving from Tertullian's apology *Against Praxeas*, one also speaks disapprovingly of 'patripassianism', which means that the Father has suffered.[48] The older view that not God the Father but his Son or Logos became man and suffered had a solution to this problem. Because the Logos, according to an old tradition, was identified with the LORD, this led to the problem of belief in 'two gods', which did not respect God's unity.

While the adoptianists could rightfully appeal to an old tradition, this cannot be said of the modalists. Their view is more of an attempt at a theological answer to the problem that was posed by belief in 'two gods'. The modalistic view did not have general approval from the church of the time, but it has always, here and there, found adherents.[49]

9.6 *Tertullian of Carthage*

For Tertullian it was not difficult to refute the modalistic view on scriptural grounds. His views stand in the Logos tradition of the second century.[50] He states that God was alone before the creation of the world, because he was everything himself, but that he did have his *ratio*, i.e. Logos or Word. Tertullian agrees that in the Scriptures the Logos is also called Wisdom. In his view, Wisdom speaks there as a *secunda persona*, a 'second figure', created by the LORD before everything else (Proverbs

46 *Against Praxeas* 27, 1–4; 29, 5.
47 Cf. *Against Praxeas* 10, 1: *monarchiani*. See Kelly, *Early Christian Doctrines*, pp. 119–123.
48 Cf. *Against Praxeas* 2, 1.
49 See, e.g., Kelly, *Early Christian Doctrines*, pp. 133–136 about modalists in Libya, in the mid third century.
50 See *Against Praxeas* 16 for the appearance of the Son, i.e. the Logos, in the Old Testament. More elaborate about Tertullian's doctrine of trinity and christology is Osborn, *Tertullian: First Theologian of the West*, pp. 116–143.

8:22–25). When God said, 'let there be light' (Genesis 1:3), this implied the birth of the Word that came forth from God. In this way this Word was the first-born of all creation (Colossians 1:15), to whom God as Father said, 'You are my son; today I have begotten you' (Psalm 2:7). Because in Psalm 33:6 God's Word and his Spirit are named parallel to one another, Tertullian concludes that the Spirit was present at the creation in the Word. Furthermore, Tertullian speaks of the Son as a *substantia* (a separate being) who has been formed by the Spirit and by Wisdom. He also calls the Son, like Wisdom, a *persona*, a separate figure.[51]

It seems as if for Tertullian Wisdom and the Word were identical at the very beginning, but he also distinguishes them. Rather inconsistently, he then conceives Wisdom as God's Spirit. He says that the Spirit came forth from the Father through the Son, and calls the Spirit a third figure besides God and the Son. For the manifestation of God as Father, Son and Spirit, he appeals to the inspiration of the Spirit who guides into the truth (John 16:13) and to the traditional rule of faith (see section 9.3). He uses Irenaeus' term *oikonomia* (plan of salvation), by which he means that God has thus, in three figures, revealed himself in the creation and the salvation of the world. He is the first to use the Latin term *trinitas* to indicate God's trinity. As opposed to the modalistic monarchians, he states that this distinction of three figures in God is not in conflict with God's *monarchia*, i.e. unity. The three figures, according to Tertullian, are distinguished indeed, but not separated.[52]

Tertullian has no problem acknowledging that the Son is subordinate to the Father. Jesus, after all, acknowledged that he did not know when the end of the world would come, which was something only the Father knew (Mark 13:32). He also said, 'the Father is greater than I' (John 14:28). Tertullian believes that the Spirit is third in order.[53] Despite the subordination of the Son to the Father he can be regarded equally well as Creator, according to Tertullian. Thus it is the Son who said, 'I am the first, and until the things that are coming, I am' (Isaiah 41:4 LXX). God has, after all, created the world through his Word, i.e. his Son.[54]

Was Jesus after all, according to Tertullian, no other than God on earth? He does not consider it this simple. The Word of the Father 'became flesh' (John 1:14), which means that in Jesus it 'clothed itself in flesh'. He

---

51 *Against Praxeas* 5, 2–7, 9. Tertullian saw no problem in the LORD creating Wisdom in Proverbs 8:22, whereas the LORD in other passages is often considered the Son who manifests himself on earth; in this text however, it does not concern an appearance of the LORD to people.
52 *Against Praxeas* 2, 1–4; 3, 1; 4, 1; 8, 7–9, 1; 11, 9–10. See Kelly, *Early Christian Doctrines*, pp. 110–115.
53 *Against Praxeas* 9, 2–3; 26, 9; cf. 14, 10.
54 *Against Praxeas* 19, 5–6.

states that as a human being, Jesus experienced his feelings of hunger, thirst and sorrow, just as he also died a human being. He concludes that Jesus is God and man, and not something between. As God he partook of God's substance, as human being he partook of human substance. Thus he says, 'We see his double status, not mixed but united in one person, God and the man Jesus (...),' and so the property of each substance is preserved.[55] About the name Christ he argues that this is not a separate figure who is to be identified with the Father. 'Christ' means after all 'Anointed', and indicates Jesus' anointment by the Father. Therefore, in the Scriptures Christ and Jesus are the same person.[56]

We see that Tertullian introduced some new terms for the relationship between God the Father and Jesus the Son. He calls the pre-existent Son and Wisdom (or Spirit) each a separate *persona* (figure) next to the Father. He speaks of a divine and a human *substantia* in Jesus, who nevertheless was one *persona*. As Theophilus of Antioch spoke in Greek of God's *trias*, so in Latin Tertullian calls the Father, the Son and the Spirit a *trinitas*.

9.7 Origen of Alexandria

Almost two decades later, Origen of Alexandria examines more closely a number of questions to which, in his judgement, the 'apostolic preaching' – another designation of the rule of faith – did not give clear answers.[57] His systematic work about the Christian faith is entitled *Peri archôn* ('On First Principles'). In addition to a large number of Greek fragments, it has been preserved in a Latin translation of Rufinus of Aquileia (of 398 CE), who sometimes presented Origen's speculative thoughts in a more orthodox way. In spite of this, Origen's systematic observations are relatively easy to recognize. Apart from this work, we will almost exclusively refer to writings that have been passed down in Greek. Origen begins his work *On First Principles* with a discourse on God the Father, the Son and the Holy Spirit (I, 1–3). He explains that God is one or, as he says, a unit (*monas*; I, 1, 6). In the tradition of Justin, Irenaeus and Tertullian, Origen relates the passage in Proverbs 8:22–25 about Wisdom, created before all other things, to Christ. That is why Christ is God's only Son and the first-born of all creation (Colossians 1:15). Origen considers it to be out

---

55 *Against Praxeas* 27, 6–11 (quote in 27, 11). Also *The Flesh of Christ* 18, 6–7 (SC 216).

56 *Against Praxeas* 28,1–13.

57 Origen, *First Principles* I *preface*; it dates from 229–230 CE (TF 24). See for this work Lothar Lies (1992), *Origenes' 'Peri Archon': Eine undogmatische Dogmatik.* Darmstadt: Wissenschaftliche Buchgesellschaft; furthermore about Origen, Kelly, *Early Christian Doctrines*, pp. 128–132; 154–158.

of the question that in the beginning God was ever without Wisdom. So, in his view, Wisdom was not created at the beginning of time, as if before that beginning there was a time when Wisdom did not yet exist. From this he concludes that God has always been the Father of his only Son. He therefore calls the begetting (or, generation) of the Son by the Father 'eternal'.[58] According to a fragment attributed to Origen's *Commentary on the letter to the Hebrews*, he thus refutes those who dared to say that there was a time when the Son was not.[59]

So Origen is the first explicitly to declare that the generation of the Son did not occur at the beginning of time, but takes place from eternity. This implies that the relationship of the Father to the Son is eternal and did not start at a certain moment in time. This manner of reasoning stems from philosophy based on Plato and Aristotle. In the same way, Alcinous (second century) considered it unthinkable that the world once did not exist. He therefore said that the world was always in a process of becoming (or, begetting, generation) from God. Alcinous also considered that the soul of the world was always there, which is why God does not create this soul, but only arranges it.[60] In this view something that has been created is perishable. Because Christ as Saviour could not be perishable, his generation had to occur from eternity, according to Origen.

Elsewhere, Origen calls the Son and Logos 'the second God'.[61] In sections 8.2 and 9.3, we saw that this term was also used by Philo and was in use in the Platonism of the time. Origen does not hesitate to speak about 'two gods' who are yet 'one God'.[62] He also speaks of the 'three hypostases', the Father, the Son and the Holy Spirit;[63] *hupostasis* is the Greek counterpart of the Latin *substantia* and here indicates something

---

58 *First Principles* I, 2, 1–4; also I, 2, 9; IV, 4, 1 (TF 24); *Homilies on Jeremiah* 9, 4 (SC 232); *Commentary on Hebrews* in Pamphilus, *Apology for Origen* 50 (SC 464).

59 J. A. Cramer (1844), *Catenae Graecorum Patrum in Novum Testamentum* VII. Oxonii: Typographeo Academico, pp. 361–362; translation in Hans Urs von Balthasar (2001), *Origen: Spirit and Fire: A Thematic Anthology of his Writings* (translated from German by Robert J. Daly), Edinburgh: T&T Clark, pp. 77–78. In a footnote Daly adds that this fragment probably originates from the Greek text of *First Principles* IV, 1, 1, but he probably means IV, 4, 1. Also in the fragment of Origen's *Commentary on Hebrews* by Pamphilus (see the previous note) he says that there never was a time in which the Son was not.

60 Alcinous, *Didaskalikos* 14 (ed. Whittaker and Louis). *Kosmos* (world) actually means 'arrangement'. Cf. Plato, *Timaeus* 27c–28b.

61 *Against Celsus* V, 39 (SC 147); *Commentary on John* VI, 202 (SC 157).

62 *Dialogue with Heracleides* 2 (SC 67). About God's unity also *First Principles* I, 1, 6 (TF 24).

63 *Commentary on John* II, 75 (SC 120).

that really and separately exists.[64] So, as opposed to the modalists, Origen emphatically distinguishes the various figures in God. He states that the Father ranks above the Son, and the Son above the Spirit.[65] From this hierarchy, Origen deduces in his book *On Prayer* that it is actually not appropriate to pray to Christ, since prayer ought to be addressed only to God the Father. Prayer is, however, addressed to God by mediation of Christ.[66] However, as opposed to the criticism of the philosopher Celsus that the Christians displayed an extravagant devotion to Jesus, Origen points to his pre-existence. He mentions the two hypostases of the Father and the Son, but also their unity. Because of their unity, Origen then considers it permissible nevertheless to worship the Father and the Son.[67] Elsewhere, he even speaks of God's *trias* to whom worship is due.[68]

Origen distinguishes between a divine and a human nature (*phusis*) in Jesus Christ,[69] although he emphasizes their mutual unity at the same time.[70] Since he is strongly influenced by Platonism, he appears, however, to have difficulty with the statement in John 1:14 that 'the Logos became flesh'. In his fundamental work *On First Principles*, he does not quote these words even once.[71] He does acknowledge, however, that Jesus Christ was a real man ('flesh'), but believes Jesus' soul to be incarnated from pre-existence into a human body. But because Origen assumes that all human souls are pre-existent before they join an earthly body, the incarnation of Christ's soul is in itself nothing special. He declares therefore that this soul in its pre-existence was the only one to hold on to God, while all other souls fell away from God. For that reason, the soul of Christ was not subject to the fall from heaven which all other souls experienced before

64 In Hebrews 1:3 the Son is called the imprint of God's *hupostasis* ('God's very being', NRSV). Hebrews 11:1 talks of faith as the assurance (*hupostasis*) of things hoped for (NRSV). See for this term Helmut Köster (1972), '*hupostasis*', in Gerhard Friedrich and Geoffrey W. Bromiley, eds, *Theological Dictionary on the New Testament* 8. Grand Rapids MI: Eerdmans, pp. 572–589, in particular 575–577; 583.
65 *Commentary on John* II, 12–18; II, 75–76; X, 246–247 (SC 120; 157).
66 *Prayer* 15, 1 – 16, 1 (GCS 3); *Against Celsus* VIII, 13 (SC 150).
67 *Against Celsus* VIII, 12–13. In his sermons Origen regularly addressed a short prayer to Christ; see P. S. A. Lefeber (1997), *Keuze en verlangen: Een onderzoek naar zin en functie van het gebed in Origenes' preken en zijn tractaat Over het Gebed*. Gorinchem: Narratio.
68 *Commentary on John* VI, 166 (SC 157). In Greek texts God's *trias* also appears in *Commentary on John* X, 270 (SC 157) and *Commentary on Matthew* XV, 31 (GCS 40).
69 *Against Celsus* III, 28 (SC 136); *Commentary on John* X, 24; XIX, 6; XXXII, 192 (SC 157; 290; 385).
70 *Commentary on John* I, 195–196 (SC 120); *Against Celsus* II, 9; III, 41; VI, 47 (SC 132; 136; 147).
71 A quote from John 1:14a appears once in Rufinus' Latin translation of *First Principles* IV, 2, 7, but it is absent in the corresponding Greek text.

their earthly life. According to Origen, the divine Logos subsequently united himself with the 'incarnate' human soul of Christ. In this sense only, he can acknowledge that the Logos 'became flesh'.[72] He repeatedly writes that Christ with his human soul and body endured the fear of death, suffered pain and died.[73] But because God cannot die, he considers it impossible for God's Logos to die on the cross. He supposes that after Christ's death, his soul and body were transformed unto God.[74]

Origen's most important contribution to the development of a view of God's trinity is that he spoke of God's 'eternal generation' of the Son. This idea sounds very speculative and theoretical in our time, but was at that time associated with the respected philosophy of the schools of Plato and Aristotle. We see that Origen, more than his predecessors, is inclined to experimental and speculative ideas in order to speak sensibly about God in his own time. His view that Jesus Christ was composed of a human soul, a human body and the divine Logos is reminiscent of some Valentinian views.[75] In comparison with the gnostic speculations of the time, his theology is, however, carefully formulated and rather well arranged. It goes without saying that there were also Christians who knew little of philosophy or did not want to use it in expressing the Christian faith. They showed little appreciation of Origen's theology. For this and other reasons a synod in Alexandria expelled him from the local church in 231–232 CE.[76] He was, however, welcomed by the bishops of Palestine, who had earlier ordained him priest. Thus he could continue his work as a scholar and teacher in Caesarea.

9.8 *Arius*

The appearance of Paul of Samosata in Antioch (section 9.4) suggests that during the entire third century there was a Christian minority that had adoptianistic views of Jesus. The same applies for Christians who thought modalistically about God and Jesus Christ. Thus Dionysius, bishop of Alexandria, had to deal with bishops in Libya who supported

---

72 *First Principles* II, 6, 3–7; IV, 4, 4 (TF 24). See Uhrig, '*Und das Wort ist Fleisch geworden*', pp. 345–466. In other works, however, Origen does quote John 1:14a without his cautious interpretation. See for example *Against Celsus* VI, 9; VI, 68 (SC 147). In *Against Celsus* IV, 15 (SC 136) he says, however, that the Logos *as it were* (*hoionei*) becomes flesh.
73 *First Principles* II, 8, 4 (TF 24); IV, 4, 4; *Against Celsus* II, 23 (SC 132).
74 *Commentary on John* XX, 85–86 (SC 290); *Against Celsus* III, 41 (SC 136).
75 See, e.g., section 2.10 about Theodotus.
76 See Joseph A. Fischer (1979), 'Die alexandrinischen Synoden gegen Origenes'. *Ostkirchliche Studien*, 28, 3–16.

the ideas of Sabellius during the sixth decade of the third century.[77] From the decades after Origen (he died about 254 CE), however, no important new theological developments are known in this field. At the beginning of the fourth century, during the reign of the emperor Diocletian, the church suffered terribly under persecutions. From that time little is known of discussions about the relationship between Jesus Christ and God the Father.[78] In 311 CE the emperor Galerius decided, however, to end the persecutions and to tolerate Christianity. Thus it obtained the status of a 'permitted religion'. An important reversal subsequently took place in 313 CE. Then Constantine, one of the four emperors of that time, became a Christian, although for the time being he was not baptized. Since then, the church in the Roman Empire received the freedom to develop and had room for affairs other than surviving and dealing with persecutions.

Great tumult arose in about 320 CE, when Arius, originating from Antioch and a priest in Alexandria, stated his view of Christ.[79] Certainly, we are only informed about this by the writings of his opponents, but they quote his views and texts sufficiently to give a good idea of them. Arius' principal point was, it seems, protest against an existing theology of his time. He indicates that he believes in one God who alone is begotten, eternal and without beginning. He disputes, however, that the Logos, who became flesh in Jesus Christ, was God's Son from eternity. He points to Proverbs 8:22, which states that in the beginning the Lord created his Wisdom. As was usual at the time, Arius identifies Wisdom with God's Logos. He argues that if the Logos was *created* by God in the beginning, he could not have been begotten by God from eternity, as Origen had proposed. Arius concludes that the Logos, i.e. the Son, was a creature and therefore not truly God like the Father. This means that God was initially alone. One of Arius' mottos was, 'there once was when he (the Son) was not'. That the Son is the first and highest of all God's creatures and is not a part of God himself Arius also deduces from Colossians 1:15, where Christ is called 'the first-born of all creation'. He thinks that the Logos cannot see and know God the Father perfectly and accurately, because in essence he is different from God himself. Arius acknowledges that the Son can indeed be called 'God', but in his view he is God in name only, because he participates in the Logos and Wisdom who belong to God's own substance. Arius distinguishes the Logos and Wisdom who

---

77 Thus Athanasius, *Defence of Dionysius* 5, 1; cf. *Defence of the Nicene Council* 26, 1 (AW II, 1). See Kelly, *Early Christian Doctrines*, pp. 133–136.

78 Lucian of Antioch, however, who died a martyr in 312 CE, was called a disciple of Paul of Samosata and influenced Arius. See Kelly, *Early Christian Doctrines*, p. 230.

79 See Rowan Williams (2001), *Arius: Heresy and Tradition* (2nd edn). London: Darton, Longman and Todd, pp. 48–66.

belong to God's own substance from the Logos and Wisdom who have
been *created* by God and became flesh in Christ. Like Origen, Arius does
speak of the three 'hypostases' (substances) of Father, Son and Spirit.
He emphasizes, however, not their unity but their mutual difference in
substance.[80]

With his theology, Arius wanted to do justice to God's unity and perfect
transcendence, which surpasses everything. He therefore considered the
Son, being the first of the creatures, subordinate to God the Father. Arius'
theology is related to that of the adoptianists, but differs from it in that
he does not hold that Jesus is adopted as God's Son at his baptism, but
in eternity before the creation of the world. Apart from Arius' polemic,
many catholic Christians of the second and third centuries probably
could have agreed with him. His theology, after all, clearly has some
archaic traits. Thus Tertullian could write in passing, in a polemic against
a philosophically reasoning Christian, '(God) could not be Father before
the Son, nor a Judge before there was sin. There was, however, a time
when there was neither sin nor the Son to make God Judge and Father.'[81]
Arius' motto, 'there once was when he (the Son) was not', appears here
inconspicuously. As we saw, Origen rejected this idea.

If one accepts that the passage about Wisdom in Proverbs 8:22–25
deals with the Logos, God's pre-existent Son, there is little to argue
against Arius' conclusion that the Son is a creature. This means that,
in his view, the Son is God's first creature in pre-existence, when God
had not yet created the material world. As we have seen in Origen, this
reasoning is derived from contemporaneous philosophy and not from the
Scriptures.[82] On the one hand Arius appealed to the Scriptures, but on the
other hand he used – like his opponents did – the philosophical categories
of the time. Because in those terms he emphatically and explicitly rejected
the idea that the Son was with the Father from eternity, he nevertheless
propagated something new. Arius' attitude, at least, challenged the church
of his time to a reaction.

This reaction came quickly from his bishop Alexander. About 321 CE
he organized a synod in Alexandria which condemned the ideas of Arius

---

80 Thus Athanasius of Alexandria, *Discourses against the Arians* I, 5–6; I, 9; II, 37; *To Bishops of Egypt* 12 (AW I, 1); *The Synods of Ariminum and Seleucia* 15–16 (AW II, 1); Epiphanius, *Panarion* 69, 6–8 (NHMS 36); Theodoret of Cyrus, *Church History* I, 5, 3 (SC 501).
81 *Against Hermogenes* 3, 3–4. See H. G. Thümmel (1999), 'ΗΝ ΠΟΤΕ ΟΤΕ ΟΥΚ ΗΝ', in W. A. Bienert and U. Kühneweg, eds, *Origeniana Septima: Origenes in den Auseinandersetzungen des 4. Jahrhunderts*. Leuven: Peeters, pp. 109–117.
82 See also Williams, *Arius*, pp. 181–229; G. C. Stead (1999), 'Philosophy in Origen and Arius', in Bienert and Kühneweg, eds, *Origeniana Septima*, pp. 101–108.

and his followers.[83] As often happens after decisions made at synods, this did not settle the case. It appeared that Arius' argument aroused much recognition. This means that many believers and their leaders did not understand or in any case did not accept the philosophical reasoning on the eternal generation of the Son. In the following section we will further examine the reaction of the Nicene Council in 325 CE, but it is worth mentioning here that afterwards many Christians remained Arians. For them, Christ was subordinate to the Father. They shared Arius' view that in the beginning, before the creation of the world, but not from eternity, Christ became God's Son. Several Germanic tribes, for instance, were initially christianized by Arians.[84]

9.9 The Nicene Council

The controversy about Arius' beliefs brought about much turmoil in the church and therefore in the Roman Empire as well. Eusebius of Caesarea remarks that a small spark had ignited a large fire.[85] Because the emperor Constantine considered it his task to further unity in the church, he besought Arius and bishop Alexander in a letter to become reconciled with each other – at least, as Eusebius reports. Constantine clearly made known that he, in fact, found the question unimportant and not worthy of so much controversy. He therefore did not regard Arius' beliefs as heresy, and thought that Christians could disagree on details.[86] Because this letter did not provide the outcome he hoped for, he convened a broad ('ecumenical') synod in 325 CE at Nicaea in Bithynia. According to Eusebius, more than 250 bishops and numerous priests, deacons and others answered his call.[87] According to another tradition, there were 318 bishops present. This synod endorsed the following creed:

> We believe in one God the Father all powerful,
> maker of all things both seen and unseen.
> And in one Lord Jesus Christ, the Son of God,
> the only-begotten from the Father,
> that is from the substance of the Father,

83 Theodoret of Cyrus, *Church History* I, 4, 6; cf. I, 3, 3 (SC 501); Williams, *Arius*, 56.
84 See for example Alain Chauvot (2001), 'Les migrations des Barbares et leur conversion au christianisme', in Jean-Marie Mayeur et al., eds, *Histoire du Christianisme: Des origines à nos jours* II. [Paris]: Desclée, pp. 861–879.
85 Eusebius of Caesarea, *Life of Constantine* II, 61, 4 (GCS Neue Folge 21).
86 *Life of Constantine* II, 62–73.
87 *Life of Constantine* III, 4–14. 'Ecumenical' here means something like 'worldwide'.

> God from God,
> light from light,
> true God from true God,
> begotten not made,
> consubstantial with the Father,
> through whom all things came to be,
> both those in heaven and those in earth;
> for us humans and for our salvation
> he came down and became incarnate,
> became human,
> suffered and rose up on the third day,
> went up into the heavens,
> is coming to judge the living and the dead.
> And in the holy Spirit.[88]

The structure of this text is similar to that of the rule of faith, which we quoted in Tertullian's version. There also, and in the baptismal confessions of that time, was successively declared what catholic Christians believed concerning the Father, the Son and the Holy Spirit. The Nicene Creed contains a few important focal points, however. Although Constantine himself – at least according to Eusebius – had made known that he had no preference for or against the beliefs of Arius, this text shows that Arius' opponents won the dispute. This is apparent from the formulation that Jesus Christ is not created, but was begotten from the substance of the Father, as God from God and Light from Light. For a moment, the creed has a hymnic character in the repetitions 'God from God, Light from Light, true God from true God'. So far, mainly biblical language has been used. This language is, however, abandoned when it is explained that Jesus Christ, as the Son of God, is from the substance (*ousia*) of the Father and consubstantial (*homo-ousios*) with the Father. These phrases underline that Christ was divine from eternity. It proves, therefore, that Origen's view of the eternal generation of the Son by the Father triumphed in Nicaea. It is not known for certain if Origen himself used the term *homo-ousios* for the relationship of the Son to God the Father.[89]

---

88 Translation by Norman P. Tanner (1990), *Decrees of the Ecumenical Councils* I. London: Sheed and Ward, Washington: Georgetown University Press, p. 5; see also the introduction on pp. 1–4. The so-called Nicene Creed which is sung or read in church services is in fact the supplemented creed which was drawn up in 381 CE by the council held in Constantinople.

89 Pamphilus, *Apology for Origen* 94; 99 (SC 464), mentions a fragment of Origen's *Commentary on Hebrews* in which the term *homo-ousios* appears to designate the relationship of the Son to the Father, but this Commentary is only known in Rufinus'

We saw that – remarkably enough – Paul of Samosata used this term. He said that the Logos was one in substance with God, but at the time the synod of Antioch had rejected this formulation (section 9.4). The followers of Sabellius in Libya had also called the Son 'one in substance' with the Father.[90]

The fact that the Holy Spirit is named without any addition proves that at that time there was no debate about it. As stated earlier, the discussion about the divinity of the Spirit did not arise until the second half of the fourth century.

In a sentence subsequent to the creed the beliefs of Arius and his followers are emphatically rejected. Anathematized are those who said about Christ, 'there once was when he was not', 'before he was begotten he was not', 'he came to be from things that were not', 'the Son of God is of another substance (*hupostasis*) or of another essence (*ousia*)' or that 'he is subject to change or alteration'.[91]

The bishops' reason for rejecting the view of Arius and his followers was that in their opinion he did not do justice to the divinity of Jesus Christ. Because the church believed in Christ as the Saviour, and salvation from sin and death could only come from God, it was necessary that the man Jesus Christ fully came from God and also was God himself. It was and is common in the Greek church to consider the salvation of people even as their deification. The argument is that only God can deify mankind. Later this was elaborately explained by Athanasius, Alexander's successor as bishop of Alexandria.[92]

9.10 *Conclusion*

Whoever in our time examines the developments which have led to the Nicene Creed, with its focused view of God's unity and trinity, is soon overcome by amazement. Whoever feels any affinity with the church of that time might regret that so much theological dispute took place regarding the identity of Jesus Christ as the Son of God. One may question whether deviant representations of his person were indeed justifiably

---

Latin translation. It is quite possible that Rufinus added this term to bring Origen, who at that time (about 400 CE) was quite controversial, more into conformity with later orthodoxy. Williams, *Arius*, pp. 132–137, concludes that Origen could not have used the term.

90 This is apparent from Athanasius, *Defence of Dionysius* 18, 2 (AW II, 1).

91 Tanner, *Decrees of the Ecumenical Councils* I, p. 5.

92 *Discourses against the Arians* I, 38–39; see also, e.g., II, 14; II, 47; II, 55–56; II, 65–70; III, 33; III, 39 (AW I, 1).

rejected. The position of Paul of Samosata, for instance, has met with sympathy from various theologians from the beginning of the twentieth century.[93] A few years ago, the Dutch systematic theologian G. D. J. Dingemans emphatically fell back on Paul of Samosata.[94] If one assumes the existence of God who is Spirit, one might say that the man Jesus was full of God's Spirit in an exceptional way. In the language of that time, one can also speak about the Spirit of God's Logos who came to live in Jesus. For the precise connection of the Logos in Jesus with God, Paul of Samosata even used the term – rejected at that time, but later adopted in Nicaea – 'consubstantial', *homo-ousios*. In a similar manner, Arius has found recognition, not only in his own time, but also in later centuries.[95] The 'orthodox' belief that Jesus was not only a human being, but also God, as eternal as God the Father, could and can not persuade every Christian.

It was not the intention of this chapter to discuss and assess the entire history of dogma up to and including the council of Nicaea; for that purpose it is much too concise. Therefore, I will stop at a few evaluating remarks about Arius. Like the adoptianists and Paul of Samosata, he regarded Jesus Christ, the Son of God, as a creature in whom God's Logos and Spirit were active. Differently from his predecessors, he situated the creation of the Son in eternity before the creation of the world. Although he thus recognized the very exalted position of Jesus Christ, the question is if, in his view, it is also justified to worship this exalted creature in hymns and prayer, as Christians were accustomed to. Because since the beginning of Christianity Jesus Christ as God's Son has been regarded as God next to God the Father, it is understandable that the church in Arius' time was not satisfied with his idea that the Son was 'God' in name only. There is a case for the reasoning of John Calvin. He was convinced that the church had to present its focused formulations about the deity of Jesus Christ because of the challenge made by Arius. If Arius had to acknowledge on the basis of Scripture that Christ was God's Son and God himself, then why did he proclaim so emphatically that Christ was in fact a creature and God in name only? – so Calvin.[96]

---

93 Van de Kamp, *Pneuma-christologie*, discusses Adolf von Harnack, Reinhold Seeberg, Friedrich Loofs, Piet Schoonenberg, Geoffry W. H. Lampe, Otto A. Dilschneider and Hendrikus Berkhof.

94 G. D. J. Dingemans (2001), *De stem van de Roepende: Pneumatheologie* (3rd edn). Kampen: Kok, pp. 21–22; 478–479.

95 See Hendrikus Berkhof (1986), *Christian Faith: An Introduction to the Study of the Faith* (revised edn). Grand Rapids MI: Eerdmans, pp. 284–296.

96 *Institution* I, 13, 4–5. This does not justify, however, Calvin's part in the conviction of the anti-trinitarian Michael Servet to be burned at the stake.

In particular, I would like to deal with the question of whether the Nicene Creed of 325 CE offers a proper interpretation of the New Testament writings. In my opinion this is definitely the case. In the first place we can refer to the prologue of the Gospel of John, where the Logos is described as God next to God the Father. The evangelist even writes that with the Logos everything came into being (1:1–3). This implies that God's Logos is considered the Creator of the world, which, by the way, corresponds with an early Jewish tradition. In that case, however, it would be very strange if a creature, even though it is the very first and highest of the creatures, became the Creator himself. In our discussion of the Gospel of John it came to light that the Logos, who 'became flesh' in Jesus Christ, is in fact equated with the LORD, the God of Israel (section 2.5). It became apparent that Jesus was considered as the LORD not only in the Gospel of John, but also in Paul and in the synoptic gospels (sections 2.1–4). This implies that this is a very ancient view on Jesus. The modalists concluded from this that God the Father, whom they considered the LORD, had become a human being in Jesus. In the Gospel of John, however, a distinction was made between Jesus as the Logos and LORD on the one hand, and God the Father on the other hand. Here God the Logos is explicitly put next to God the Father. In this gospel, nothing points to the idea that the Logos is actually a creature. To be sure, Arius did not conclude this from the Gospel of John, but from Proverbs 8:22.

We saw that it was common in catholic Christianity of the second and third centuries to make this distinction between God the Father and God the Logos. This evoked the criticism that Christians believed in 'two gods'. Origen introduced a solution to this problem, which implied that God eternally generates his Son. In this way, he wanted to do justice to God's unity – the Son is after all eternally the Son of the Father, and therefore they are one – and to the distinction between the Father and the Son. In our time, Origen's proposal comes across as alienating. Nevertheless, it can be established that the authors of the Nicene Creed tried to do justice both to the distinction in God, and to God's unity. Aside from the terms they used, they stood in an old Jewish tradition of 'logos theology'.[97]

This does not mean that we can establish historically that Jesus considered himself the eternal Son of God and the LORD. To be sure, various testimonies from the gospels do indeed point to this, but it is inevitable that these testimonies are biased by the faith of Jesus' disciples after his death and appearances. Although Jesus certainly had a high awareness of his own calling and mission, and may have considered himself to be the unique Son of God, this does not prove that he considered himself the

---

97 See Boyarin, *Border Lines*, pp. 89–147.

second person of the triune God.[98] Yet we can conclude that Jesus himself gave ample cause to the exalted view of his person. But since we do not have his personal testimonies, the question of Jesus' view of himself cannot be definitely answered on the basis of historical arguments.

Neither can we conclude from our biblical-theological and dogma-historical overview that after Jesus' life on earth it became apparent that he *is* the 'incarnate' Logos and the eternal Son of God. In historical respect, we can only determine that this view, which is expressed in the Nicene Creed, stands in an old tradition. One can either accept this tradition, or reject it – but that is a question of faith, about which one can reflect theologically. We can, however, demonstrate on historical grounds that this theological belief has old, even Jewish roots.

---

98 An interesting, but not convincing attempt to prove that Jesus did regard himself as such was made by J. C. O'Neill (1995), *Who Did Jesus Think He Was?*. Leiden: Brill.

CHAPTER 10

Conclusions and Evaluation

In section 5.1 we drew some preliminary conclusions from chapters 2 to 4 with regard to the relationship between Jesus and the gnosis of the gnostics. We concluded there that a greater degree of historical reliability must be attributed to the New Testament testimonies about Jesus than to the various gnostic views on him. According to the New Testament gospels, Jesus was in line with the Old Testament and relied on the God of Israel. He preached the coming of God's kingdom and acted with divine authority. He considered himself the Messiah, the Son of Man and God's Son. His death on a cross did not end the movement which he started. His disciples experienced that he had been raised from the dead, appeared to them and instructed them again. In their view, his place was henceforth in heaven at God's right hand. There he could be called upon, which points to the divine status attributed to him.

In comparison to this, it became apparent that most gnostic testimonies offered far more complex blueprints to explain Jesus' origin and divine status. Gnostics distinguished between various gods and knew a greater number of heavenly powers from which the person of Jesus Christ came forth. It is very important that, in their view, he did not act on behalf of the Old Testament God, but proclaimed a higher God. For gnostics, Jesus' death was problematic since in their view, as divine figure he could not suffer and die. They therefore thought that the divine element in him had already withdrawn from him before he died a human being. Afterwards, he again appeared to his disciples and initiated them more fully into his secret teaching. In spite of some similarities with the beliefs of 'catholic' Christianity, we concluded that many of the gnostic views on Jesus were secondary to the older testimonies which were preserved in the New Testament.

In chapters 6 to 9, we broadened our examination, and 'Jewish Christianity' was the first to be discussed. We saw that different factions existed among Jewish Christians and that people of other nations also felt attracted to their beliefs. In these groups, Jesus was seen as Messiah and Son of God, but not as God alongside God the Father. Sometimes his pre-existence was acknowledged, although more often it was not mentioned. Jesus' baptism in the river Jordan was considered an important event, because at that time the Spirit of God descended upon him and he was proclaimed Son of God or Son of the Spirit. Jewish Christians usually did not attribute a redemptive value to Jesus' death and resurrection, although the Nazoreans seemed closer to the catholic Christians in this respect. From the second century onward, the Jewish forms of Christianity had a marginal position in Christianity in its broader sense and remained primarily limited to Syria. Nevertheless, Jewish Christianity still influenced the church as a whole, because during the first centuries there have always been catholic believers – including a bishop such as Paul of Samosata – who were inspired by it. They came to adoptianistic (or, dynamic monarchianistic) ideas about Jesus as an exceptional human being who was inspired by God's Spirit.

It is very possible that this Jewish Christianity, with its simple view on Jesus Christ as an exceptional prophet who was filled with God's Spirit, goes back to the beginning of Christianity. At the same time, we must establish that besides this, other views of Jesus also existed quite early, as is apparent from the New Testament writings. From a historical perspective we cannot say that these other views were more true or more valuable because later on they were included in the New Testament. This would be a circular argument, because the New Testament reflects precisely that form of Christianity which saw in Jesus much more than an exceptional prophet who was inspired by God's Spirit. However, on the basis of our investigation of the Old Testament and early Judaism in chapter 8, we can establish that those Christians who saw in Jesus Christ the incarnate Logos or the LORD and the Son of God could draw on an old Jewish pattern. Besides Christians who saw Jesus as an exceptional human being who was inspired by the Spirit, there appeared to be even more or at least more influential Christians who considered Jesus as LORD and God alongside God the Father. We can establish that Jesus apparently left behind this impression, and that the New Testament holds evidence of this. So, from a historical perspective, Jewish Christianity can indeed appeal to ancient ideas about Jesus, but from a theological perspective, the question arises whether this branch of Christianity does justice to the way in which he manifested himself. In any case, the proclamation of Jesus as God's Logos, God's Son and as God alongside God has reached and appealed far more people than Jewish Christianity, which remained orientated to the Mosaic law. Certainly, the majority is not necessarily right from a theological viewpoint. However, because the majority of those who believed in Jesus as the Saviour coming from God and also being God himself could draw on the Old Testament and early Jewish traditions, their conviction can be called justifiable not only on historical but also on theological grounds.

If Jesus Christ was rightly called upon as God and one could believe in him as God, then his relationship with God the Father still had to be described in more detail. This is exactly what took place from the second to the fourth centuries. During that time the modalistic, or modalistic monarchianistic view arose, which implies that Jesus Christ *is* God the Father. This was an attempt to do justice to God's unity and clearly and plainly to express the position of Jesus – an attempt which has been rejected by the church as being too simple.

We are not only concerned about an evaluation of the Jewish Christian, the adoptianistic, the modalistic and the catholic views on Jesus, but we also want to include the gnostic movement. It is striking that gnostics were often very interested in the origin of the heavenly world and of the creation of the material world. They spoke of numerous heavenly powers by whose doing the physical world came into being. They had their own ideas about the figures of Jesus and Christ and about the gods from whom they originated. It proves that not only catholic Christians occupied themselves with the beginning of the world and with what happened in the timeless eternity which preceded the creation of the material world. At that time, it was assumed that what had occurred at the primordial beginning determined life on earth and the end of the existing order. Whoever examines gnostic myths must conclude that in comparison with these, the view on Jesus Christ in catholic Christianity was much less complicated. So, we see on the one hand the Jewish Christian, adoptianistic and modalistic views, with their very elementary forms of theology and Christology. On the other hand, there were the complicated gnostic views of God and Christ and the many other heavenly powers. It proves that the catholic church took a position in the middle of these two extremes. It acknowledged that the questions about Christ's origin and his relation to God the Father preceding the creation of the world were legitimate, but it rejected the far-reaching mythological speculations of the gnostics. For this position, the church appealed to the Old Testament, to the oral tradition of the apostles, and to those written testimonies about Jesus which it acknowledged as being authoritative, i.e. the – ultimately canonized – New Testament. On the basis of this, the church also dissociated itself from the views of the Jewish Christians, the adoptianists and the modalists, which it regarded as too simplistic.

In comparison with the gnostic speculations, the Nicene Creed is a concise, orderly account of the catholic faith. Too orderly, gnostic Christians would say; after all, nothing is said about the origin of evil and about the imperfection of the world. They found it implausible that the one God created heaven and earth. In their view, the story of creation and salvation was more complex – even very complex, as is evident from various complicated myths and discourses. For the Jewish Christian, the adoptianistic and the modalistic believers, the Nicene Creed was, however, too highly engrafted on philosophical distinctions that were not found in the Scriptures.

If we now pose the question of the continuity between Jesus, the gnostic gnosis and the dogma of God's trinity, we must establish an important discontinuity between Jesus and 'gnosis'. Although there were gnostic groups who continued to attribute a certain importance to the Old Testament, nevertheless in various degrees gnostics cut Jesus Christ off from his Old Testament and Jewish background. Although the Old Testament and early Jewish books testify to a plurality in the one God, the gnostics went much further and introduced a contrast between a lower and a higher God. They believed that Jesus' preaching implied how the soul of a human being can return to the heaven of the high God from which it once fell. In this persuasion, the influence of Platonic philosophy is clearly recognizable. Here we see a Hellenistic interpretation and adaptation of Jesus' preaching of the coming of God's kingdom.

With regard to catholic Christianity, it is not easy to determine the continuity or discontinuity between Jesus and the dogma of God's trinity. In any case, Jesus was not a philosophically schooled theologian who thought in categories of eternity and time. One problem is that it can no longer be determined with complete certainty how Jesus saw himself exactly. We may assume that he considered himself as the Son of Man, as Messiah and as God's Son, in addition to which must be remarked that the title 'God's Son' can be understood in various ways. If Jesus indeed considered himself the Son of Man, this means that he was conscious of his heavenly provenance. The Son of Man was, after all, a heavenly figure. In that case, it can be assumed that Jesus was in some way aware of his heavenly pre-existence. If he also considered himself the Son of God, this can be interpreted as one of the sons of God, the angels, in whose midst he was the Son of God par excellence. This title, then, points to Jesus' heavenly origin. It is quite doubtful whether he also saw himself as the LORD, and therefore as God. This can not be recovered with certainty, but considering the accumulation of other titles which he already had – Son of Man, Messiah, i.e. Christ, Son of God – it is not probable; many scholars will say that it is out of the question. Yet we do see that in the earliest written testimonies, which have been preserved in the New Testament, he is described in terms of the LORD and God. We established earlier, that Jesus in any case left this impression behind. If Jesus as the Son of God could, at the same time, be called God's Logos and the LORD, he was not only pre-existent, but also God alongside God the Father.

Initially, the catholic Christians lived with a somewhat naïve view of God's trinity. No speculation was made about the question how the Son was begotten by the Father. In reaction to some who said that the Son once, in the beginning, was not, Origen proposed to speak about the eternal generation of the Son. With this he meant that God's pre-existent Logos is the Son of the Father from eternity. This argumentation is based upon contemporaneous philosophical categories, which were derived from Plato and Aristotle. Not until Arius distinguished between the Logos and Wisdom of God's own substance and another Logos and Wisdom which God created and whom he also called his Son did the church take a position on this matter. One may regret that Arius, after he came forward with his protest against the eternal divinity of the Son, did not reconcile himself with his bishop Alexander as – according to Eusebius' report – the emperor Constantine had hoped. Since his view of a twofold Logos had an artificial character and he wanted to acknowledge the Son, as a creature, only as God in name, he evoked the reaction of the Nicene Council. The creed that was formulated there declared that the Lord Jesus Christ is God from God, born from the substance of the Father and consubstantial with the Father. Since Jesus was early on considered as the LORD, and – in the conceptions of that time – it was inconceivable that the LORD had ever been begotten and therefore was not eternal, the decision of the Nicene Council is understandable. There is an important degree of continuity between these early beliefs about Jesus and the dogma of God's trinity. What is more, these beliefs have their roots in the Old Testament and in early Judaism.

However, this conclusion does not alter the fact that we nevertheless have to speak of a broken continuity, much as a stick stuck in the water optically no longer seems to be straight. Perhaps it would have been desirable if the church had retained its initially more naïve belief in God's trinity. In Nicaea, however, it felt compelled to a more precise and more speculative formulation. Yet, on the basis of the New Testament writings the theological motive of the council of Nicaea can be called justifiable. In the creed then formulated it was stated that the one God has manifested himself in Jesus Christ, who took the way of the cross and resurrection. Thus, God himself came in the person of Jesus, however paradoxical this may sound. In its confession of God's trinity, the council pointed to the plurality of God and rejected rigid monotheism. This implies that God not only resides in a high heaven, but counts as the Creator of heaven and earth, knows what it is like to be a human being and with his Spirit wants to live in people. If one accepts the oldest written testimonies about Jesus of Nazareth, who, filled with the Spirit, acted on behalf of God, then it is justified in the terms of that time to speak of him in the way the Nicene Council has done.[1]

This conclusion raises the question of whether it is still necessary in our time to speak about God and Jesus in the way the council of Nicaea did. The answer is in part dependent on one's evaluation of the history of the church and of the tradition that was formed at that time. To be sure, not every tradition from the history of so many centuries of Christianity has to be maintained forever. With regard to speaking about the trinity of the one God, however, we have seen that this goes back to the oldest traditions in the New Testament. Since its beginning after all the church has believed in Jesus as the Son of God who himself is also LORD and God. That is why since the beginning of the church, prayer was not only offered in the name of Jesus Christ to God the Father, but also to Christ himself. This means that in life and death it is possible to trust in Christ. This conviction is solidly anchored in the Christian religious life and is expressed in hymns and confessions.[2] Whoever would like to remove this tradition from Christian spirituality also touches the heart of the New Testament testimony.

The question of whether it is still necessary in our time to speak about God and Jesus in the way the council of Nicaea did calls for a personal answer. Obviously, this answer is intended as a recommendation to the church at large. As for myself, I consider the value of these ancient formulations, the intention of which goes back to early traditions of the New Testament, great enough to hold them in esteem. Otherwise the ties with the church of all ages would be broken. A person who no longer wants to sing hymns to the Father, the Son and the Holy Spirit positions himself on the edge of the world-wide catholic church. We must at the same time realize, however, that – paradoxically enough – it was never the intention of such formulations to define God to the last detail. Human words are not adequate to that purpose, because God is always greater and escapes our expressions and formulations – as the church fathers of the first centuries knew very well.[3] This does not mean, however, that Christians should no longer say anything about the mystery by which

---

1   Cf. Gerald Bray (1997), *Creeds, Councils and Christ* (2nd edn). Fearn: Mentor.
2   See, e.g., the beginning of the Heidelberg Catechism (of 1563), 'What is thy only comfort in life and death? – That I with body and soul, both in life and death, am not my own, but belong unto my faithful Saviour Jesus Christ; who, with his precious blood, has fully satisfied for all my sins, and delivered me from all the power of the devil; and so preserves me that without the will of my heavenly Father, not a hair can fall from my head; yea, that all things must be subservient to my salvation, and therefore, by his Holy Spirit, He also assures me of eternal life, and makes me sincerely willing and ready, henceforth, to live unto him.'
3   Vladimir Lossky (1957), *The Mystical Theology of the Eastern Church*. Cambridge, London: James Clarke & Co, pp. 7–66.

they have been touched, or that it does not matter what is said about it. This mystery concerns the man from Nazareth who proves not to be a gnostic teacher and inexpressibly more than an inspired rabbi. That is why Stephen, the first martyr, for his belief in Jesus, could die with the invocation 'Lord Jesus, receive my spirit' on his lips.[4]

Gloria Patri et Filio et Spiritui Sancto

4   Acts 7:60.

Bibliography

Primary literature

Bible
Elliger, K. and Rudolph, W., eds. (1984), *Biblia Hebraica Stuttgartensia: Editio minor*. Stuttgart: Deutsche Bibelgesellschaft (Masoretic Text, MT).
Rahlfs, A., ed. (1979), *Septuaginta: Id est Vetus Testamentum graece iuxta* LXX *interpres: Editio minor*. Stuttgart: Deutsche Bibelgesellschaft (LXX).
Aland, Kurt and Barbara et al., eds (1993), *Novum Testamentum Graece* (27th edn). Stuttgart: Deutsche Bibelgesellschaft.
The Holy Bible containing the Old and New Testaments: Authorized King James Version (without date). London: Collins (KJV).
The Holy Bible containing the Old and New Testaments with the Apocryphal/Deuterocanonical Books: New Revised Standard Version (1995, Anglicized edn). Oxford: Oxford University Press (NRSV).

Writings of the Dead Sea Scrolls
García Martínez, F. and Tigchelaar, E. J. C. (1997), *The Dead Sea Scrolls: Study Edition* 1–2, Leiden: Brill.

Pseudepigrapha
A large number of translations of early Jewish pseudepigraphical writings have been collected by Charlesworth, J. H., ed. (1983–1985), *The Old Testament Pseudepigrapha* 1–2. London: Darton, Longman & Todd (OTP).

Philo of Alexandria
Colson F. H. and Whittaker, G. H. (1929–1962), *Philo in Ten Volumes (and Two Supplementary Volumes)* (Loeb Classical Library 226; 227; 247; 261; 275; 289; 320; 341; 363; 379), London: Heinemann, Cambridge MA: Harvard University Press.
Marcus, R. (1953), *Philo in Ten Volumes (and Two Supplementary Volumes): Supplement* 1–2 (Loeb Classical Library 380; 401), London: Heinemann, Cambridge MA: Harvard University Press.

Coptic gnostic writings
The writings of the Nag Hammadi Library and the Berlin Codex have been published and translated in *The Coptic Gnostic Library* 1–5 (2000), Leiden: Brill, which includes the previous volumes of the series Nag Hammadi Studies.
Kasser, R. and Wurst, G. et al., eds (2007), *The Gospel of Judas together with the Letter of Philip, James, and a Book of Allogenes from Codex Tchacos: Critical Edition*. Washington DC: National Geographic.
Robinson, J. M., ed. (1996), *The Nag Hammadi Library in English* (4th edn). Leiden: Brill.
Meyer, M., ed. (2007), *The Nag Hammadi Scriptures*. New York: HarperCollins.

Targums
Díez Macho, A. (1968), *Neophyti 1: Targum Palestinense: Ms de la Biblioteca Vaticana I*. Madrid, Barcelona: Consejo Superior de Investigaciones Científicas.
Klein, M. L. (1980), *The Fragment-Targums of the Pentateuch According to their Extant Sources* 1–2. Roma: Biblical Institute Press.
Maher, Michael (1992), *Targum Pseudo-Jonathan: Genesis*. Edinburgh: T&T Clark.
Martin McNamara, Robert Hayward and Michael Maher (1994), *Targum Neofiti 1: Exodus. Targum Pseudo-Jonathan: Exodus*. Edinburgh: T&T Clark.

Abbreviations of collections of early Christian sources used in the notes
ANF   Ante-Nicene Fathers, Grand Rapids MI: Eerdmans
AW   Athanasius Werke, Berlin: Walter de Gruyter
CCSL   Corpus Christianorum Series Latina, Turnhout: Brepols
GCS   Die Griechischen Christlichen Schriftsteller der ersten Jahrhunderte, Berlin: Akademie Verlag
LCL   Loeb Classical Library, London: Heinemann, Cambridge MA: Harvard University Press

NHS   Nag Hammadi Studies, Leiden: Brill
NHMS   Nag Hammadi and Manichaean Studies, Leiden: Brill
PTS   Patristische Texte und Studien, Berlin: Walter de Gruyter
SC   Sources Chrétiennes, Paris: Cerf
TF   Texte zur Forschung, Darmstadt: Wissenschaftliche
        Buchgesellschaft

For other editions of early Christian sources the names of the editors or translators have been added to the references. For editions and translations of early Christian writings one may consult: Döpp, S. and Geerlings, W., eds (2002), *Lexikon der antiken christlichen Literatur* (3rd edn). Freiburg: Herder.

Secondary literature

Attridge, H. W. and Pagels, E. H. (1985), 'The Tripartite Tractate: Introduction', in Harold W. Attridge, ed., *Nag Hammadi Codex I (The Jung Codex)*. Leiden: Brill, pp. 159–190.
Baarda, T. (1969), 'Als engelen …'. *Voorlopig* 1, 238–241.
────── (1982), '2 Clement and the Sayings of Jesus', in J. Delobel, ed., *Logia. Les Paroles de Jésus – The Sayings of Jesus*. Leuven: Peeters, pp. 529–556.
────── (1983), *Early Transmission of Words of Jesus. Thomas, Tatian and the Text of the New Testament: A Collection of Studies*. Amsterdam: Free University Press.
────── (1994), *Essays on the Diatessaron*. Kampen: Kok Pharos.
Ball, D. M. (1996), *'I Am' in John's Gospel: Literary Function, Background and Theological Implications*. Sheffield: Sheffield Academic Press.
Barbel, J. (1941), *Christos Angelos: Die Anschauung von Christus als Bote und Engel in der gelehrten und volkstümlichen Literatur des christlichen Altertums: Zugleich ein Beitrag zur Geschichte des Ursprungs und der Fortdauer des Arianismus*. Bonn: F. J. Dölger-Institut.
Barker, M. (1992), *The Great Angel: A Study of Israel's Second God*. London: SPCK.
Barrett, C. K. (1978), *The Gospel according to St John: An Introduction with Commentary and Notes on the Greek Text* (2nd edn). London: SPCK.
Bauckham, R. (2003), 'The Origin of the Ebionites', in P. J. Tomson and D. Lambers-Petry, eds, *The Image of Judaeo-Christians in Ancient Jewish and Christian Literature*. Tübingen: J. C. B. Mohr, pp. 162–181.

——— (2006), *Jesus and the Eyewitnesses: The Gospels as Eyewitness Testimony*. Grand Rapids MI, Cambridge: Eerdmans.

Berger, K. (1997), *Im Anfang war Johannes: Datierung und Theologie des vierten Evangeliums*. Stuttgart: Quell.

——— (1995), *Theologiegeschichte des Urchristentums. Theologie des Neuen Testaments* (2nd edn), Tübingen, Basel: Franke Verlag.

——— (2002), *Sind die Berichte des Neuen Testaments wahr? Ein Weg zum Verstehen der Bibel*. Gütersloh: Gütersloher Verlagshaus.

Berkhof, H. (1986), *Christian Faith: An Introduction to the Study of the Faith* (revised edn; translated from the Dutch by Sierd Woudstra). Grand Rapids MI: Eerdmans.

Bertrand, D. A. (1973), *Le baptême de Jésus: Histoire de l'exégèse aux deux premiers siècles*. Tübingen: J. C. B. Mohr.

——— (1980), 'L'Evangile des Ebionites: une harmonie évangelique antérieure au *Diatessaron*', *New Testament Studies* 26, 548–563.

Bienert, W. A. (1993), 'Sabellius und Sabellianismus als historisches Problem', in H. C. Brennecke, E. L. Grasmück and C. Markschies, eds, *Logos: Festschrift für Luise Abramowski zum 8. Juli 1993*. Berlin, New York: Walter de Gruyter, pp. 124–139.

Black, M. (1985), *The Book of Enoch or I Enoch: A New English Edition*. Leiden: Brill.

Bonnard, P. (1963), *L'Évangile selon Saint Matthieu*. Neuchâtel: Delachaux et Niestlé.

Bonnard, P.-E. (1972), *Le Second Isaïe: Son disciple et leurs éditeurs: Isaïe 40–66*. Paris: Gabalda.

Bons, E. (2003), 'Die Septuaginta-Version von Psalm 110 (Ps 109 LXX): Textgestalt, Aussagen, Auswirkungen', in D. Sänger, ed., *Heiligkeit und Herrschaft: Intertextuelle Studien zu Heiligkeitsvorstellungen und zu Psalm 110*. Neukirchen-Vluyn: Neukirchener Verlag, pp. 122–145.

Boring, M. E. (1995), 'The Gospel of Matthew: Introduction, Commentary, and Reflections', in L. E. Keck et al., eds, *The New Interpreter's Bible* VIII. Nashville TN, pp. 87–505.

Bovon, F. (1989), *Das Evangelium nach Lukas (Lk 1,1–9,50)*. Zürich, Düsseldorf: Benzinger Verlag, Neukirchen-Vluyn: Neukirchener Verlag.

——— (1996), *Das Evangelium nach Lukas (Lk 9,51–14,35)*. Zürich, Düsseldorf: Benzinger Verlag, Neukirchen-Vluyn: Neukirchener Verlag.

——— (2001), *Das Evangelium nach Lukas (Lk 15,1–19,27)*. Düsseldorf, Zürich: Patmos Verlag, Benzinger Verlag, Neukirchen-Vluyn: Neukirchener Verlag.

Boyarin, D. (2004), *Border Lines: The Partition of Judaeo-Christianity*. Philadelphia: University of Pennsylvania Press.

Bray, G (1997), *Creeds, Councils and Christ* (2nd edn). Fearn: Mentor.

Brown, D. (2003), *The Da Vinci Code*, London: Bantam Press.

Brown, R. E. (1970), *The Gospel according to John (xiii–xxi)*. Garden City NY: Doubleday.

—— (1979), *The Community of the Beloved Disciple: The Life, Loves, and Hates of an Individual Church in New Testament Times*. New York, Mahwah: Paulus Press.

Brunson, A. C. (2003), *Psalm 118 in the Gospel of John: An Intertextual Study on the New Exodus Pattern in the Theology of John*. Tübingen: J. C. B. Mohr.

Büchsel, F. (1969), '*monogenês*', in G. Kittel and G. W. Bromiley, eds, *Theological Dictionary of the New Testament* 4. Grand Rapids MI: Eerdmans, pp. 737–741.

Bultmann, R. (1953), *Das Evangelium des Johannes*. Göttingen: Vandenhoeck & Ruprecht.

—— (1970), *Die Geschichte der synoptischen Tradition* (8th edn). Göttingen: Vandenhoeck & Ruprecht.

Burchard, C. (1985), 'Joseph and Aseneth: A New Translation and Introduction', in J. H. Charlesworth, ed., *The Old Testament Pseudepigrapha* 2. London: Darton, Longman & Todd, pp. 177–247.

Capes, D. B. (1992), *Old Testament Yahweh Texts in Paul's Christology*. Tübingen: J. C. B. Mohr.

Carlson, S. (2005), *The Gospel Hoax: Morton Smith's Invention of Secret Mark*. Waco TX: Baylor University Press.

Carotta, F. (2005), *Jesus was Caesar: On the Julian Origin of Christianity*. Soesterberg: Aspekt.

Carratelli, G. P. (2003), *Les lamelles d'or orphiques: Instructions pour le voyage d'outre-tombe des initiés grecs*. Paris: Les belles lettres.

Chae, Y. S. (2006), *Jesus as the Eschatological Davidic Shepherd: Studies in the Old Testament, Second Temple Judaism, and in the Gospel of Matthew*. Tübingen: J. C. B. Mohr.

Chauvot, A. (2001), 'Les migrations des Barbares et leur conversion au christianisme', in Jean-Marie Mayeur et al., eds, *Histoire du Christianisme: Des origines à nos jours* II. [Paris]: Desclée, pp. 861–879.

Cirillo, L. and Schneider, A. (1999), *Les Reconnaissances du pseudo Clément: Roman chrétien des premiers siècles*. Turnhout: Brepols.

Cockerill, G. L., 'Cerinthus', in D. N. Freedman, ed. (1992), *The Anchor Bible Dictionary* 1. New York: Doubleday, p. 885.

Colpe, C. (1972), '*ho huios tou anthrôpou*', in G. Friedrich and G. W.
	Bromiley, eds, *Theological Dictionary of the New Testament* 8.
	Grand Rapids MI: Eerdmans, pp. 400–477.
Craigie, P. C. and Tate, M. E. (2004), *Psalms 1–50* (2nd edn). Waco TX:
	Word Books.
Cullmann, O. (1957), *Die Christologie des Neuen Testaments*. Tübingen:
	J. C. B. Mohr.
Dahl, N. A. (1962), 'The Johannine Church and History', in W.
	Klassen and G. Snyder, eds, *Current Issues in New Testament
	Interpretation: Essays in Honor of Otto A. Piper*. New York:
	Harper, pp. 124–142.
Daniélou, J. (1958), *Philon d'Alexandrie*. Paris: Fayard.
——— (1958), *Théologie du Judéo-Christianisme*. Paris: Desclée.
——— (1961), *Message évangélique et culture hellénistique aux IIe et
	IIIe siècles*. Paris: Desclée.
De Boer, E. A. (2004), *The Gospel of Mary: Beyond a Gnostic and a
	Biblical Mary Magdalene*. London, New York: T&T Clark.
DeConick, A. D. (2001), *Voices of the Mystics: Early Christian Discourse
	in the Gospels of John and Thomas and Other Ancient Christian
	Literature*. Sheffield: Sheffield Academic Press.
——— (2006), 'Corrections to the Critical Reading of the *Gospel of
	Thomas*'. *Vigiliae Christianae*, 60, 201–208.
——— (2007), *The Original Gospel of Thomas in Translation: With
	a Commentary and New English Translation of the Complete
	Gospel*. London, New York: T&T Clark.
——— (2007), *The Thirteenth Apostle: What the Gospel of Judas Really
	Says*. London, New York: Continuum.
Denaux, A. (1999), 'The Theme of Divine Visits and Human
	(In)hospitality in Luke-Acts: Its Old Testament and Graeco-Roman
	Antecendents', in J. Verheyden, ed., *The Unity of Luke-Acts*.
	Leuven, pp. 255–279.
De Jonge, H. J. (1989), 'Ontstaan en ontwikkeling van het geloof in
	Jezus' opstanding', in F. O. van Gennep et al., *Waarlijk opgestaan!
	Een discussie over de opstanding van Jezus Christus*. Baarn: Ten
	Have, pp. 31–50.
Dingemans, G. D. J. (2001), *De stem van de Roepende: Pneumatheologie*
	(3rd edn). Kampen: Kok.
Dodd, C. H. (1963), *The Interpretation of the Fourth Gospel*.
	Cambridge: University Press.
Dunderberg, I. (2006), *The Beloved Disciple in Conflict? Revisiting the
	Gospels of John and Thomas*. Oxford: Oxford University Press.
Dunn, J. D. G. (1980), *Christology in the Making: An Inquiry into the
	Origins of the Doctrine of Incarnation*. London: SCM Press.

—— (1988), *Romans 1–8*. Dallas TX: Word Books.

—— (1998), *The Theology of Paul the Apostle*. London, New York: T&T Clark.

—— (2003), *Jesus Remembered*. Grand Rapids MI, Cambridge: Eerdmans.

Ehrman, B. D. (1993), *The Orthodox Corruption of Scripture: The Effect of Early Christological Controversies on the Text of the New Testament*. New York, Oxford: Oxford University Press.

Eissfeldt, O. (1956), 'El and Yahweh', *Journal of Semitic Studies*, 1, 25–37.

Elliott, J. K. (2005), *The Apocryphal New Testament: A Collection of Apocryphal Christian Literature in an English Translation* (reprint). Oxford: Clarendon Press.

Evans, C. A. (2001), *Mark 8:27–16:20*. Nashville TN: Word Books.

Fantino, J. (1994), *La théologie d'Irénée: Lecture des Écritures et réponse à l'exégèse gnostique: Une approche trinitaire*. Paris: Cerf.

Fee, G. D. (1987), *The First Epistle to the Corinthians*. Grand Rapids MI: Eerdmans.

—— (1995), *Paul's Letter to the Philippians*. Grand Rapids MI: Eerdmans.

Fieger, M. (1991), *Das Thomasevangelium: Einleitung, Kommentar und Systematik*. Münster: Aschendorff.

Fischer, J. A. (1979), 'Die alexandrinischen Synoden gegen Origenes'. *Ostkirchliche Studien*, 28, 3–16.

Fitzmyer, J. A. (1979), *A Wandering Aramean: Collected Aramaic Essays*. Missoula: Scholars Press.

—— (1981), *The Gospel according to Luke (I–IX)*. New York: Doubleday.

—— (1985), *The Gospel according to Luke (X–XXIV)*. New York: Doubleday.

—— (1993), '4Q246: The "Son of God" Document from Qumran'. *Biblica* 74, 153–174.

—— (1995), 'The Palestinian Background of "Son of God" as a Title for Jesus', in T. Fornberg and D. Hellholm, eds, *Texts and Contexts in their Textual and Situational Contexts*. Oslo: Scandinavian University Press, pp. 567–577.

Fossum, J. E. (1995), *The Image of the Invisible God: Essays on the Influence of Jewish Mysticism on Early Christology*. Freiburg, Switzerland: Universitätsverlag, Göttingen: Vandenhoeck & Ruprecht.

—— (1999), 'Son of God', in K. van der Toorn, B. Becking and P. W. van der Horst, eds, *Dictionary of Deities and Demons in the Bible* (2nd edn). Leiden: Brill, pp. 788–794.

Fox, R. L. (1986), *Pagans and Christians*, London: Penguin Books.

Franzmann, M. (1996), *Jesus in the Nag Hammadi Writings*. Edinburgh: T&T Clark.

Fredrikson, M. (2003), *According to Mary Magdalene* (translated from the Swedish by Joan Tate). Charlottesville VA: Hampton Roads.

Frickel, J. (1993), 'Hippolyts Schrift Contra Noetum: ein Pseudo-Hippolyt', in H. C. Brennecke, E. L. Grasmück and C. Markschies, eds, *Logos: Festschrift für Luise Abramowski zum 8. Juli 1993*. Berlin, New York: Walter de Gruyter, pp. 87–123.

Frid, B. and Svartvik, J. (2004), *Thomasevangeliet med Jesusorden från Oxyrhynchus* (2nd edn). Lund: Arcus.

Funk, R. W. and Hoover, R. W. (1993), *The Five Gospels: The Search for the Authentic Words of Jesus*. New York: Macmillan.

García Martínez, F. and Van der Woude, A. S. (2007), *De rollen van de Dode Zee* (2nd edn). Kampen: Ten Have.

Gärtner, B. (1961), *The Theology of the Gospel of Thomas* (translated from the Swedish by Eric J. Sharpe). London: Collins.

Gathercole, S. J. (2006), *The Preexistent Son: Recovering the Christologies of Matthew, Mark, and Luke*. Grand Rapids MI, Cambridge: Eerdmans.

——— (2007), *The Gospel of Judas: Rewriting Early Christianity*. Oxford: Oxford University Press.

Geoltrain, P. (2005), 'Roman pseudo-clémentin: Introduction', in P. Geoltrain and J.-D. Kaestli, eds, *Écrits apocryphes chrétiens* II. [Paris]: Gallimard, pp. 1175–1187.

Gerhardsson, B. (2005), 'The Secret of the Transmission of the Unwritten Jesus Tradition'. *New Testament Studies* 51, 1–18.

Gnilka, J. (1986), *Das Matthäusevangelium* 1. Freiburg: Herder.

——— (1988), *Das Matthäusevangelium* 2. Freiburg: Herder.

——— (1994), *Theologie des Neuen Testaments*. Freiburg: Herder.

——— (1998), *Das Evangelium nach Markus (Mk 1–8,26)* (5th edn). Zürich, Düsseldorf: Benzinger Verlag, Neukirchen-Vluyn: Neukirchener Verlag.

——— (1999), *Das Evangelium nach Markus (Mk 8,27–16,20)* (5th edn). Zürich, Düsseldorf: Benzinger Verlag, Neukirchen-Vluyn: Neukirchener Verlag.

Goodenough, E. R. (1935), *By Light, Light: The Mystic Gospel of Hellenistic Judaism*. New Haven CT, reprint (1969) Amsterdam: Philo Press.

Gourgues, M. (1978), *A la droite de Dieu: Résurrection de Jésus et actualisation du Psaume 110:1 dans le Nouveau Testament*. Paris: Gabalda.

Gray, J. (1967), *Joshua, Judges and Ruth*. London: Nelson.

Guelich, R. A. (1989), *Mark 1–8:26*. Dallas TX: Word Books.

Gutbrod, W. (1967), '*nomos*', in G. Kittel and G. W. Bromiley, eds, *Theological Dictionary of the New Testament* 4. Grand Rapids MI: Eerdmans, pp. 1022–1091.

Hadas-Lebel, M. (2003), *Philon d'Alexandrie: Un penseur en diaspora*. [Paris]: Fayard.

Hanson, A. T. (1976), 'John i. 14–18 and Exodus xxxiv'. *New Testament Studies*, 23, 90–101.

—— (1980), *New Testament Interpretation of Scripture*. London: SPCK.

—— (1991) *The Prophetic Gospel: A Study of John and the Old Testament*. Edinburgh: T&T Clark.

Hay, D. M. (1973), *Glory at the Right Hand: Psalm 110 in Early Christianity*. Nashville TN: Abingdon Press.

Hayward, C. T. R. (1978), 'The Holy Name of the God of Moses and the Prologue of St John's Gospel'. *New Testament Studies*, 25, 16–32.

Heiligenthal, R. (2006), *Der verfälschte Jesus: Eine Kritik moderner Jesusbilder* (3rd edn). Darmstadt: Wissenschaftliche Buchgesellschaft.

Helderman, J. (2004), 'Logion 50 des Thomasevangeliums', in M. Immerzeel and J. van der Vliet, eds, *Coptic Studies on the Threshold of a New Millennium* I. Leuven: Peeters, pp. 759–768.

Hengel, M. (1976), *The Son of God: The Origin of Christology and the History of Jewish-Hellenistic Religion*. Philadelphia: Fortress Press.

Hindley, J. C. (1967–1968), 'Towards a date for the Similitudes of Enoch: An Historical Approach'. *New Testament Studies* 14, 551–565.

Hofrichter, P. L. (1987), 'Das Verständnis des christologischen Titels "Eingeborener" bei Origenes', in L. Lies, ed., *Origeniana Quarta*. Innsbruck: Tyrolia-Verlag, pp. 186–193.

——, ed., (2002), *Für und wider die Priorität des Johannes-evangeliums*. Hildesheim: Olms.

—— (2003), *Logoslied, Gnosis und Neues Testament*. Hildesheim: Olms.

Hogeterp, A. L. A. (2005), 'The *Gospel of Thomas* and the Historical Jesus: The Case of Eschatology', in A. Hilhorst and G. H. van Kooten, eds, *The Wisdom of Egypt: Jewish, Early Christian, and Gnostic Essays in Honour of Gerard P. Luttikhuizen*. Leiden: Brill, pp. 381–396.

Horbury, W. (2004), 'Jewish and Christian Monotheism in the Herodian Age', in L. T. Stuckenbruck and W. E. S. North, eds, *Early Jewish and Christian Monotheism*. London: T&T Clark, pp. 16–44.

Hübner, R. M. (1993), 'Der antivalentinianische Charakter der Theologie des Noët von Smyrna', in H. C. Brennecke, E. L. Grasmück and C.

Markschies, eds, *Logos: Festschrift für Luise Abramowski zum 8. Juli 1993*. Berlin, New York: Walter de Gruyter, pp. 57–86.

——— (1999), *Der Paradox Eine: Antignostischer Monarchianismus im zweiten Jahrhundert*. Leiden: Brill.

Hurtado, L. W. (1998), *One Lord, One God: Early Christian Devotion and Ancient Jewish Monotheism* (2nd edn). Philadelphia: Fortress Press.

——— (2003), *Lord Jesus Christ: Devotion to Jesus in Earliest Christianity*. Grand Rapids MI, Cambridge: Eerdmans.

Isaac, E. (1983), '1 (Ethiopic Apolcalypse of) Enoch', in J. H. Charlesworth, ed., *The Old Testament Pseudepigrapha* 1. London: Darton, Longman & Todd, pp. 5–89.

Jeffery, P. (2007), *The Secret Gospel of Mark Unveiled: Imagined Rituals of Sex, Death, and Madness in a Biblical Forgery*. New Haven CT: Yale University Press.

Jeremias, J. (1971), *Neutestamentliche Theologie* I. Gütersloh: Gerd Mohn.

Johnson, A. R. (1961), *The One and the Many in the Israelite Conception of God* (2nd edn). Cardiff: University of Wales Press.

Johnson, S. E. and Buttrick, G. A. (1951), 'The Gospel according to Matthew', in G. A. Buttrick et al., eds, *The Interpreter's Bible* VII. New York/Nashville TN, pp. 229–625.

Kasser, R., Meyer, M. and Wurst, G., eds. (2006), *The Gospel of Judas from Codex Tchacos*. Washington DC: National Geographic.

Kelly, J. N. D. (1972), *Early Christian Creeds* (3rd edn). New York: Longman.

——— (1977), *Early Christian Doctrines* (5th edn). London: Adam & Charles Black.

Khalidi, T. (2001), *The Muslim Jesus: Sayings and Stories in Islamic Literature*. Cambridge MA: Harvard University Press.

King, K. L. (2006), *The Secret Revelation of John*. Cambridge MA: Harvard University Press.

Kleinknecht, H. (1967), 'The Logos in the Greek and Hellenistic World', in G. Kittel and G. W. Bromiley, eds, *Theological Dictionary of the New Testament* 4. Grand Rapids MI: Eerdmans, pp. 77–91.

Klijn, A. F. J. and Reinink, G. J. (1973), *Patristic Evidence for Jewish-Christian Sects*. Leiden: Brill.

Koole, J. L. (1998), *Isaiah Part 3, Volume 2: Isaiah 49–55* (translated from the Dutch by Anthony P. Runia). Leuven: Peeters.

Koschorke, K. (1978), *Die Polemik der Gnostiker gegen das kirchliche Christentum*. Leiden: Brill.

Köster, H. (1972), '*hupostasis*', in G. Friedrich and G. W. Bromiley, eds, *Theological Dictionary on the New Testament* 8. Grand Rapids MI: Eerdmans, pp. 572–589.

Kraus, H.-J. (1978), *Psalmen 1–2* (5th edn). Neukirchen-Vluyn: Neukirchener Verlag.

Kroeze, J. H. (1968), *Het boek Jozua verklaard*. Kampen: Kok.

Krüger, R. (2003), *Arm und reich im Jakobusbrief von Lateinamerika aus gelesen: Die Herausfordeung eines profetischen Christentums* (Ph.D. thesis, Vrije Universiteit Amsterdam).

Kuitert, H. M. (1998), *Jezus, nalatenschap van het christendom: Schets voor een christologie*. Baarn: Ten Have.

Lane, W. L. (1974), *The Gospel according to Mark: The English Text with Introduction, Exposition and Notes*. London: Marshall, Morgan & Scott.

Lang, B. (1999), 'Wisdom', in K. van der Toorn, B. Becking and P. W. van der Horst, eds, *Dictionary of Deities and Demons in the Bible* (2nd edn). Leiden: Brill, pp. 900–905.

Lefeber, P. S. A. (1997), *Keuze en verlangen: Een onderzoek naar zin en functie van het gebed in Origenes' preken en zijn tractaat Over het Gebed*. Gorinchem: Narratio.

Lelyveld, M. (1987), *Les Logia de la vie dans l'Évangile selon Thomas: À la recherche d'une tradition et d'une rédaction*. Leiden: Brill.

Lies, L. (1992), *Origenes' 'Peri Archon': Eine undogmatische Dogmatik*. Darmstadt: Wissenschaftliche Buchgesellschaft.

Lietaert Peerbolte, B. J. (2006) 'The Name above all Names (Philippians 2:9)', in G. H. van Kooten, ed., *The Revelation of the Name YHWH to Moses: Perspectives from Judaism, the Pagan Graeco-Roman World, and Early Christianity*. Leiden: Brill, pp. 187–206.

Logan, A. H. B. (1996), *Gnostic Truth and Christian Heresy: A Study of the History of Gnosticism*. Edinburgh: T&T Clark.

Lohmeyer, E. (1967), *Das Evangelium des Markus* (17th edn). Göttingen: Vandenhoeck & Ruprecht.

Löhr, W. A. (1996), *Basilides und seine Schule: Eine Studie zur Theologie- und Kirchengeschichte des zweiten Jahrhunderts*. Tübingen: J. C. B. Mohr.

Lossky, V. (1957), *The Mystical Theology of the Eastern Church* (translated from the French). Cambridge, London: James Clarke & Co.

Luttikhuizen, G. P. (2002), *De veelvormigheid van het vroegste christendom*. Delft: Eburon.

Luz, U. (1997), *Das Evangelium nach Matthäus (Mt 18–25)*. Zürich, Düsseldorf: Benzinger Verlag, Neukirchen-Vluyn: Neukirchener Verlag.

——— (2002), *Das Evangelium nach Matthäus (Mt 1–7)* (5th edn). Düsseldorf, Zürich: Benzinger Verlag, Neukirchen-Vluyn: Neukirchener Verlag.

―――― (2002), *Das Evangelium nach Matthäus (Mt 26–28)*. Düsseldorf, Zürich: Benzinger Verlag, Neukirchen-Vluyn: Neukirchener Verlag.

McDonald, L. M. (2007), *The Biblical Canon: Its Origin, Transmission, and Authority*. Peabody MA: Hendrickson.

Mach, M. (1999), 'Michael', in K. van der Toorn, B. Becking and P. W. van der Horst, eds, *Dictionary of Deities and Demons in the Bible* (2nd edn). Leiden: Brill, pp. 569–572.

Marjanen, A. (1998), 'Is *Thomas* a Gnostic Gospel?', in R. Uro, ed., *Thomas at the Crossroads: Essays on the Gospel of Thomas*. Edinburgh: T&T Clark, pp. 107–139.

―――― (1998), '*Thomas* and Jewish Religious Practices', in R. Uro, ed., *Thomas at the Crossroads: Essays on the Gospel of Thomas*. Edinburgh: T&T Clark, pp. 163–182.

Meier, J. P. (1991), *A Marginal Jew: Rethinking the Historical Jesus I: The Roots of the Problem and the Person*. New York: Doubleday.

Ménard, J.-É. (1975), *L'Évangile selon Thomas: Traduction et commentaire*. Leiden: Brill.

Menken, M. J. J. (1996), *Old Testament Quotations in the Fourth Gospel: Studies in Textual Form*. Kampen: Kok Pharos.

Metzger, B. M. (1994), *A Textual Commentary on the Greek New Testament* (2nd edn). Stuttgart: Deutsche Bibelgesellschaft, United Bible Societies.

Meyer, M., ed. (2007), *The Nag Hammadi Scriptures: The International Edition*. New York: HarperCollins.

Michel, O. (1977), *Der Brief an die Römer* (14th edn). Göttingen: Vandenhoeck & Ruprecht.

Milik, J. T. (1976), *The Books of Enoch: Aramaic Fragments of Qumrân Cave 4*. Oxford: Clarendon Press.

Mimouni, S. C. (1998), *Le judéo-christianisme ancien: Essais historiques*. Paris: Cerf.

―――― (1998), 'Les Nazoréens: recherche étymologique et historique'. *Revue Biblique*, 105, 208–262.

Moody, D. (1953), 'God's Only Son: The Translation of John 3:16 in the Revised Standard Version'. *Journal of Biblical Literature*, 72, 213–219.

Moore, G. F. (1927), *Judaism in the First Centuries of the Christian Era: The Age of the Tannaim* I (reprint). Cambridge, reprint New York: Schocken Books.

Müller, U. B. (1974), 'Vision und Botschaft: Erwägungen zur prophetischen Struktur der Verkündigung Jesu'. *Zeitschrift für Theologie und Kirche*, 74, 416–448.

Mussner, F. (1974), *Der Galaterbrief*. Freiburg: Herder.

———— (1987), *Der Jakobusbrief* (5th edn). Freiburg: Herder.

Nodet, E. (2002), *Le Fils de Dieu: Procès de Jésus et Évangiles*. Paris: Cerf.

Nordsieck, R. (2004), *Das Thomasevangelium: Einleitung – Zur Frage des historischen Jesus – Kommentierung aller 114 Logien*. Neukirchen-Vluyn: Neukirchener Verlag.

O'Neill, J. C. (1995), *Who Did Jesus Think He Was?*. Leiden: Brill.

Osborn, E. (1997), *Tertullian: First Theologian of the West*. Cambridge: Cambridge University Press.

Pagels, E. (2003), *Beyond Belief: The Secret Gospel of Thomas*. New York: Vintage Books.

Pagels, E. and King, K. (2007), *Reading Judas: The Gospel of Judas and the Shaping of Christianity*. London, New York: Allen Lane.

Painchaud, L. (1982), *Le deuxième traité du Grand Seth (NH VII, 2)*. Québec: Laval.

Palmer, M. (2001), *The Jesus Sutras*. New York: Ballantine Publishing Group.

Parker, S. B. (1999), 'Sons of (the) Gods', in K. van der Toorn, B. Becking and P. W. van der Horst, eds, *Dictionary of Deities and Demons in the Bible* (2nd edn). Leiden: Brill, pp. 794–800.

Perkins, P. (1980), *The Gnostic Dialogue: The Early Church and the Crisis of Gnosticism*, New York: Paulist Press.

Perler, O. (1966), *Méliton de Sardes: Sur la Pâque et fragments* (SC 123). Paris: Cerf.

Pesch, R. (1976), *Das Markusevangelium* 1. Freiburg: Herder.

Pesch, R. (1977), *Das Markusevangelium* 2. Freiburg: Herder.

Petersen, W. L. (2001), 'Constructing the Matrix of Judaic Christianity from Texts', in S. C. Mimouni and F. S. Jones, eds, *Le judéo-christianisme dans tous ses états: Actes du colloque de Jérusalem 6–10 juillet 1998*. Paris: Cerf, pp. 126–144.

Pines, S. (1966), *The Jewish Christians of the Early Centuries According to a New Source*. Jerusalem: The Israel Academy of Sciences and Humanities.

Pixner, B. (2001), 'Nazoreans on Mount Zion (Jerusalem)', in S. C. Mimouni and F. S. Jones, eds, *Le judéo-christianisme dans tous ses états: Actes du colloque de Jérusalem 6–10 juillet 1998*. Paris: Cerf, pp. 289–316.

Pouderon, B. (2001), 'Aux origines du roman clémentin: Prototype païen, refonte judéo-hellénistique, remaniement chrétien', in S. C. Mimouni and F. S. Jones (eds), *Le judéo-christianisme dans tous ses états: Actes du colloque de Jérusalem 6–10 juillet 1998*. Paris: Cerf, pp. 231–256.

Rankin, D. I. (1995), *Tertullian and the Church*. Cambridge: Cambridge University Press.

Ratzinger Benedictus XVI, J. (2007), *Jesus of Nazareth*. New York:
    Doubleday.
Reim, G. (2001), 'Wie der Evangelist Johannes gemäß Joh 12,37ff. Jesaja
    6 gelesen hat'. *Zeitschrift für die neutestamentliche Wissenschaft*,
    92, 33–46.
Ridderbos, H. N. (1953), *The Epistle of Paul to the Churches of Galatia:
    The English Text with Introduction, Exposition and Notes*. Grand
    Rapids MI: Eerdmans.
——— (1992), *The Gospel according to John: A Theological
    Commentary*. Grand Rapids MI: Eerdmans.
Riley, G. (1996), 'Second Treatise of the Great Seth', in B. Pearson, ed.,
    Nag Hammadi Codex VII. Leiden: Brill, pp. 129–199.
Robertson, R. G. (1985), 'Ezekiel the Tragedian', in J. H. Charlesworth,
    ed., *The Old Testament Pseudepigrapha* 2. London: Darton,
    Longman & Todd, pp. 803–819.
Robinson, J. M. (2005), *The Gospel of Jesus: In Search of the Original
    Good News*. San Francisco: HarperSanFrancisco.
Robinson, J. M., Hoffmann, P. and Kloppenborg, J. S., eds. (2000), *The
    Critical Edition of Q: Synopsis including the Gospels of Matthew
    and Luke, Mark and Thomas with English, German, and French
    Translations of Q and Thomas*. Leuven: Peeters, Minneapolis:
    Fortress.
Roukema, R. (1999), *Gnosis and Faith in Early Christianity: An
    Introduction to Gnosticism*. London: SCM Press, Harrisburg:
    Trinity Press.
——— (2002), 'Le Fils du Très-Haut: sur les anges et la christologie'.
    Études Théologiques et Religieuses, 77, 343–357.
——— (2003), 'Les anges attendant les âmes des défunts: une
    comparaison entre Origène et quelques gnostiques', in L. Perrone,
    P. Bernardino and D. Marchini, eds, *Origeniana Octava: Origen
    and the Alexandrian Tradition. Papers of the 8th International
    Origen Congress, Pisa 27–31 August 2001*. Leuven: Peeters, pp.
    367–374.
——— (2004), 'La tradition apostolique et le canon du Nouveau
    Testament', in A. Hilhorst, ed., *The Apostolic Age in Patristic
    Thought*. Leiden, Boston: Brill, pp. 86–103.
——— (2005), 'Paul's Rapture to Paradise in Early Christian Literature',
    in A. Hilhorst and G. H. van Kooten, eds, *The Wisdom of Egypt:
    Jewish, Early Christian, and Gnostic Essays in Honour of Gerard
    P. Luttikhuizen*. Leiden: Brill, pp. 267–283.
——— (2006), 'De Messias aan Gods rechterhand', in G. C. den Hertog
    and S. Schoon, eds, *Messianisme en eindtijdverwachting bij joden
    en christenen*. Zoetermeer: Boekencentrum, pp. 92–107.

—— (2006), 'Jesus and the Divine Name in the Gospel of John', in George H. van Kooten, ed., *The Revelation of the Name YHWH to Moses: Perspectives from Judaism, the Pagan Graeco-Roman World, and Early Christianity*. Leiden: Brill, pp. 207–223.

—— (forthcoming), 'Jesus Tradition in Early Patristic Writings', in T. Holmén and S. E. Porter, eds, *Handbook for the Study of the Historical Jesus* 3. Leiden: Brill.

Rowe, C. K. (2006), *Early Narrative Christology: The Lord in the Gospel of Luke*. Berlin, New York: Walter de Gruyter.

Sagnard, F. (1970), *Clément d'Alexandrie: Extraits de Théodote* (SC 23). Paris: Cerf.

Sauer, G. (2000), *Jesus Sirach / Ben Sira*. Göttingen: Vandenhoeck & Ruprecht.

Schaper, J. (1995), *Eschatology in the Greek Psalter*. Tübingen: J. C. B. Mohr.

Schippers, R. and Baarda, T. (1960) *Het evangelie van Thomas: Apocriefe woorden van Jezus*. Kampen: Kok.

Schmithals, W. (1979), *Das Evangelium nach Markus Kapitel 1–9,1*. Gütersloh: Mohn, Würzburg: Echter Verlag.

Schnackenburg, R. (1979), *Das Johannesevangelium* 1 (4th edn). Freiburg: Herder.

—— (1975), *Das Johannesevangelium* 3. Freiburg: Herder

Schniewind, J. (1968), *Das Evangelium nach Matthäus*. Göttingen: Vandenhoeck & Ruprecht.

Schrage, W. (1991), *Der erste Brief an die Korinther (1Kor 1,1–6,11)*. Düsseldorf: Benzinger Verlag, Neukirchen-Vluyn: Neukirchener Verlag.

—— (1995), *Der erste Brief an die Korinther (1Kor 6,12–11,16)*. Solothurn, Düsseldorf: Benzinger Verlag, Neukirchen-Vluyn: Neukirchener Verlag.

—— (2001), *Der erste Brief an die Korinther (1Kor 15,1–16,24)*. Düsseldorf: Benzinger Verlag, Neukirchen-Vluyn: Neukirchener Verlag.

Schucman, H. (1976), *A Course in Miracles*. Mill Valley: Foundation for Inner Peace.

Schürmann, H. (1994), *Das Lukasevangelium* 2. Freiburg: Herder.

Schweitzer, A. (1977), *Geschichte der Leben-Jesu-Forschung* (reprint). Gütersloh: Gerd Mohn, pp. 442–444 (2nd edn 1913: Tübingen: Mohr Siebeck).

Sevenster, G. (1948) *De Christologie van het Nieuwe Testament* (2nd edn). Amsterdam: Holland.

Smith, J. Z. (1985), 'Prayer of Joseph', in J. H. Charlesworth, ed., *The Old Testament Pseudepigrapha* 2. London: Darton, Longman & Todd, pp. 699–723.

Smith, M. (1973), *Clement of Alexandria and a Secret Gospel of Mark*.
Cambridge MA: Harvard University Press.
Spanneut, M. (1994), '*Apatheia* ancienne, *apatheia* chrétienne: Ière partie:
L'*apatheia* ancienne', in W. Haase, ed., *Aufstieg und Niedergang
der Römischen Welt* II, 36, 7. Berlin, New York: Walter de
Gruyter, pp. 4641–4717.
Stead, G. C. (1999), 'Philosophy in Origen and Arius', in W. A. Bienert
and U. Kühneweg, eds, *Origeniana Septima: Origenes in den
Auseinandersetzungen des 4. Jahrhunderts*. Leuven: Peeters, pp.
101–108.
Strack, H. L. and Billerbeck, P. (1974), *Kommentar zum Neuen
Testament aus Talmud und Midrasch* II (6th edn). München:
Beck'sche Verlagsbuchhandlung.
Strecker, G. (1958), *Das Judenchristentum in den Pseudoklementinen*.
Berlin: Akademie-Verlag.
——— (1989), *Die Johannesbriefe*. Göttingen: Vandenhoeck &
Ruprecht.
Stroumsa, G. G. (1996), *Hidden Wisdom: Esoteric Traditions and the
Roots of Christian Mysticism*. Leiden: Brill.
Stuckenbruck, L. T. (1995), *Angel Veneration and Christology: A Study
in Early Judaism and in the Christology of the Apocalypse of John*.
Tübingen: J. C. B. Mohr.
——— (2004), '"Angels" and "God": Exploring the Limits of Early
Jewish Monotheism', in L. T. Stuckenbruck and W. E. S. North,
eds, *Early Jewish and Christian Monotheism*. London: T&T
Clark, pp. 45–70.
Tanner, N. P. (1990), *Decrees of the Ecumenical Councils* I. London:
Sheed and Ward, Washington: Georgetown University Press.
Tardieu, M. (1975), 'ΨΥΧΑΙΟΣ ΣΠΙΝΘΗΡ: Histoire d'une métaphore
dans la tradition platonicienne jusqu'à Eckhart'. *Revue des Études
Augustiniennes* 21, 225–255.
Taylor, V. (1959), *The Gospel according to St. Mark*. London: MacMillan
& Co.
Theissen, G. and Merz, A. (1997), *Der historische Jesus. Ein Lehrbuch*
(2nd edn). Göttingen: Vandenhoeck & Ruprecht.
Thomassen, E. (2006), *The Spiritual Seed. The Church of the
"Valentinians"*. Leiden: Brill.
Thomassen, E. and Painchaud, L. (1989), *Le Traité Tripartite (NH I, 5):
Texte établi, introduit et commenté*. Québec: Laval.
Thrall, M. E. (2000), *The Second Epistle to the Corinthians II*. London,
New York: T&T Clark.
Thümmel, H. G. (1999), 'ΗΝ ΠΟΤΕ ΟΤΕ ΟΥΚ ΗΝ', in W. A. Bienert
and U. Kühneweg, eds, *Origeniana Septima: Origenes in den*

Auseinandersetzungen des 4. Jahrhunderts. Leuven: Peeters, pp. 109–117.

Tobin, T. H. (1992), 'Logos', in D. N. Freedman, ed., *The Anchor Bible Dictionary* 4. New York: Doubleday, pp. 348–356.

Tomson, P. J. (2001), *'If this be from Heaven ...': Jesus and the New Testament Authors in their Relationship to Judaism.* Sheffield: Sheffield Academic Press.

Uhrig, C. (2004), *'Und das Wort ist Fleisch geworden': Zur Rezeption von Joh 1,14a und zur Theologie der Fleischwerdung in der griechischen vornizänischen Patristik.* Münster: Aschendorff.

Uro, R. (2003), *Thomas: Seeking the Historical Context of the Gospel of Thomas.* London, New York: T&T Clark.

Van de Kamp, G. C. (1883), *Pneuma-christologie: een oud antwoord op een actuele vraag?*. Amsterdam: Rodopi.

Van der Vliet, J. (2006), 'Judas and the Stars: Philological Notes on the Newly Published Gospel of Judas (*GosJud*, Codex Gnosticus Maghâgha 3)'. *The Journal of Juristic Papyrology* 36, 137–152.

Van de Sandt, H. and Flusser, D. (2002), *The Didache: Its Jewish Sources and its Place in Early Judaism and Christianity.* Assen: Van Gorcum, Minneapolis: Fortress Press.

Van Iersel, B. M. F., (1961), *'Der Sohn' in den synoptischen Jesusworten: Christusbezeichnung der Gemeinde oder Selbstbezeichnung Jesu?*. Leiden: Brill.

Van Kooten, G. H. (2005), 'The "True Light which Enlightens Everyone" (*John* 1:9): John, *Genesis*, the Platonic Notion of the "True, Noetic Light," and the Allegory of the Cave in Plato's *Republic*', G. H. Van Kooten, ed., *The Creation of Heaven and Earth: Re-interpretations of Genesis 1 in the Context of Judaism, Ancient Philosophy, Christianity, and Modern Physics.* Leiden: Brill, pp. 149–194.

Van Os, L. K. (forthcoming), *Baptism in the Bridal Chamber: The Gospel of Philip as a Valentinian Baptismal Instruction* (Ph.D. thesis, University of Groningen 2007). Leiden: Brill.

Verheyden, J. (2003), 'Epiphanius on the Ebionites', in P. J. Tomson and D. Lambers-Petry, eds, *The Image of Judaeo-Christians in Ancient Jewish and Christian Literature.* Tübingen: J. C. B. Mohr.

Von Balthasar, H. U. (2001), *Origen: Spirit and Fire: A Thematic Anthology of his Writings* (translated by Robert J. Daly), Edinburgh: T&T Clark.

Vos, J. S. (2000), '"The Letter of Simon to Amion": A Hotly Debated Antipauline Document'. *Gereformeerd Theologisch Tijdschrift*, 100, 184–189.

Williams, C. H. (2000), *I am He: The Interpretation of 'Anî Hû in Jewish and Early Christian Literature.* Tübingen: J. C. B. Mohr.

Williams, M. A. (1996), *Rethinking "Gnosticism": An Argument for Dismantling a Dubious Category*. Princeton NJ: Princeton University Press.

Williams, R. (2001), *Arius: Heresy and Tradition* (2nd edn). London: Darton, Longman & Todd.

Zahn, T. (1913), *Das Evangelium des Lucas*. Leipzig: Deichert.

Internet

Dunn, J. D. G., review of Simon J. Gathercole (2006), *The Preexistent Son: Recovering the Christologies of Matthew, Mark, and Luke*. Grand Rapids MI: Eerdmans, http://www.bookreviews.org/pdf/5607_6160.pdf.

Index of Passages[1]

Bible

Old Testament

Genesis

1–3	57
1:3	149, 178
1:26	169
1:26–27	21, 75, 152–3
1:31	57
2:21–23	75
3	49
3:5	21
6:2	146
6:4	146
14:18–20	160
14:22	148
16:7–13	148
18:2	151
18:17	154
22:11	148
22:15	148
32:24–30	153, 156
32:28	156
32:30	153
41:45	158

Exodus

3:2	148, 154
3:6	62
3:14	11, 30, 43, 48, 151
4:22	152, 157
4:22–23	151
7:1	154
12	90
12:3–13	98
12:10	98
12:12–13	155
12:29	98, 155
12:46	98
20:5	117
20:12	61
20:12–16	61
23:20	28, 153
23:20–23	148
24:8	93
25:22	152
29:38–46	98
32:34	148
33:2	148
34:6	41

---

[1] This index is based on references in the main text. Only some of the references in the footnotes have been included.

217

Leviticus
16:5–28   98
19:18   62
24:16   48

Numbers
9:12   98
20:16   148

Deuteronomy
4:35   146
5:9   117
6:4   146
6:4–5   62
14:1   154
32:6   170, 171
32:8–9   147–8
32:39   43, 146

Joshua
5:13–15   147, 169

1 Samuel
14:17   151
14:20   151
19:27   151

1 Chronicles
17:14   151
28:5   151
29:20   151
29:23   151

2 Chronicles
9:8   151

Job
1:6   146
2:1   146
16:19–21   146
38:7   146

Psalms
2:7   37–8, 150, 178
8:4   27
8:5   38
22:2   94
24:1   24
29:1   146
31:6   96
33:6   149, 170, 178
45:6–7   150, 167
45:7   150
47:3   148
82   146–7
82:1   151, 160
83:19   148
89:6   146
89:8   151
89:27–28   150
97:9   148
107:20   149
110:1   30, 45, 91
110:3   150, 169
110:4   160
118:22   47, 48
118:26   30, 41
147:15   149

Proverbs
8:22   153, 178, 183,
         189
8:22–23   149
8:22–25   177–8, 179, 184
8:22–31   169
8:27–31   149

Isaiah
6:1–7   42
6:10   41–2
7:14   33
9:5   150–1
28:10   48
40:3   28, 36, 41
40:3–5   36

40:13	24
41:4	178
45:5	146
45:23	23
53	90, 97
53:4	98
53:7	98
53:11–12	93
53:12	90
55:11	149
56:7	62
61:1–2	65

Jeremiah

7:11	62
9:22–23	24
23:5	37

Ezekiel

34:11–16	33
34:12–22	43
34:23	33, 43

Daniel

7:13	27
8:11	147
10:13	147
10:20–21	147
12:1	147

Hosea

6:6	64
11:1	33, 151
12:5	156–7

Joel

| 2:32 | 23 |
| 3:5 | 92 |

Zephaniah

| 3:14–15 | 41 |

Zechariah

3:8	37
6:12	37, 153
13:7	93

Malachi

| 3:1 | 28, 36 |

Deuterocanonical books

Wisdom of Solomon

2:13	157
2:16–18	157
9:1	154
18:14–16	155

Wisdom of Jesus ben Sirach

4:10	157–8
17:17	148
42:15	154

New Testament

Matthew

1:1–17	33
1:18–23	33
1:23	33, 95
2:6	33
2:15	33
3:3	41
3:13–17	6
3:13–4:17	18
3:16	142
3:16–17	32, 165
3:17	123, 124
4:3	34
4:5	34
4:17	63
4:23	63
5–7	63
5:3	122

5:3–10	64	24–25	138
5:17	32	24:3–25:46	64
5:17–20	63, 130	24:29–31	134
5:21–48	63–4	24:30	8
5:31–32	64	24:34	8
5:34	5	24:36	34
5:37	5	24:48	64
9:13	64	24:49	8
9:36	33	25:5	8, 64
10:5–42	138	25:31–46	33
10:6	33	26:2	95
10:16	33	26:28	7, 95
10:34–35	32	26:31	33, 95
10:37	64	26:32	106
11:25–27	34	26:64	8
11:27	26, 69, 166	27:5	95
12:7	64	27:25	95
12:28	64	27:50	118
12:32	47	27:52–53	95
12:49–50	138	28:1–10	95
13:10	138	28:18	95
13:11	138	28:19	84, 95–6, 130,
13:24–30	138		165, 166, 168
13:36–43	138	28:20	95
13:55	14		
14:33	32	*Mark*	
15:24	33, 124	1:1	25, 30
16:13–16	10	1:1–8	24
16:16	32	1:2–3	28
16:21	95	1:3	28, 41
16:24	102, 105	1:8	29, 41
16:28	8	1:9	25
17:1–5	142	1:9–11	6, 165
17:22–23	95	1:9–15	18
18	138	1:10	134, 142
19:3–9	64	1:11	7, 24, 37, 123,
20:17–19	95		124
20:28	7, 95	1:12–15	25
21:3	37	1:14	31
22:41–46	32	1:15–16	61
23:3	63, 130	1:16–20	62, 136
23:34–37	34–5	1:24	25, 31
23:37–39	35	1:24–25	137

1:29	136	9:7	25
1:38	31	9:31	62, 92, 137
2:1–12	29	9:33–35	62
2:10	27	10:2–9	48, 61, 66
2:17	31	10:17–19	61
2:23–28	61	10:21–31	62
2:28	27	10:32	136
3:6	92	10:32–34	62
3:11	25, 134	10:33–34	92, 137
3:11–12	137	10:35–44	62
3:13–19	136	10:45	7, 31, 62, 92
3:19	104	10:47	25
3:29	47	11:1–11	30
4:1–9	136	11:3	30, 37
4:10–11	135, 136	11:15–18	62
4:10–12	61	12:1–8	93
4:13–20	137	12:26–27	62
4:33–34	136	12:27	47
4:37–41	29	12:28–31	62
5:7	25, 29, 134	12:35–37	30, 48
5:37–43	136	13	62
6:1–3	25	13:3–37	136–7
6:3	14, 25, 134	13:20	62–3
6:4	128	13:22	62–3
6:34	33	13:24–27	143
6:47–51	29	13:26	8, 26, 27
6:50	29, 42, 70	13:27	62–3
7:1–15	61	13:30	8
8:27–29	10	13:32	5, 26, 34, 178
8:27–30	13	13:32–36	63
8:29	30, 50–1, 62	14:1	94
8:29–30	137	14:12	94
8:30	62, 137	14:13	136
8:31	27, 62, 92, 105	14:17	136
8:31–33	12	14:22–24	93
8:31–38	137	14:24	7
8:34	102, 105	14:24–25	62
8:34–38	62	14:25	93
8:37	92	14:27	33, 93
8:38	27, 63	14:32–33	136
9:1	8	14:32–36	93
9:2–8	134, 142	14:43–15:20	93–4
9:2–10	136	14:61	26

14:62	8, 26–7, 42, 70	7:27	36, 65
14:67	25	8:1–3	65–6, 139
15:6–15	93–4	8:9	139
15:21	109, 110	8:10	139
15:21–22	94, 110	9:18–20	10
15:21–24	109	9:22	96
15:26–37	94	9:23	102, 105
15:28	106	9:27	8
15:37	118	9:28–32	142
15:39	27	9:44	96
15:40–41	94, 136	9:54–55	38
15:42	94	10:18	134, 141
15:42–46	94	10:21–22	34
16:1–8	94	10:22	26, 69, 166
16:6	25	10:25–28	65
		10:38–42	139
Luke		10:41–42	139
1:17	36, 41	11:20	66
1:26–34	36	11:49–51	34–5, 65
1:32	22, 158	12:10	47
1:35	54	12:49	38
1:68	38	13:33	128
1:76	36, 41, 128	13:34	35
1:78	36–7, 38, 153	14:20	65–6
2:11	37	14:26	65, 139
2:22–52	35	14:27	105
3:1–7	36	16:18	66
3:4–6	41	17:20–21	66–7
3:21–22	6, 37, 165	17:21	72
3:21–4:15	18	17:22–37	67, 139
3:22	7, 37–8, 123,	17:27	66
	124, 165, 174	18:20	65, 66
3:23	18	18:29	65–6
3:23–31	22	18:31–33	96
3:23–38	38	19:44	38
4:3	34	20:34–35	66
4:9	34	20:38	47
4:16–30	65	20:41–44	36
4:18–19	65	21:5–36	67
4:43	65	21:25–27	143
6:17–49	65	21:27	8
6:20	65, 122	21:32	8
7:16	38, 128	22:19–20	96

23:43	96	3:11–12	142
23:46	96, 105, 118	3:13	40, 142
23:55–24:11	96	3:13–14	68, 98
24:5	102	3:16	166
24:26–27	96	3:18	40, 68, 166
24:31	96	3:18–20	69
24:36–37	96	3:29	41
24:39–43	96–7	3:34	165
24:44–47	96	3:36	69
		4:22	69
John		4:24	165
1:1	44, 167, 170	4:25–26	40, 68, 139
1:1–3	39, 44, 161, 189	4:42	139
1:1–18	40, 53, 59, 166,	4:44	128
	167	5:43	43
1:3	46, 170	6:20	42
1:4–9	43	6:35	139
1:5–9	46	6:38	134, 142
1:9	116	6:44	68
1:12	68, 108	6:51	134
1:14	39, 40, 42, 46,	6:62	68, 142
	53, 161, 166,	6:67–69	12–13
	178, 181, 182	6:69	25
1:14–18	39, 40	6:70–71	104
1:15	40	8:12	43, 46, 68, 69,
1:17	40–1		139
1:18	40, 108, 161,	8:23	134
	166, 167	8:23–24	69
1:23	41	8:24	42–3
1:29	97, 139	8:28	40, 42–3, 68, 98
1:30	40	8:56	161
1:32–34	7, 165	8:58	40
1:33	41	10:1–16	139
1:34	40, 139	10:11	43
1:36	97	10:11–18	98
1:41	40, 68, 139	10:25	43
1:49	40	10:25–28	68
1:51	40, 69, 142	10:25–38	139
2:1–11	69	10:30	43, 165
2:22	99	10:30–31	48
3:3	67	11:16	9
3:3–5	74	11:25–26	68, 99
3:5	67	11:25–27	68

11:50–52	98	18:36	67
12:13	41	19:14	98–9
12:13–15	69	19:30	99, 118
12:28	43	19:36	98
12:32	68–9, 98	20:1–8	99
12:37–40	69	20:9	99
12:40	41–2	20:11–18	99
12:41	42, 161	20:17	68, 99
12:44–50	139	20:19–23	99
12:47–48	69	20:19–25	9
13–16	69, 139	20:22	140
13:1	139	20:24–29	99
13:5	139	20:26–29	9
13:13	43–4	20:27–29	99
13:26–30	139	20:28	43, 167
13:34–35	69, 78–9, 83	20:31	68, 141
14:5	9	21:1–19	99
14:6	69	21:9–13	99
14:16–17	69, 140	21:25	141
14:26	69, 140, 165		
14:28	178	*Acts of the Apostles*	
15:1–10	69	1:1–8	97
15:6	69	1:11	8
15:12–13	69	2:36	44, 174
15:13	98	7:56	97
15:15	140	7:59–60	97
15:18–16:4	69	7:60	197
15:26	69, 135, 140, 165	8:9–24	126
16:7	135	8:32–33	97
16:7–15	69, 140	11:26	129
16:13	135, 178	13:33	44, 174
16:25	140	15:13	14
16:29	139, 140	20:28	97
17	139–40	21:18	14
17:3	68	24:5	123
17:5	42		
17:6	43	*Romans*	
17:12	69, 104	1:3–4	21, 174
17:24	42	3:25–26	89
17:26	43	4:25	89, 90
18:5–6	42–3	8:3	19, 23
18:8	42–3	8:9–10	165
18:20	141	8:34	91

9:5	167	*Galatians*	
10:9	23, 91	1:16	20
10:12–14	92	1:19	14, 134
10:13	23	2:9	14
14:8–9	23	2:12	14
14:11	23	2:20	20, 89, 90
		3:1	90
1 Corinthians		3:13	89
1:2	91–2	4:4	19
1:9	23	4:5	20
1:18	89, 106		
1:31	24	*Ephesians*	
2:16	24	1:3–14	165
5:7	89, 90	4:13	23
6:20	89		
7:22	89	*Philippians*	
8:6	22, 40, 44, 46,	2:1–5	91
	161, 166	2:6–8	20
10:4	22, 129, 161	2:6–11	91
10:26	24	2:7	54
11:2	135	2:9	91
11:24–25	89	2:9–11	23, 29
12:4–6	165		
15	91	*Colossians*	
15:3	90	1:13	23
15:3–5	88	1:15	178, 179, 183
15:4	91	1:15–17	166–7
15:6–7	88	2:18	162
15:7	14, 134		
15:23–28	26, 91	*1 Thessalonians*	
15:28	23	1:10	23, 91
15:44	90	4:13–17	142
15:45–49	90	4:14	91
15:51–57	142	4:15–17	8, 60
16:22	92		
		2 Thessalonians	
2 Corinthians		2:15	135
1:19	23		
8:9	22	*1 Timothy*	
12:2–4	76, 142	1:4	171
13:13	165	3:16	46
		4:1	8
		6:15	8

Titus		*Gospel of Mary*	
2:13	8	7	82
		8	132
Hebrews		8–9	83
1:2–3	167	10	83, 132
1:3	181	15–17	84
1:8–9	150, 167	17–18	84
11:1	181		
		Gospel of Thomas	
James		Heading	47, 71, 102, 132
2:1	129–30	1	71
5:7–8	130	2	71
5:8	8	3	71–2, 73, 76, 79, 83, 102
		4	72–3, 74, 75
2 Peter		5	77
1:1	167	6	48
3:4	8	11	8–9, 74, 75, 76
		12	13, 14, 128
1 John		13	10, 11, 13, 14, 48, 132, 148
4:2	46	14	48, 73
4:9	166	16	74
5:7	165–6	18	77
5:20	167	19	73
		21	77
Revelation		22	74, 75
1:4	157	23	74
1:7	8	24	78
1:18	102	25	78
6:14	77	27	71, 78, 79
22:20	8, 92	28	46–7
		29	73
		30	167
Some other early Christian writings		37	77, 102
		39	80
		43	48
Gospel of Judas		44	47, 167
33	81	46	46, 47, 80
33–35	52	48	79
38–41	81	49	73, 74, 76
39–41	104	50	73–4, 84 102
43	81	51	76
47–52	52		
56	81, 104		

52	47, 80, 102	85	47, 80
53	48	87	73
54	78	95	78
55	79, 102, 105	97	143
59	79, 102	98	143
60	80	99	79
61	46	101	46, 102, 124
62	132	102	80
63	78	104	48, 78
64	78	106	74
65	102	108	8, 77–8
66	47	110	78
67	72	111	8–9, 76–7, 102
70	79	112	73
75	74	113	72, 76
77	46, 78, 80	114	72, 73

Index of Names and Subjects

adoptianism   44, 173–5, 177, 182, 188, 192, 193, 194
Alcinous   82, 172, 180
Alexander of Alexandria   184, 185, 187, 195
Angel of the Lord   148, 155, 169
Aphrahat   127, 148
Aristotle   180, 182, 195
Arius   182–9, 195
Athanasius of Alexandria   183, 184, 187

Barbelo   2, 52
Barnabas   125–6, 133–4
Basilides   108–9, 111
Basil of Caesarea   135

Callistus   176
Calvin, John   188
Canon   16–17
Celsus   17, 162, 175, 181
Cerinthus   15, 49–51, 58, 60–1, 103, 106, 110, 116, 122
Clement of Alexandria   15, 53, 66, 105, 106, 133–5, 137, 138, 141, 168
Clement of Rome   47, 125–7
Constantine   9, 183, 185, 186, 195

Corpus Hermeticum   72, 75

Didache   96, 130
Dionysius of Alexandria   182–3

Ebionites (also: Gospel of the)   6, 122–5
Enoch (also: Book of)   27–8, 35, 50, 142, 146, 154, 157
Epiphanius of Salamis   122, 123, 124, 174, 175, 176
Eusebius of Caesarea   123, 124, 133, 134, 154, 173, 174, 185, 186, 195
Ezekiel the Tragedian   154, 155, 159

Flavius Josephus   14

Hebrews (Gospel of the)   124
Hippolytus of Rome   48, 173, 174, 175, 176

Ignatius of Antioch   47, 168
Irenaeus of Lyons   15, 48, 49, 50, 51, 53, 54, 60, 84, 103, 106, 107, 108, 122, 132, 133, 170–2, 178, 179

James (brother of Jesus)   13–14,
    25, 88, 133–4
Jerome   123, 124
John the Baptist   10, 18, 24,
    28, 29, 36, 37, 39, 40, 41,
    45–6, 50, 80, 97–8, 123,
    128, 156, 165
Joseph and Aseneth   158–9
Judas (also: Gospel of)   2, 15,
    25, 51–2, 58, 80–2, 86, 95,
    104, 110, 111, 112, 116,
    132, 133, 139–40, 144
Justin Martyr   122, 123, 169,
    170, 179

Lucian of Antioch   183

Marcion   66, 126, 172, 173
Mary, mother of Jesus   25, 33,
    36, 38, 49, 50, 54, 122,
    123, 171, 173–4, 175, 176
Mary Magdalene (also: Gospel of)
    1, 15, 61, 72, 77, 82–4, 85,
    87, 94, 99, 132, 140
Matthew   10–12, 14
Melchizedek   160
Melito of Sardes   90, 169–70
Michael   147, 160
modalism   175–7, 178, 181, 182,
    189, 193–4

Nazarenes, Nazoreans   123–4,
    128, 192
Nicaea (council of)   3, 16, 119,
    120, 121, 164, 185–7, 188,
    189, 190, 193, 194, 195–6
Noetus of Smyrna   175–7
Novatian of Rome   174
Numenius   172

Ophites   15, 49–51, 53, 54–5,
    58, 60–1, 103, 106, 110,
    112, 116

Origen of Alexandria   116, 122,
    123, 124, 156, 179–82,
    183, 184, 186, 187, 189,
    195

Papias of Hierapolis   133
Paul   8, 13–14, 15, 18–24, 31,
    40, 44, 45, 48, 58–9, 60,
    83, 88–92, 94, 97, 100,
    101, 111, 113, 114, 115,
    117, 122, 126, 128, 129,
    130, 135, 142, 143, 161,
    165, 166, 167, 189
Paul of Samosata   174–5, 182–3,
    187, 188, 192
Peter   9–14, 25, 32, 50–1, 62,
    65–6, 82, 83–4, 92, 99,
    125–7, 133–4, 136
Philip (Gospel of)   48, 167–8
Philo of Alexandria   75, 107,
    151–4, 155, 156, 157, 161,
    172, 173, 180
Plato, Platonism   75, 82 106–7,
    112–13, 116, 117, 152,
    172, 173, 180, 181, 182,
    194, 195
Pliny the Younger   168–9
Praxeas   176–7
pseudo-Clementine writings
    125–7, 131
Ptolemaeus (the Valentinian)   53

Qumran   27, 148, 157, 158,
    159, 160, 162

Rufinus of Aquileia   125, 179,
    181, 186–7

Sabellius   176, 177, 183, 187
Saklas   81, 85
Satan   12, 141, 146
Satornilus of Antioch   107
Secret Gospel of Mark   137–8

Simon of Cyrene 15, 94,
   108–10, 111, 113, 118
Simon the Magician 126
Sophia (see also: Wisdom)
   49–50, 53–5, 57, 58, 85,
   103, 105, 116
Stoic philosophy 83, 172, 173

Talmud 158
Targum 155–6
Tertullian of Carthage 134–5,
   171–2, 176, 177–9, 184,
   186
Theodotus (the leather merchant)
   173–4
Theodotus (the Valentinian) 15,
   53–5, 57, 58, 60, 104–7,
   110–11, 116, 168, 182
Theophilus of Antioch 170, 179
Thomas (also: Gospel of) 2, 8,
   9–14, 15, 43–4, 45–9, 58,
   71–80, 83, 84, 85, 86–7,
   99, 102, 105, 110, 111–12,
   115–16, 124, 128, 132,
   143, 144, 167–8

Tripartite Tractate 15, 55–8, 84,
   87, 107–8, 110, 112, 116,
   162, 168
Trypho the Jew 122

Uriel 156–7

Valentinus, Valentinians 17,
   53–5, 57–8, 59, 102,
   104–6, 110–11, 112,
   167–8, 176, 182
Victor of Rome 174

Wisdom (see also: Sophia) 34–5,
   49, 123, 149, 153, 154,
   161, 169, 170–1, 177–9,
   180, 183–4, 195

Yaldabaoth 49–50, 52, 55, 85,
   103, 109, 110

Zephyrinus 176